The
7
Hidden
Powers
of Effective
Managers

Unlock Your Influence,
Make Smarter Decisions,
and Build High-Performing Teams

Stephen J. McIntyre

Echo Enterprise
An Imprint of Echo Story Media LLC

First published in 2025.

Cover and interior design by Stephen J. McIntyre.
Published by Echo Story Media LLC

ECHO
STORY
MEDIA

Echo Story Media LLC
30 N Gould St Ste R
Sheridan, WY 82801

ISBN: 979-8-9998500-0-3 (paperback)

For permissions requests, speaking inquiries, and bulk order purchase options, email info@echostorymedia.com or use our contact page https://echostorymedia.com/contact.

Lead With Confidence™ Series and The 7 Hidden Powers™ are trademarks of Echo Story Media LLC.

Disclaimer

This is a work of fiction. Names, characters, businesses, brands, places, events, locales, and incidents are either the product of the author's imagination or used in a fictitious manner. Any resemblance to actual persons, living or dead, or actual events is purely coincidental.

Dedication

To Jaime - for the patient listening, thoughtful feedback, and steady presence.

To Harper - for the joy, perspective, and reminders to play.

To our family milestone list - for making space each year to celebrate what we've built together.

Here's one more for the record.

Table of Contents

Unifying Map

The 7 Hidden Powers → 3 Phases

Stabilise → Accelerate → Sustain

- **Stabilise** (stop the slide)
  - **Convene** - meet on purpose; decisions have a home and a cadence.
  - **Presence** - calm under load; signal, not noise.
  - **Process** - small, repeatable rituals (Momentum Board; Rule of Three).

- **Accelerate** (go faster, safely)
  - **Calculated Risk** - guardrails, risk budget, rollback signal.
  - **Perspective** - Street → Skyline → Systems (change altitude).

- **Sustain** (make wins boring)
  - **Ownership** - one owner, outcome not tasks.
  - **Team Synergy** - make momentum visible; recognition, growth, no brilliant jerks.

Failure modes (spot the missing power):
Paralysis (no Convene) · Panic (no Presence) · Heroics (no Process) · Stall (no Calculated Risk) · Misalignment (no Perspective) · Bounce (no Ownership) · Burnout (no Team Synergy).

Map where you are. Fix the missing power first. Don't skip phases.

Quickstart for Managers in Crisis

If you only have today and tomorrow - do this.

Today (≤60 min, no prior reading)

1. **Name the mission**: *Choose* **X** *now so* **Y** *can move*; or, *Agree* **A/B/C** *by* **time** *so* **next team** *can start, etc.*
2. **Start a Momentum Board**: Draw *Today | Blocked | Cleared.* Create 3-7 tasks in *Today* column.
3. **Run a stand-up (15 min)**: One round only: *Today* (one task), *Blocked* (name the blocker and an owner), *Cleared* (commit to one cleared before lunch). No extra updates.
4. **Log one decision (needed and/or made)**: Decision, Context (1 line), Options (A/B), Owner, Decision revisit date.

Tomorrow

1. **Pick one risky change (run a 30 min pre-brief)**: One goal. One **risk budget** (e.g., 4 hrs, test account only). One **rollback signal** (e.g., errors >0.5% or p95>300 ms for 5 min → revert). Name the **rollback owner**. Decide **Go/Test/No-Go**; record it.
2. **Assign single owner to the most critical task**: Say out loud: "*I own <the outcome> until <date>.*" Post the update channel and daily check-in time.
3. **Targeted reading (~60 min total)**: Read the end of chapter summary boxes for Ch2, Ch5, Ch6, Ch3.

Reminder: You don't need everything - just the **missing** thing **now**. *See the 'Failure modes' on the previous page.*

Prologue

Marcia stared out at the glistening cityscape; her reflection superimposed over Puget Sound. Rivulets of rain on the tenth-floor windows of Alpha's headquarters blurred the now familiar Space Needle. Three years ago, she would have been fixated on the code in front of her, not panoramic views from a corner office.

"Congratulations on the promotion, Marcia." Robert Miller's voice pulled her back to the moment. The founder and CEO of Alpha Consulting leaned against his polished walnut executive desk, its rich grain catching the soft grey light filtering through the windows. Arms crossed, his salt-and-pepper hair perfectly styled despite Seattle's notorious humidity. "I believe you're exactly what the Global Financial Partners project needs right now."

Marcia settled into a visitor chair, unable to shake the feeling that she'd been called to the principal's office. "Thank you, Robert. I'm honoured, but…"

"But you're wondering why we're moving you from Practice Lead to Delivery Manager so quickly?" Robert smiled. "Especially for our most high-profile project?"

She nodded. Ever since the crisis with her previous team, she'd known this moment was coming - she just didn't expect it to arrive so soon. Being offered the role now wasn't just a promotion; it felt like the fulcrum where everything she'd learned would be tested.

Marcia felt the old sense of stepping into something just

beyond her certainty. She didn't fear the work; she feared disappointing the people who were trusting her with it. But she steadied herself with the habits she'd built over the past few years: start with clarity, build from connection.

After her successful stint as Team Leader three years ago, her rise to Practice Lead in the Team Excellence group had been logical - a natural progression that let her leverage her technical expertise while developing her leadership skills across increasingly complex projects.

Marcia cleared her throat and shifted a little. But Delivery Manager? That was different. She'd be responsible for the entire relationship with Global Financial Partners, overseeing multiple teams across offices, managing client expectations, and ultimately being accountable for a multi-million-dollar contract.

Robert tapped his laptop, bringing up a dashboard on the wall screen. Red indicators dominated the display. "GFP is behind schedule, over budget, and our client satisfaction score is, concerning."

A cold flutter ran through Marcia's stomach. If she couldn't turn this around, the fallout wouldn't just hit the company - it would reinforce every fear she still carried from her earlier failures. What if this was the moment her leadership finally buckled? The thought lodged sharply, threatening to drain the confidence she'd fought hard to build.

"I've heard rumblings," Marcia admitted. "But I thought Brett had it under control."

"Brett resigned Friday." Robert's expression tightened. "Family emergency - his mother's health has taken a turn. He's moving back to Chicago."

"I'm sorry to hear that," Marcia said, genuinely concerned for her colleague but also suddenly understanding why she'd been summoned. "And the project can't wait for a traditional hiring process."

"Six months ago, we were a team of three hundred with three offices," Robert said. "Now we're pushing five hundred across five locations. Our growth is outpacing our ability to develop leaders internally."

Marcia met the point with a small smile, remembering the champagne toast just last month when they'd opened the Toronto office. Alpha Consulting's meteoric rise from a boutique Seattle firm to a multi-city operation had been both exhilarating and dizzying.

"We need someone who understands our methods and can turn this around quickly," Robert continued. "Your work in New York last quarter was exceptional. The client specifically mentioned your structured approach to problem-solving."

"That was a much smaller engagement," Marcia pointed out. "GFP is implementing core banking systems across their entire North American operation. It's at least five times the complexity."

Robert spread his hands apart, palms facing each other. "And that's exactly why I need you, Marcia. You see the complexity clearly. Most people would either oversimplify or get overwhelmed. You map it out and create systems to manage it."

Outside, the Seattle rain intensified, drumming against the windows. Marcia fought the fluttering sensation in her stomach. This wasn't imposter syndrome - this was rational concern about stepping into a management role that typically required years more experience than she had.

"The team is demoralised," Robert continued, swiping through slides showing declining velocity and increasing defect rates. "The client is threatening to cancel if we don't right the ship immediately. I need someone who can both manage upward with Elizabeth Parker at GFP and rebuild the team's confidence."

Marcia recognised the name. Elizabeth Parker had been a demanding stakeholder on her very first leadership project three years ago. The fact that she was GFP's executive sponsor added another layer of pressure.

"I've already spoken with James Anderson," Robert added, referring to the VP of Development who had mentored Marcia through her first leadership role. "He thinks you're ready."

Marcia took a deep breath. "When would I start?"

"Tomorrow morning." Robert slid a folder across the table. "There's a steering committee meeting at 10 am. Elizabeth will be there, along with their CIO."

Marcia opened the folder, scanning the executive summary. The situation was worse than she'd heard. Critical integrations failing, missed deliverables, and team attrition that had left key roles unfilled.

"I know it's a lot to ask," Robert said, his tone softening. "But I wouldn't put you in this position if I didn't believe you could handle it."

Marcia stared at the project dashboard again, the red indicators seeming to pulse with urgency. Part of her wanted to decline - to suggest someone with more experience. But another part, the part that had thrived on building systems when she first became a Team Leader, saw the challenge clearly. A struggling project, a demoralised team, a demanding client - all the elements that would require her to level up again.

"I'll need full authority to make changes," she said finally. "And access to resources if I need to bring in specialists."

Robert's face broke into a relieved smile. "Done and done. Whatever you need. James has already cleared his calendar to support you through the transition."

"And the team? Have they been told?"

"I wanted to confirm with you first. We'll announce it this afternoon. Most of them are in Seattle, but you've got people in New York and a couple working remotely from Chicago."

Marcia pressed her lips together in assent, mentally preparing for the reactions. She'd be younger than most of the senior team members, and her rapid rise might raise eyebrows.

"One more thing," Robert said, pulling a small box from his top drawer. "Alpha tradition."

He opened it to reveal a sleek silver business card holder engraved with her name and new title: *Marcia Hughes, Delivery Manager - Enterprise Solutions.*

"Thank you," she said, taking the gift. The weight of the metal in her hand made her new reality sink in. "I'll do my best not to let you down."

She ran her thumb over the engraving and managed a smile, but inside she felt a jolt of fear. If this went badly, that title could be short-lived - or worse, a mark against her career.

"I know you will," Robert said, standing and extending his hand. "The question isn't whether you can do this, Marcia. It's what you'll learn about management along the way."

As Marcia shook his hand, she glanced again at the Seattle skyline and took a deep breath. She tucked the business card holder into her bag and straightened her shoulders. She had weathered difficult meetings before, and with proper preparation and trusting her instincts, she knew she would get through the next one too.

✦ ✦ ✦

Marcia's condo was quiet except for the steady rhythm of rain against the glass. She'd moved here after her promotion to Practice Lead - a small luxury she'd allowed herself, with floor-to-ceiling windows offering an uninterrupted view of the city. Tonight, however, it was more like a barrier. The world beyond shimmered and wavered, distorted by the streaks of water threadding down the window.

She placed the sleek business card holder on her kitchen counter and stared at it. *Delivery Manager*. The title still felt foreign, like someone else's clothes that didn't quite fit.

Her phone buzzed with a text from James: *Heard the news. Coffee tomorrow before the steering committee? 8:30 at Analog Capitol Hill?*

A little tension eased. James had been her lifeline when she'd first stepped into leadership, guiding her through those uncertain early months with patience and wisdom. She remembered the Team Leader Toolbox folder James gave her years ago. His continued mentorship had been instrumental in her growth from Senior Developer to reluctant Team Leader to confident Practice Lead.

See you there, she typed back. *I have a feeling I'll need your advice more than ever.*

She opened her laptop and navigated to the project dashboard Robert had shown her. With her elevated access, she could now see all the details that had been hidden before. The situation was even worse than Robert had indicated.

The team had missed the last three deliverables. Defect count was rising weekly. Two senior developers had resigned last month. Customer satisfaction scores plummeted from 9.2 to 5.7 in just six weeks.

And the timeline... Marcia winced. The original go-live date was in three months, but at the current velocity, they'd need at least six.

Marcia shut her eyes as the scope of the disaster hit her. *What if I can't fix this?* The thought came ice-cold. Her pulse hammered at her temples, and for a heartbeat she imagined calling Robert back to say he'd chosen the wrong person. Months of missed deadlines, a team on the brink - it felt like a tidal wave about to break over her. She forced one slow inhale, then another, grounding herself. *No. They can't see fear.* If she was going to lead them out of this, she had to push through the panic.

She pulled up the team roster. Seventeen people total, spread across three offices. She recognised a few names from previous projects, but most were strangers. One name stood out: Liam Everett, Principal Architect. She'd worked with him briefly when she first joined Alpha. Brilliant but notoriously difficult to manage, with a reputation for pushing back against leadership.

Her phone buzzed again. A company-wide email had just gone out announcing her promotion, effective immediately.

Great, she thought. *The team will find out through a form email.*

As if on cue, her phone rang. The caller ID showed Tessa Tanaka, a business analyst who had relocated from the New York office last year.

"Hey, Tessa," Marcia answered, trying to sound casual. "I guess you saw the announcement?"

"I did," Tessa said. "Congratulations! Though I suspect with the GFP project, it's more of a 'good luck' situation."

Marcia laughed. "That obvious, huh?"

"Brett was a good guy, but he was drowning," Tessa said bluntly. "We haven't had clear direction in weeks. The client is furious, and honestly, the team is falling apart."

Marcia grabbed a notepad. "Tell me what you're seeing from your perspective."

Over the next half hour, Tessa painted a picture that made Marcia's stomach tighten. Technical debt piling up. Communication breakdowns between the Seattle and New York teams. A client who kept changing requirements but still expected the original timeline.

"The worst part," Tessa concluded, "is that nobody wants to make decisions anymore. Brett was so overwhelmed that everything became a committee discussion. We spend hours in meetings and nothing gets resolved."

Marcia jotted down *decision paralysis* and underlined it twice. "Who else should I talk to before tomorrow's steering committee?"

"Noah in New York has the best grasp of the integration issues," Tessa suggested. "And Liam... well, Liam should be in the loop, but be prepared. He's not exactly thrilled about another leadership change."

After hanging up, Marcia realised her hands were trembling. *This project might be impossible*, she thought, the weight of Tessa's words pressing down on her. Part of her wanted to shut her laptop and walk away. *Maybe I'm not cut out for this*, a small voice whispered. She imagined the team's sceptical faces and felt a stab of fear - were they already dismissing her as just another failing manager? For a fleeting instant, she wished she'd never accepted the role. But had she really had a choice? Turning Robert down would have branded her as unreliable. Accepting meant staking everything - her credibility, her career, and Alpha's largest client. If she failed, GFP could be lost.

But she clenched her fists, forcing the doubt back. *If I give in now, nothing will improve. They need me to be stronger than my fear*, she reminded herself, opening her eyes and refocusing on the messy plan she'd have to fix.

Forcing herself to start with small practical steps, Marcia sent brief introduction emails to the key team members Tessa had mentioned.

She went to her small home office, hauling out her old whiteboard that she propped against the living room wall. This had been her method since her first leadership role - visualising the problem before jumping to solutions.

In blue marker, she began mapping out what she knew:

Team - Demoralised, fragmented, decision-paralysed
Client - Frustrated, losing confidence
Project - Behind schedule, quality issues
Technology - Integration problems, technical debt

Around midnight, her whiteboard was covered with notes, arrows, and questions. The rain had finally stopped, and the city lights reflected in wet patches below. Marcia stood back, tapping the marker against her chin.

The situation was challenging, certainly. But underneath the chaos, she could see patterns - the same fundamental leadership issues she'd faced before, just at a larger scale. People needed clarity. Processes needed structure. Communication needed consistency.

She thought back to her first days as a Team Leader, how overwhelmed she'd felt by the responsibility. James had told her something that stuck with her: "Leadership isn't about knowing all the answers. It's about asking the right questions and bringing people together to find solutions."

Marcia erased a section of the whiteboard and wrote in capital letters:

WHAT DO THEY NEED FROM ME?

Her phone buzzed with a calendar alert. The steering committee was just nine hours away. She needed sleep if she was going to face Elizabeth Parker and the GFP executives with any clarity.

As she got ready for bed, Marcia spotted a well-worn notebook on her nightstand - a gift from James when she'd completed her first successful project as Team Leader. Most of the pages were already filled with notes, diagrams, and lessons from the past two years. She thought about the systems and approaches she'd developed over that time. They had worked for small teams and medium-sized projects, but would they work for something of this scale and complexity?

Marcia closed her eyes. Tomorrow she would step into a room filled with frustrated executives and a demoralised team. They would all be looking to her for answers she didn't yet have.

But what she did have was an approach - a way of breaking down the complex into manageable pieces, of bringing structure to chaos, of aligning people toward a common goal.

As she drifted toward sleep, her mind kept cycling through the day's events. Robert's confidence in her abilities. Tessa's blunt assessment of the project state. The weight of the new business card holder in her hand.

Delivery Manager.

Maybe the title would feel more natural tomorrow. Maybe not. Either way, she had a steering committee to face and a team to rebuild. Somehow, she would find a path forward.

Outside her window, the Seattle skyline glittered against the night sky, flashes of lighting in the distance. Like the city itself, Marcia would weather this latest downpour. She just needed to remember the tools and systems that had served her well before.

As she rolled over, one thought remained: James would be there tomorrow, just as he had been at the start of her leadership journey. She knew James would have her back.

And yet, as the room dimmed, a knot tightened in her chest. What if this project was bigger than her abilities? What if she failed a team already bruised by dysfunction? The familiar insecurity whispered from deep inside: maybe she wasn't good enough to lead people through something this broken. She exhaled slowly, wishing doubt didn't follow her so faithfully.

✧ ✧ ✧

Analog Coffee buzzed with morning energy. The scent of fresh roasts mingled with the lingering dampness from yesterday's rain. Through the window, Marcia could see puddles reflecting the brightening sky - Seattle's version of a promising day.

"You look like you didn't sleep much," James said, sliding a large latte across the reclaimed wood table. At fifty-two, the VP of Development had the relaxed confidence of someone who'd weathered countless corporate storms. His button-down shirt was crisp, but he'd skipped the tie - Alpha's concession to West Coast casual.

"Is it that obvious?" Marcia cupped the warm ceramic mug, grateful for the caffeine.

"Only to someone who's known you as long as I have." James smiled. "The night before a big challenge, your brain tends to run laps."

Marcia took a sip of her latte. "I mapped out the entire project on my whiteboard last night. It's... not great."

"Brett was drowning," James said with a grim half-smile. "Good guy, excellent technical skills, but…"

"But he couldn't say no to the client," Marcia finished. "Tessa filled me in. Sounds like Elizabeth Parker has been expanding scope while holding firm on deadlines."

James leaned back in his chair. "Elizabeth is tough but fair. She pushes hard because her own leadership is pushing her. GFP's competitors are eating into their market share with more modern banking apps."

"So, she's under pressure to deliver digital transformation

yesterday," Marcia said. "And we're the bottleneck."

"From her perspective, yes." James took a bite of his blueberry scone. "The steering committee today won't be pretty. She'll want reassurance that you can turn things around."

"And can I?" Marcia asked plainly. "Robert seems to think so, but the team's fractured, the New York and Seattle offices aren't coordinating, and we're at least three months behind."

James studied her, then asked. "Do you remember your first week as a Team Leader? When the FreshWorks project was imploding?"

Marcia groaned. "How could I forget? I was sure I'd be fired."

"But you weren't. You pulled it together. Started with those daily stand-ups, implemented that tracking system."

"That was six people in one office," Marcia pointed out. "This is seventeen across three locations, a multi-million-dollar contract, and a client who's ready to walk."

"True," James said simply. "The scale is different. The principles aren't."

He reached into his messenger bag and pulled out a small notebook. "I was going to save this for your official promotion celebration, but you need it now."

Marcia took the notebook, running her fingers over the smooth leather cover.

"When you became a Team Leader," James said, "you discovered you had certain... abilities. Powers, really, that you didn't know you possessed as an individual contributor."

"Like the power to annoy Liam with process changes?" Marcia joked.

James laughed. "Like the power to bring order to chaos. To see patterns others miss. To build systems that scale."

"Those worked for small teams," Marcia said, flipping

through the lined pages of the notebook.

"They'll work for larger ones too," James assured her.

Reaching the front, she noticed he'd written inside the cover:

Remember: the tools that got you here will serve you at the next level too. Just use them more deliberately.

He glanced at his watch. "We've got thirty minutes before you need to head upstairs. Let's talk tactics for the steering committee."

Marcia opened the notebook and turned the first page. "Elizabeth will want a revised timeline, I assume?"

"Don't give her one," James said firmly.

"What?" Marcia looked up, surprised.

"Not yet." James leaned forward. "The worst thing you can do is commit to a deadline you haven't verified. Brett's mistake was promising what the team couldn't deliver."

"So, what do I say when she demands a date?"

"You tell her you need one week to properly assess the situation," James said. "That you've already begun the evaluation and will provide a detailed recovery plan, including a revised timeline, after you've had time to work with the team."

Marcia frowned. "She won't like that."

"No, she won't," James agreed. "But she'll respect you for it, especially if you demonstrate that you understand the business impact of the delays."

He took another sip of his coffee. "Elizabeth respects honesty more than optimism, as you know. Show her you grasp the severity of the situation but need time to create a realistic plan. Then deliver that plan exactly when you promised."

Marcia jotted this down, then looked up. "What about

the team? I'm walking into a room of people who've never worked with me, taking over from a leader who just disappeared overnight."

"This is where you have a hidden advantage," James said. "Most of them know the project is struggling. They're expecting changes. Your job today isn't to present solutions - it's to demonstrate that you're listening."

"Listening," Marcia repeated, underlining the word in her notes.

"Your instinct will be to jump in and fix things immediately," James continued. "Resist that urge. For the first few days, ask questions. Lots of them. Show the team you value their expertise."

Marcia thought about the roster she'd reviewed last night. "Even Liam?"

James's eyes warmed knowingly. "Especially Liam. He's brilliant but proud. If he thinks you're dismissing his concerns, he'll undermine you at every turn. If he believes you're listening, he can become your strongest ally."

They spent the next twenty minutes discussing key stakeholders, potential quick wins, and communication strategies. As they prepared to leave, James held the door for her.

"One more thing," he said as they stepped into the crisp morning air. "Remember that you have powers most new managers don't."

Marcia raised an eyebrow. "What powers are those?"

"For one, you have the power to convene," James said as they walked toward Alpha's building. "You can put a meeting on anyone's calendar - client executives, developers, even Robert - and they'll show up."

"That's just a calendar invite," Marcia laughed.

"No, it's more than that," James insisted. "It's the ability to bring people together, to create deadlines, to drive collaboration through strategic scheduling. Most new managers don't realise how powerful that is."

Marcia mulled it over as they approached the gleaming glass entrance of Alpha's headquarters. It seemed too simple, yet she remembered how effective her daily stand-ups had been in her first leadership role. She recalled sharing a note about convening the team with her mentee Lila. Perhaps James was right.

"There are other powers you'll discover," James said as they entered the lobby. "But for today, focus on listening and understanding. The solutions will come."

The elevator doors opened, revealing several members of the GFP project team waiting to ascend. Marcia recognised Tessa Tanaka, who gave her a subtle nod of encouragement.

"Looks like your team is gathering," James said quietly. "Ready?"

Marcia took a deep breath and stepped into the elevator. "As ready as I'll ever be."

As the doors closed and the elevator began its ascent, she noticed a tall man in the corner watching her with undisguised scepticism. From last time they worked together, she recognised Liam Everett, the brilliant but difficult developer who would likely be her biggest challenge.

Marcia met his gaze steadily, offering a small smile. His expression didn't change, but he gave a barely perceptible nod - acknowledgment, not acceptance.

The elevator chimed at the tenth floor. As the doors opened, Marcia could see the conference room at the end of the hall, already filling with people. Through the glass walls, a woman in a tailored suit was setting up a presentation - Elizabeth Parker had arrived early and was clearly ready for battle, the same executive Marcia had first worked with during the FreshWorks rollout before Elizabeth moved to

GFP.

James lightly touched Marcia's forearm, a steadying gesture from someone who'd guided her through countless turning points. "Remember," he said, keeping his voice low. "Listen first. Solutions later."

James paused with her in the corridor. "You'll get through this," he said. Then, with an assured tone, "One day, you'll be the one guiding someone else before an important steering committee."

Marcia managed a faint grin at the thought. It was hard to imagine ever being that seasoned and confident, but James's faith in her planted a small seed of hope.

With the team walking the corridor ahead of her, Marcia stood tall and took her first steps toward the conference room.

But as she walked, her pulse kicked up. This meeting could either pull the offices together or widen every fracture beyond repair. A tremor of panic rose - what if she couldn't hold the room when it mattered most? What if all the progress so far collapsed under pressure? She steadied her breath, reminding herself that courage wasn't the absence of fear but the decision to move anyway

With James's guidance and her own experience to draw on, she at least had a starting point.

As the elevator slid shut behind them, there was no turning back.

Chapter 1
From Leader to Manager

The conference room fell silent as Marcia entered. Twelve faces turned toward her - some curious, others sceptical, a few openly hostile. Through the floor-to-ceiling windows, Seattle's skyline provided a dramatic backdrop, the sky had cleared to a surprising blue, with the Olympic Mountains just visible past Elliott Bay.

"Good morning, everyone," Marcia said, setting her laptop on the table. "I know this is unexpected. For all of us."

Elizabeth Parker stood at the head of the table, arms crossed. Her crisp navy suit and sleek silver bob projected authority. She'd aged a bit since Marcia had last worked with her, but her penetrating gaze hadn't changed.

"Marcia," Elizabeth's tone made it less greeting than summons. "I was just explaining to the team that while Brett's departure is unfortunate, perhaps a change in leadership is exactly what this project needs."

The implied criticism hung in the air like a storm cloud. From the corner of her eye, Marcia caught James Anderson's subtle head shake. *Listening mode. Not defending mode.*

"Before we dive into project status," Marcia said, "I'd like to take a moment to acknowledge something." She looked around the table, making brief eye contact with each person. "I'm new to this role. You all have been living with this project for months. You understand its complexities in ways

I don't yet."

She noticed Liam's eyebrow raise slightly. Tessa, seated near the middle of the table, gave an encouraging nod.

"My first priority is to understand - from your perspective - where we are, what's working, and what isn't. I'm not here to sweep in with ready-made solutions before I understand the problems."

Elizabeth tapped her pen impatiently. "That's commendable, Marcia, but GFP has serious concerns about timeline and quality. We need answers, not more questions."

A man Marcia didn't recognise - presumably from GFP's executive team - leaned forward. "We're already three months behind. Our competitors are eating our lunch while we're stuck in implementation hell." His British accent gave the criticism extra weight.

James cleared his throat. "If I may, Malcolm. Marcia brings a structured approach that's proven effective on complex projects. Alpha didn't make this leadership change lightly."

Malcolm - who Marcia now recognised from her briefing as GFP's CIO - looked unconvinced. "Structured approach or not, we need to know when we'll be back on track."

Marcia felt the pressure mounting. Every instinct screamed to offer reassurance, to promise a quick recovery. Swallowing that spike of panic, she steadied her voice.

"Malcolm, Elizabeth - I understand completely. Three months behind means you're losing market share daily. That's real money and real opportunity cost."

Marcia felt her heart thud against her ribs - if she overpromised now and failed to deliver, her credibility would be shot. Every instinct screamed at her to play it safe and tell them what they wanted to hear. Instead, she remembered James's advice.

She opened her notebook. "I won't insult you by making

promises I can't keep. What I can commit to is this: by the end of the week, you'll have a comprehensive recovery plan with realistic timelines based on a thorough assessment, not wishful thinking."

Elizabeth's expression hardened. "One week just to make a plan? Brett told us yesterday he could get us back on track by the end of the month."

"And did you believe him?" Marcia asked quietly.

The room went perfectly still. Elizabeth and Malcolm exchanged glances.

"No," Elizabeth admitted finally. "We didn't."

Marcia inclined her head. "Then let me earn your trust by being honest from day one. I need time to work with the team, understand the technical blockers, and develop a plan that's aggressive but achievable."

She glanced at the team members. Some looked relieved at her candour; others remained wary.

"In the meantime," Marcia continued, "I'd like to hear from the team about our most critical issues. Not to problem-solve today, but to make sure I understand what we're facing."

For the next thirty minutes, Marcia facilitated a frank discussion. Noah, joining virtually from New York, detailed integration challenges with GFP's legacy systems. Tessa highlighted requirements inconsistencies that had led to rework. A Senior Quality Analyst named Sarah described test environment instabilities.

Liam remained silent until Marcia directly asked his assessment.

"The fundamental architecture has flaws," he said bluntly. "We're building on quicksand because we rushed the design phase to meet an arbitrary deadline."

Malcolm bristled. "That deadline wasn't arbitrary. It aligned with our quarterly reporting to shareholders."

"Which is exactly my point," Liam replied, his tone just shy of insubordinate. "Technical realities were sacrificed for a financial calendar."

Marcia sensed the conversation derailing. "This is exactly the kind of honest feedback I need," she interjected smoothly. "Liam's concerns about the architecture need to be addressed in our recovery plan."

She turned to a whiteboard and began categorising the issues they'd raised:

1. Technical challenges (integration, architecture)
2. Process issues (requirements, testing)
3. Communication gaps (cross-office, client-team)
4. Resource constraints (key roles unfilled)

"This isn't comprehensive," she acknowledged, "but it gives us a starting framework. My plan for this week is to dive deeper into each area with the relevant team members."

Elizabeth checked her watch. "We have quarterly earnings next month. The board is expecting a progress update on digital transformation."

"I understand," Marcia said. "Which is why I'll deliver the recovery plan on Friday, not a day later."

As the meeting wrapped up, Marcia noticed something surprising: the tension in the room had shifted. It wasn't gone, but it had transformed from defensive hostility to cautious assessment. They were taking her measure, waiting to see if she would be different from Brett.

Elizabeth lingered as others filed out. "Bold move," she said once they were alone. "Most new managers would have promised the world to make a good first impression."

"Would you have believed them?" Marcia asked.

"Not for a second." Elizabeth's stern expression relaxed slightly. "I remember you from the FreshWorks project. You were just a Team Leader then, but you never sugar-coated the challenges."

Marcia's lips curved in a faint, acknowledging smile. "I learned that lesson early."

"Your recovery plan," Elizabeth said, gathering her things, "needs to be exceptional. My leadership is questioning whether Alpha can deliver."

"Understood."

Elizabeth paused at the door. "This project is too important to fail, Marcia. I'm putting my reputation on the line by giving you this window of opportunity."

After Elizabeth left, Marcia sank into a chair, exhaling shakily. The adrenaline that had carried her through the meeting drained, leaving her hands trembling slightly. She allowed herself a wry, whispered remark to the empty room, "Welcome to management." She'd survived her first trial by fire by staying truthful.

After seeing Elizabeth out, James returned with two cups of coffee.

"You did well," he said, setting one in front of her. "Especially with Liam."

"He wasn't wrong about the architecture," Marcia said.

"No, but his timing could have been better. You redirected without dismissing his concerns - that was smart."

Marcia took a sip of coffee. "Elizabeth is giving me just enough rope to hang myself."

James chuckled. "That's how she operates. But she respects your honesty. That's a starting point."

Through the glass walls, Marcia could see the team gathering in small clusters, undoubtedly discussing the meeting. Liam stood alone, typing rapidly on his phone, his expression unreadable.

"What now?" she asked, looking at James.

"Now," James said, "you start exercising that first power

we discussed. Book one-on-ones with every key team member. Create a daily stand-up. Schedule architecture reviews with Liam and the technical leads. Use your authority to convene people in ways that will surface the truth quickly."

Marcia's eyes sharpened with focus, already drafting a calendar in her mind. "I'll need access to the New York team too."

"Book a flight for early next week," James suggested. "Some things need to be done in person."

As they left the conference room, Marcia felt the weight of expectation from both the client and the team. She had one week to develop a plan that would save the project, satisfy Elizabeth, and unite a fractured team.

One thing was becoming clear: the approach that had worked for her as a Team Leader would need to evolve. The tools were similar - structured communication, clear accountability, systematic problem-solving - but the application had to be more strategic, more deliberate.

The Power to Convene, as James called it, would be her first test. How she brought people together, what questions she asked, and how she used those interactions would set the tone for everything that followed.

Marcia opened her calendar and began to schedule the conversations that would give her the insights she needed. Her time was now her most valuable resource, and she intended to use it wisely.

✧   ✧   ✧

Marcia's office - Brett's old space - still felt like someone else's territory. Family photos had been removed, but ghostly rectangles on the wall marked where they'd hung. A forgotten Seattle Seahawks mug sat on the credenza, a thin film of coffee residue at the bottom.

She set her laptop on the desk and opened her calendar. A growing array of one-on-one meetings stared back at her, meticulously scheduled over the next three days. First up: Tessa Tanaka.

A soft knock at the door pulled her attention away from the screen.

"Got a minute?" It was Tessa, punctual as always, a tablet tucked under her arm.

"Perfect timing," Marcia said, gesturing to the chair across from her desk. "and thanks for the call last night."

Tessa sat down, her posture perfect. "Everyone's talking about the steering committee. You handled Elizabeth better than Brett ever did."

"That remains to be seen," Marcia said with a small smile. "I've bought us a week, that's all."

"One week of honesty is worth more than a month of false promises." Tessa tapped her tablet. "I've prepared some notes on the requirements issues I mentioned. Would you like me to walk you through them?"

For fifteen minutes, Tessa detailed how GFP's business stakeholders had been adding features without adjusting timelines. Each requirement change triggered a ripple effect through the development process, but Brett had been reluctant to push back.

"He was afraid of confrontation," Tessa explained. "Every time Elizabeth or Malcolm asked for something, he'd say yes without consulting the technical team."

Marcia jotted notes in her new leather notebook. "How's the team's morale been affected by all this?"

Tessa hesitated. "It's... not good. The Seattle team feels overwhelmed. The New York team feels disconnected. And there's a lot of finger-pointing."

"Between offices?"

"Between everyone." Tessa's usual composure cracked

slightly. "QA blames development for quality issues. Development blames analysis for unclear requirements. Everyone blamed Brett for poor planning. It's toxic."

Marcia underlined *team fragmentation* in her notebook and kept her void even. "Who on the team has the most influence - not just by title, but who do people actually listen to?"

"Liam, for technical matters," Tessa said without hesitation. "He can be difficult, but he knows the system architecture better than anyone. People respect his expertise, even when they don't like his delivery."

Marcia added to her earlier notes:

Liam - keep in the loop - knows system - expertise respected.

"And for process or team dynamics?"

Tessa paused. "Probably Noah in New York. He's a senior developer but also a natural mediator. When tensions rise, he's often the one who calms things down."

Again, she expanded her notes on Noah:

Noah - understands integration issues - natural mediator.

"And you?" Marcia asked. "Where do you fit in all this?"

A look of surprise crossed Tessa's face. "Me? I'm just a business analyst."

"Just?" Marcia raised an eyebrow. "You seem to have a pretty clear view of the whole situation."

Tessa shrugged. "I work with everyone - business stakeholders, developers, QA. It gives me perspective. But I'm not in a leadership position."

"Formal leadership and influence aren't always the same thing," Marcia noted. "Who brings the team together for lunch? Who organises the happy hours? Who do people vent to when they're frustrated?"

Tessa looked down at her tablet. "I guess I do some of that."

"That's influence," Marcia said. "and it's valuable."

Their conversation shifted to specific requirements issues. Tessa had meticulously documented each change request, along with its impact on the development timeline. The pattern was clear: GFP kept moving the goalposts, and Alpha kept trying to score on an increasingly impossible field.

"This is incredibly helpful," Marcia said as their time drew to a close. "One last question - what's one thing you would change immediately if you were in my position?"

Tessa didn't hesitate. "I'd create a change control process that includes impact analysis. Right now, changes come in, and we just absorb them without pushing back."

Marcia wrote this down. "Consider it on the list." She stood up, extending her hand. "Thank you, Tessa. I appreciate your candour."

After Tessa left, Marcia had just enough time to review her notes before her next meeting. Liam had been scheduled for 11:30 am, but at 11:25 am, her phone buzzed with a message from him: *In the middle of debugging a critical issue. Need to reschedule.*

Marcia took a moment, then typed back: *I'll come to you. Which floor?*

Three dots appeared, disappeared, then appeared again. Finally: *8th floor, northeast corner. But I'm not stopping what I'm doing.*

"Wouldn't expect you to," Marcia murmured to herself as she gathered her notebook.

The eighth floor was a stark contrast to the executive level. Instead of glass-walled offices and sleek conference rooms, it was a sprawling open space filled with developers, multiple monitors at each station, and a handful of standing desks. The energy was different too - less polished, more intense.

Liam wasn't hard to spot. In the corner, surrounded by two large screens displaying code, sat a man with uncombed hair and a Seattle University sweatshirt, headphones clamped over his ears. His fingers moved across the keyboard in rapid bursts, pausing occasionally as he squinted at the screen.

He reminded Marcia of Victor from the FreshWorks team, who didn't like his environment changing or unexpected surprises.

Marcia approached but didn't interrupt. She stood a respectful distance away, waiting for him to notice her.

After nearly a minute, Liam glanced up, frowned, then reluctantly removed his headphones.

"I said I needed to reschedule," he said, his tone making it clear that her presence was an unwelcome interruption.

"You did," Marcia agreed, pulling over a nearby empty chair. "But I thought it might be more productive to see what you're working on. Sometimes context matters more than formal meetings."

Liam looked at her sceptically, then shrugged and turned back to his screen. "Authentication service is failing intermittently. Been trying to reproduce the error for three hours."

Marcia stooped forward slightly, watching as he navigated through the code. "Mind if I ask a few questions while you work?"

"Depends on the questions," Liam muttered, his eyes not leaving the screen.

"Fair enough." Marcia opened her notebook. "In the steering committee, you mentioned architectural flaws. What specifically concerns you?"

Liam's typing slowed. He glanced at her, seemingly surprised by the technical nature of her question.

"We're using a distributed architecture that's too complex for what we need," he said after a moment. "Three separate authentication services when we could have used one. Microservices where monoliths would be simpler. It's overengineered."

"Why was it designed that way?"

Liam snorted. "Because it looked good in PowerPoint slides. GFP wanted a 'modern cloud-native architecture' without understanding what that actually means for their legacy systems."

His fingers resumed their dance across the keyboard as he spoke. "Brett didn't push back. He just said yes to whatever the client wanted, then told us to make it work."

Marcia watched as he navigated through log files. "And now you're dealing with integration issues?"

"Integration nightmares," Liam corrected. "The New York team built their services assuming one authentication model. We built ours assuming another. Now nothing talks to anything else properly."

A line of red text appeared on his screen. Liam leaned in, suddenly focused. "There it is," he murmured, more to himself than to Marcia. "Token expiration handling is inconsistent."

He began typing rapidly, adding comments to the code. Marcia remained silent, recognising the flow state of a developer onto something important.

After a few minutes, Liam sat back, a look of grim satisfaction on his face. "Confirmed. Timing mismatch - that's the cause."

"Can it be fixed?" Marcia asked.

"Of course it can be fixed," Liam said with mild irritation. "That's not the point. The point is we shouldn't have had this problem in the first place. A simpler architecture would have avoided it entirely."

He turned to face her fully for the first time. "Look, I know you're doing your rounds, trying to understand the project. But here's what you need to know: the foundation is shaky. We can patch it up, make it work, but it's going to be brittle. And brittleness means bugs, maintenance headaches, and ultimately, an unhappy client."

Marcia's outer eyes tightened, recognising the genuine concern beneath his prickly exterior. "If you could redesign parts of the architecture now, what would you prioritise?"

Liam looked surprised at the question. Most managers, Marcia guessed, had probably told him to just make the current design work.

"Authentication and identity management," he said after a moment. "Consolidate the services, create a single source of truth. It would take two weeks to rebuild, but save months of debugging later."

Marcia wrote this down. "What else?"

For the next fifteen minutes, Liam outlined architectural changes that could improve system stability. His initial reluctance gave way to engagement as he realised Marcia actually understood what he was talking about.

"You've got a technical background," he observed finally.

"I was a developer before I moved into management," Marcia confirmed. "Not as senior as you, but I understand the fundamentals."

Liam's expression lightened, a hint of respect edging in. "Brett was a project manager through and through. Gantt charts and status reports. Never understood why some things took longer than others."

A notification popped up on his screen. "I need to get back to this," he said, already reaching for his headphones.

"Of course," Marcia stood. "Thanks for making time."

As she turned to leave, Liam called after her. "If you're serious about fixing the architecture, I can put together a proposal. Trade-offs, timelines, the works."

Marcia turned back. "I'd appreciate that. When could you have it ready?"

"Monday," Liam said. "I'll need to coordinate with Noah in New York."

"Perfect," Marcia said. "I'm flying there Tuesday. Perhaps the three of us could review it together."

Liam nodded and slipped his headphones back on, already reimmersed in his code.

As Marcia made her way back to the elevator, she reflected on the conversation. Beneath Liam's abrasive exterior was a deeply knowledgeable engineer who cared about building the right solution. His frustration stemmed not from difficulty, but from seeing potential problems that others ignored.

Reaching her desk, she released a slow breath. Liam's blunt assessment had been daunting, but she'd glimpsed the passion behind his frustration. Marcia rubbed her neck, thinking, "If I can earn his trust and channel that intensity in a productive way, we might stand a chance." The thought was equal parts encouraging and intimidating.

Her phone buzzed with a calendar notification: lunch with James, followed by five more one-on-ones this afternoon. She had scheduled eight tomorrow and three early Thursday. Then the New York trip Tuesday and Wednesday.

The Power to Convene was already showing its value. Each conversation was filling in pieces of the puzzle, helping her understand not just the technical challenges but the human dynamics at play.

Tessa's diplomacy. Liam's technical brilliance and frustration. The cross-office tensions. The client's changing requirements.

Patterns were emerging, and with them, the beginnings of a plan. But she would need more than understanding to turn this project around. She would need to transform how these different personalities worked together - starting with healing the rift between Seattle and New York.

Marcia made a mental note: before she left for New York, she needed to set up a video call with Noah. If he was indeed the mediator Tessa described, he might be the key to bridging the divide between the teams, and perhaps between Liam's technical vision and Elizabeth's business imperatives as well.

✧   ✧   ✧

"So, you've met the dragon in his lair and lived to tell the tale," James said, joining Marcia at the end of an industrial style table at Pike Street Coffee, a small café two blocks from Alpha's headquarters. Rain had returned, pattering against the windows and sending lunchtime crowds scurrying inside.

Marcia smiled, warming her hands around a bowl of clam chowder. "Liam's not a dragon. Just a brilliant developer who's tired of being ignored."

"Spoken like someone who's never been on the receiving end of one of his code reviews." James unwrapped his sandwich. "Brett used to avoid him entirely."

"Which probably made everything worse," Marcia observed. "He actually opened up once we started talking about architecture."

"That doesn't surprise me. Liam wants to build things right. When managers focus only on timeline, he gets... prickly."

Marcia took a bite of her chowder, savouring the warmth. "I'm flying to New York on Tuesday. I need to understand what's happening in that office."

"Great, you got it booked," James dipped his head. "Brett tried to manage them remotely. Never really got a handle on the cross-office dynamics."

"Tessa mentioned someone named Noah who seems to be a calming influence. I've got a video call with him this afternoon."

James's eyebrows rose. "You've been busy."

"The Power to Convene, remember?" Marcia mouth quirked. "I've booked seventeen one-on-ones in three days. My calendar looks like a game of Tetris."

"Any patterns emerging yet?"

Marcia pulled out her notebook. "Several. The requirements process is broken - GFP keeps changing things without understanding the impact. The architecture has fundamental flaws. And there's a rift between the Seattle and New York teams."

"That's a lot to tackle in one week," James said.

"I don't need to solve everything by Friday. I just need a credible plan that Elizabeth and Malcolm will accept."

James took a sip of his coffee. "Speaking of Elizabeth, Robert mentioned she called him after the steering committee."

Marcia froze mid-bite. "What did she say?"

"That you were either impressively honest or setting up excuses for failure." James said, his voice mild. "Robert told her to trust the process."

"That's not exactly a ringing endorsement," Marcia said, putting down her spoon.

"It's better than you think. Elizabeth respects boundaries. Brett never set any."

Marcia's phone lit up - Sarah, the QA tester she was meeting at 1:30 pm. *Can we push back 30 minutes? Dealing with a critical bug.*

Marcia quickly responded: *No problem. Do you need help?*

The reply came seconds later: *Surprised you asked. Yes, actually. Liam's fix broke something else. Could use a buffer between dev and QA.*

"Everything okay?" James asked, noticing her frown.

"Integration issues," Marcia said. "Liam fixed an authentication problem, but it broke something downstream. Sarah needs a buffer."

James checked his watch. "You should go. First week as Delivery Manager, you need to be visible during crises. Even small ones."

"What about our lunch?"

"We've covered the essentials," James said, wrapping up the remainder of his sandwich. "Besides, this is how you build credibility - being present when the team needs support."

Marcia glanced at James, gathering her things. "I owe you a lunch."

"You can buy next time," James said cheerfully. "Go be the leader they need."

✧ ✧ ✧

The QA area on the seventh floor was less spacious than the development section above. Sarah Okoro - a woman in her forties with auburn hair and glasses on a chain - was standing over a younger tester's shoulder, pointing at something on his screen.

"The error only appears when you submit the form with special characters," she was saying. "Try an ampersand."

"Marcia," she said, looking up. "Thanks for coming down. This is Lucas, our newest team member."

The young man offered a tentative smile, clearly uncomfortable having a manager observe his work.

"What are we looking at?" Marcia asked, keeping her tone casual.

Sarah sighed. "Liam's authentication fix addressed the

token expiration, but now form submissions with special characters are failing. It's blocking our regression testing."

Marcia studied the screen. "Is Liam aware of the issue?"

"I sent him a message twenty minutes ago," Sarah said, frustration edging her voice. "No response. Typical."

Lucas shifted uncomfortably in his chair.

"Mind if I try something?" Marcia asked him.

"Uh, sure," Lucas said, sliding his chair to the side.

Marcia leaned over and examined the error message, then opened the browser console. After checking a few logs, she said, "Character encoding issue."

"Liam's fix is probably doing proper validation now, but something in the form submission isn't handling special characters correctly," she added.

Marcia straightened up. "Let's go talk to him together."

Sarah looked surprised. "You want to go up there now?"

"Unless you have a better idea for getting this resolved quickly?"

"No, it's just..." Sarah hesitated. "Brett would have had us file a ticket and wait."

"And how long would that typically take?"

"Days, sometimes."

Marcia gestured toward the elevator. "Then let's try something different."

Upstairs, they found Liam still at his workstation, headphones on, oblivious to their approach. Marcia tapped him gently on the shoulder.

He turned, irritation flashing across his face until he recognised Marcia. His eyes narrowed when he spotted Sarah.

"Let me guess," he said, removing his headphones. "My fix broke something."

"Character encoding in form submissions," Marcia said before Sarah could respond. "Special characters are causing validation errors."

Liam's irritation shifted to interest. "You checked the console logs?"

Marcia tilted her head. "UTF-8 encoding issue, looks like. I thought a quick conversation might be faster than ticket ping-pong."

Liam regarded her briefly, then turned to his computer. "Show me the exact error."

Sarah stepped forward, more cautiously than Marcia had expected. "Lucas reproduced it with an ampersand in the name field," She entered an ampersand, submitted the form, and reproduced the error.

They worked together on the issue for ten minutes. Liam quickly identified the problem - his authentication fix had tightened input validation, but the form processing assumed a different encoding standard.

"Easy fix," he said finally, fingers zipping over the keyboard. "We need to standardise the encoding across all services."

Marcia noticed how Liam's demeanour changed when focusing on a technical problem. The prickliness faded, replaced by focus and clarity. Sarah, too, became more engaged and less defensive as they worked through the solution.

"That should do it," Liam said, pushing his chair back. "Try it now."

Sarah messaged Lucas, who ran the test again.

"It worked," Sarah confirmed, genuine relief in her voice. "Thanks, Liam."

He nodded, already reaching for his headphones. "Next time, just come up and show me. Tickets take too long."

After they left Liam's workspace, Sarah turned to Marcia in the hallway by the elevators.

"That was unexpectedly productive," she admitted.

"Usually, there's a lot more friction between dev and QA."

"Sometimes the medium is the message," Marcia said. "Ticket systems have their place, but face-to-face communication cuts through barriers."

Sarah thought it over. "Brett was big on 'following process.' Everything had to go through proper channels."

"Processes should serve people, not the other way around," Marcia said. "For critical issues, direct communication is often faster."

As they returned to the QA area, Sarah seemed to relax. "I've been at Alpha for six years," she said. "Seen a lot of managers come and go. Your approach is different."

Marcia wasn't sure if that was a compliment. "Different good or different concerning?"

Sarah smiled for the first time. "Good, I think. You're hands-on without being controlling. Most managers swing too far in either direction."

Back at Lucas's desk, the young tester had completed several more tests successfully.

"No more encoding errors," he reported. "Everything's passing now."

"Great work, everyone," Marcia said. "Sarah, let's reschedule our one-on-one for later this afternoon?"

"Actually," Sarah said, "I think we just had it. You learned more about how we work in the last thirty minutes than you would have in a formal meeting."

Marcia lifted a hand, conceding the point. "Fair point. But I'd still like to hear your thoughts on the QA process more broadly. How about 4:30 pm?"

"Works for me," Sarah agreed.

As Marcia headed back to her office, she reflected on what had just happened. An impromptu collaboration had accomplished in minutes what might have taken days through formal channels. More importantly, she'd witnessed firsthand the tension between development and QA - and a potential path to improving it.

Her calendar showed a video call with Noah from the New York office at 3 pm. If Liam was the technical anchor in Seattle, Noah might be the key to understanding the New York team's perspective.

She had one more meeting before then - a check-in with James to prepare for her New York trip. As she walked into his office, she found him reviewing GFP's contract.

"Perfect timing," he said, looking up. "I was just double-checking something about the New York deliverables."

"Find anything interesting?" Marcia asked, settling into a chair.

"The New York team is responsible for customer-facing components. Seattle handles the back-end services." James pushed the contract aside. "Classic divide that creates natural tension."

"When front-end features don't work, users blame the interface," Marcia said, understanding the dynamic. "Even if the problem is in the back-end."

"Exactly. And from what I've gathered, the New York team has been taking the heat for integration issues they didn't cause."

Marcia thought about Liam's authentication fix and its ripple effects. "That tracks with what I just saw with an encoding issue."

James dipped in agreement. "Your trip to New York is more important than I realised. The division isn't just geographical - it's architectural and cultural."

"Noah might help bridge that gap," Marcia said. "I'm speaking with him in an hour."

"Good." James handed her a folder. "These are the key New York stakeholders. I've highlighted the ones you should prioritise while you're there."

Marcia opened the folder, scanning the names and roles on the People Map James had assembled. "Any political landmines I should know about?"

"Their office director, Alan Prescott," James pointed to a name near the top. "He's protective of his team and wasn't thrilled when Brett managed them remotely from Seattle. He might see your visit as interference."

"How should I handle him?"

"Be transparent about your goals. Make it clear you're there to understand, not to blame or take over."

Marcia jotted it down. "Anything else?"

"One more thing," James said, his expression growing serious. "Robert wants an update on your recovery plan. Just to make sure you're on track for Friday's deadline with Elizabeth."

Marcia felt a twinge of anxiety. She'd made progress, but so far interviews had raised more questions than answers.

"I'll pull together what I have so far," she said. "When does he want to meet?"

"Wednesday end-of-day." James held her gaze, reassuringly. "Don't worry. He doesn't expect a finished plan yet. Just a clear direction."

As Marcia left James's office, she mentally composed what she'd tell Robert. The project faced significant challenges: architectural flaws, process breakdowns, team divisions. But there were also strengths: Liam's technical expertise, Tessa's organisational skills, Sarah's quality focus, and potentially Noah's mediation abilities.

Back in her office, Marcia began organising her notes. The whiteboard from her condo now stood against one wall, covered with categories and connections. She added new insights from her conversation with Sarah and the interaction with Liam.

Patterns were emerging more clearly now. The project

wasn't failing because of a single fatal flaw, but from a series of compounding issues:

1. Requirements constantly changed but timelines didn't
2. Architecture was more complex than necessary
3. Teams were divided by geography, function, and communication style
4. Previous leadership avoided difficult conversations

As she prepared for her call with Noah, Marcia felt both the weight of the challenge and the first stirrings of a plan. What she needed now was to strengthen bridges between teams while removing barriers to progress.

Her phone buzzed with a calendar reminder: fifteen minutes until her call with New York.

A knock at the door. Liam hovered in the doorway, a printout in hand. "QA's flagged another regression in the overnight build. They're saying the auth changes are brittle."

Marcia checked the time. "Log the path and the steps to reproduce. I'll speak to Sarah after my call with New York. For now, let's avoid tickets ping-pong - just capture the specifics."

"Right," he said, already turning back. The interruption left a faint pulse of tension behind - noise she couldn't ignore for long.

She shut her door, set her phone to silent, and laid out her notes and notebook for the call. For the next hour, the regression would have to wait.

✧ ✧ ✧

Marcia adjusted her webcam and checked the time: 2:58 pm in Seattle, 5:58 pm in New York. She'd deliberately scheduled the call for the end of Noah's workday, hoping he might be more candid when not surrounded by colleagues.

Her screen flickered as the video call connected. Noah Vasques appeared, backlit by Manhattan's early evening glow. He was younger than Marcia had expected - early thirties at most - with dark hair pulled back in a short ponytail and a neatly trimmed beard. A worn Yankees cap sat on his head, and behind him, the New York office looked markedly different from Seattle's - more compact, with city skyscrapers pressing close to the windows providing a haze of office lights and reflections of neon from the streets below.

"Hello from the East Coast," he said with a slight smile. "You're the talk of both offices, you know."

"Good talk or concerned talk?" Marcia asked, grinning.

"Bit of both." Noah adjusted his cap. "The New York team is... cautiously optimistic. Brett wasn't exactly a frequent visitor."

"So I've heard. Which is why I'm coming on Tuesday. I'd like to understand the New York perspective firsthand."

Noah's eyebrows rose slightly. "That's, great. Brett's approach was more 'send me your status reports.'"

"Reports don't tell the whole story," Marcia said. "Especially when there are cross-office challenges."

Noah's expression shifted, becoming more guarded. "What have you heard about our challenges?"

"That Seattle builds the back-end services, you build the customer-facing components, and when things don't integrate properly, your team takes the blame from users." Marcia kept her tone matter-of-fact, not accusatory.

Noah leaned back in his chair, studying her. "Well, you've done your homework. Yes, that's the core issue. It's been frustrating."

"Tell me more," Marcia said, opening her notebook.

For the next twenty minutes, Noah outlined the New

York team's experience. Unlike Liam's blunt criticism, Noah's assessment was measured and diplomatic, but the underlying frustrations were clear. The Seattle team made architectural decisions without consulting New York. Changes to APIs weren't communicated in advance. When bugs appeared in the user interface, GFP blamed the front-end team, even when the root cause was in the back-end services.

"It sounds like a communication breakdown more than a technical issue," Marcia observed.

"Precisely." Noah didn't hesitate. "We have talented developers here. So does Seattle. But we're not working as one team."

"I spoke with Liam earlier today," Marcia said, watching for Noah's reaction.

A flicker of tension crossed his face. "Ah, Liam. Brilliant developer. Not always the easiest collaborator."

"He mentioned you two might work on an architectural proposal. Something about consolidating the authentication services?"

"He reached out about that, yes." Noah sounded surprised. "I didn't expect him to follow through."

"Would you be willing to collaborate with him on it? I'd like to review it with both of you when I'm in New York."

Noah thought it over. "I can make that work. It would be a good starting point for better cross-office collaboration."

Marcia jotted this down, then asked, "You've been described as someone who calms tensions when they arise. Is that a fair assessment?"

Noah laughed, looking slightly embarrassed. "I suppose so. In this industry, technical skills are common. The ability to work well with others is rarer."

"That's an insight many managers miss," Marcia said.

"From what I've gathered, the technical solutions exist for most of our problems. It's the human dynamics that are complicated."

"Exactly." Noah leaned forward, warming to the topic. "Take Liam, for example. His architectural concerns are valid. But his delivery puts people on the defensive, so they resist his ideas on principle."

"And you've been bridging that gap?"

"Trying to." Noah shrugged. "I translate 'Liam-speak' into something less confrontational. He knows the right solutions; he just hasn't mastered presenting them in a way that builds consensus."

Marcia set her pen down, seeing the dynamic more clearly. "What's your relationship like with Alan Prescott?" she asked, referring to the New York office director James had mentioned.

Noah's expression shifted again, becoming more careful. "Alan is... protective of the New York team. He respects our technical skills, but he's frustrated with how the project has been managed from Seattle."

"Will he see my visit as interference?"

"That depends on your approach," Noah said diplomatically. "If you come to impose Seattle's vision, yes. If you come to understand and address our concerns..." He left the sentence unfinished.

"I'm not coming with preconceived solutions," Marcia assured him. "My goal is to understand both perspectives, then develop a plan that works for everyone."

Noah seemed satisfied. "Then I think Alan will be receptive. He just wants the New York team to be treated as equal partners, not order-takers."

"That's completely reasonable," Marcia said. "Any advice for my visit?"

"Meet with the team as a group, but also make time for

one-on-ones," Noah suggested. "Some people won't speak openly in front of colleagues. And try to join us for lunch or after-work drinks. The informal conversations are often more revealing than the official meetings."

"I'll keep that in mind," Marcia said, making a note. "One last question: if you were in my position, what one change would you make immediately to improve the project?"

Noah had an immediate answer. "Create joint architecture and design sessions between the offices. Twice a week, video call, mandatory attendance from tech leads in both locations. We need to be making decisions together, not in silos."

"Consider it done," Marcia said, writing this down. "I'll set up the first one for next week."

As they wrapped up the call, Noah's manner had become noticeably more open. "I'm looking forward to meeting in person on Tuesday," he said. "The team will appreciate that you made the trip."

"I'll see you then," Marcia said. "And thank you for your candour. It's been incredibly helpful."

After the call ended, Marcia sat back and reviewed her notes. The picture was becoming clearer. The Seattle and New York teams had fallen into a classic pattern of office tribalism, exacerbated by distance and distinct roles. Each side saw the other as the problem, creating a cycle of blame rather than collaboration.

Brett's remote management style had widened the gap. By failing to bring the teams together regularly, he'd allowed separate cultures and processes to develop. And by avoiding difficult conversations with both the client and Liam, he'd created an environment where real issues festered rather than being resolved.

Marcia checked the time. She had her one-on-one with Sarah in twenty minutes, then two more team members after that. Tomorrow would bring another full day of interviews, followed by her end-of-day update with Robert.

Her phone vibrated with a text from James: *How did the call with Noah go?*

Well, she typed back, kicking herself that she forgot to take her phone off silent. *He's as diplomatic as advertised. Confirms the Seattle-NY divide is our biggest team issue.*

James replied almost immediately: *No surprise there. Have you thought about your approach for the Robert update meeting?*

Marcia hadn't, not fully. She had pages of notes but no coherent plan yet. *Working on it tonight,* she responded. *Need to synthesize everything I've learned so far.*

Don't stay up too late, came James's reply. *This is a marathon, not a sprint.*

Marcia set the phone aside, appreciating his concern. She was already feeling the weight of responsibility. The GFP project wasn't just a technical challenge; it was a complex human system with competing priorities, personalities, and perspectives.

She turned to her whiteboard, adding new insights from her conversation with Noah. The New York team's frustrations mirrored Seattle's, just from a different angle. Both sides felt unheard and undervalued. Both had valid concerns about the project's direction.

The question wasn't which side was right - it was how to get them working together toward a common goal.

Marcia stood back, markers in hand. The chaos of notes - complaints, failure points, ideas - swirled in her mind. *There's too much... how do we tackle it all?* she thought, massaging her temple. Then slowly, she began grouping the problems: immediate fires in one cluster, systemic issues in another, future improvements in a third. A pattern emerged.

She capped the marker, uncertain. *We don't have to solve everything at once... but what do I call this?*

A knock at her door interrupted her thoughts. "Got a minute?" James asked. "Thought I could help with synthesis."

"Sure, come in - though I'm expecting Sarah any moment," she cautioned.

He studied the board for thirty seconds, then took a marker and wrote three words across the top:

Stabilise → Accelerate → Sustain

"Here's the language for what you've already mapped," he said, underlining each. "First we stop the bleeding and make the work visible. Then we build safe speed. Then we make the gains boring."

Marcia exhaled; the clusters clicked into place.

"I'll pop back to walk through these phases," James added, capping the marker.

"That would be great - thanks James," Marcia said as Sarah arrived in her doorway, exactly on time for their rescheduled meeting.

"I'll leave you two to catch up." James gave a small nod and slipped out.

"Ready for round two?" Sarah asked with a smile.

Marcia set her notes aside and straightened, energy returning to her posture. "Absolutely. Come on in."

Sarah stepped in with a printout. "The core module still has a few critical defects. If Malcolm or Elizabeth ask about quality, I'm not sure we can honestly say everything's on track." Her voice dropped.

"Good you told me," Marcia said. "If they ask, I need you to speak up about the bugs - and say what we're doing to fix them."

"Really?" Sarah hesitated. "I thought we might downplay it until it's fixed. I don't want to get blamed for bad news."

Marcia shook her head. "Silence is riskier. We owe them the truth and a plan. I'll back you - and it should come from the person who knows the details best."

Sarah drew a breath, then nodded. "Okay. I'll say it plainly, and outline the fix steps."

"Good," Marcia said. "That's how we build trust."

Sarah settled into the chair opposite.

"So," Marcia said, "tell me about the quality challenges you're seeing, and what you think we should do about them."

Sarah rubbed her eyes and admitted, "My team is pretty burned out. We've been running on fumes - working weekends, late nights - and it still feels like we're always behind." A tired smile. "Right now, most of us are just bracing for the next hit."

Marcia listened, adding another piece to the puzzle. Wednesday's meeting with Robert loomed, but for now, she focused entirely on the conversation in front of her.

One meeting at a time. One insight at a time. That was how she would turn this project around.

The sheer weight of what lay ahead pressed on her. Every conversation had revealed another fracture - burnout, distrust, technical instability, a team stretched past its limits. She could already feel the expectations tightening around her. What if she couldn't pull this back together? What if one week wasn't enough to prove she belonged in a role this visible, this unforgiving?

I've bought us one week, she thought - *now I have to earn it.*

Chapter 2
The Power to Convene

Every leader has a hidden superpower: the ability to gather people. A simple calendar invite can shift momentum, mend divides, or spark breakthroughs. Convening isn't scheduling - it's summoning the right voices into the same room, at the right time, for the conversations that change everything.

✧ ✧ ✧

Make the room smaller so decisions get bigger.

✧ ✧ ✧

Marcia noticed a few guarded glances as everyone joined the hybrid morning stand-up - some in-person and some online. Daily cross-office check-ins weren't the norm here. The atmosphere was frosty - developers huddled virtually on one side, QA staff on the other, each group eyeing the other warily. She could almost feel the invisible wall between them.

The politeness cracked when Sarah mentioned that several recent builds had failed overnight.

"We're testing the same fixes again and again," she said, trying to keep her tone neutral.

Liam folded his arms. "Maybe if the requirements stopped changing mid-sprint, the builds would hold."

He didn't say it aloud, but a flicker of worry crossed his face - the old fear resurfacing: that he'd let the team down again.

"They change because of your design shortcuts," Sarah shot back before she could stop herself.

The room fell silent.

Marcia stepped in, recognising a turning point. "Let's take a breath," she said evenly. "Liam's right that clarity matters. Sarah's right that we can't stabilise something still shifting underneath. This isn't about fault - it's about flow. We'll fix it together."

The group relaxed slightly. It wasn't the first time Sarah and Liam had clashed, but it was the first time they'd done so openly - and for Marcia, that honesty was progress.

She offered a warm grin. "Alright, everyone," she said, deliberately bridging the divide, "we're all here to solve the same puzzle."

Marcia continued, "Our mission: name one in-progress item in the *Today* column each, each *Blocked* has an owner, and together move one to *Cleared* before lunch so testing can resume."

At the side wall, Marcia rolled out a portable whiteboard she'd labelled Momentum Board. Three columns:

Today | Blocked | Cleared

"Let's start with a quick round: what's the biggest headache you need solved today?" She said lightly, uncapping a marker.

A few people looked startled by the informal opener.

Liam called out the login bug; Marcia jotted the fix under Today. When Sarah flagged a test harness issue, Marcia slid its card under Blocked and wrote *Owner: Sarah* beneath it.

As the mood shifted, a murmur of cross-team conversation replaced the tension.

"Visibility beats guesswork," Marcia said. "Small things. Done well. Every day." Heads tilted toward the board; a low buzz softened. Work had somewhere obvious to go.

As the team dispersed, Marcia caught Lucas, a junior analyst, hovering near the doorway with a discouraged look.

"I know that stand-up felt rough," she said, walking alongside him. "Do you know why we hold these every day?"

Lucas shrugged. "To give status updates, I guess."

"Partly." Marcia kept her tone steady, inviting rather than corrective. "We want to make sure every voice is heard and problems surface early."

Lucas's frown eased. "Hadn't thought of it like that."

"It isn't about giving *me* updates," she said. "It's about sharing with each other so we can act as a team. Next update, try flagging one thing that's blocking you or someone else."

"Thanks," Lucas said, nodding.

If convening could surface the truth, she'd need air cover to act on it. Robert would get the honest read next.

"Small room, clear mission."

"Decide X by Y so Z can move."

✧ ✧ ✧

Robert Miller's corner office made Marcia's new space look utilitarian by comparison. Floor-to-ceiling windows offered a stunning panorama of the Sound, with ferries gliding across the water like toys in a bathtub. A collection of antique maps decorated one wall - Pacific Northwest territories from the 1800s, each one showing how understanding of the region had evolved with more exploration.

"Thanks for making time," Robert said, gesturing for Marcia to take a seat at his small conference table. "James tells me you've been quite thorough in your assessment. Seventeen one-on-ones in two days?"

"Fourteen so far," Marcia corrected. "Three more tomorrow."

"Impressive," Robert said, settling into his chair. "Most new managers would still be decorating their office."

Marcia gave a small shrug. "My office still has Brett's sports memorabilia. I've been a bit busy."

"So I've heard." Robert's expression grew more serious. "The team says you've been hands-on. Jumping in to solve technical issues, facilitating conversations between development and QA. Even Liam Everett seems cautiously impressed."

"It's early days," Marcia cautioned. "But I'm starting to see the patterns."

"That's what I wanted to discuss." Robert glanced at his watch. "I've got thirty minutes before my evening call with the board. Walk me through your preliminary findings and your approach for Friday's presentation to Elizabeth."

Marcia opened her laptop, pulled up a simple slide deck, and shared it to the room's display. The first slide showed just four categories: Technical, Process, People, and Client.

"I've organised my assessment into four areas," she explained. "Each has distinct challenges, but they're all interconnected."

Robert scanned the categories. "Good framework. Start with technical, since that's usually the most straightforward."

"Actually, it's not," Marcia said. "The technical issues are just symptoms of deeper problems."

Robert raised an eyebrow, intrigued. "Go on."

Marcia clicked to the next slide, which showed a simplified architecture diagram. "The system is more complex than it needs to be. Three separate authentication services instead of one unified approach. Microservices where monoliths would work better. The complexity isn't serving any business purpose - it's creating integration nightmares."

"Why was it designed this way?"

"Because GFP asked for a 'modern cloud-native architecture' without understanding what that meant for their legacy systems. And Brett said yes without pushing back."

Robert's expression darkened slightly. "We're not in the business of saying no to clients, Marcia."

"I'm not suggesting we should have," Marcia clarified. "But we should have educated them on the trade-offs and proposed alternatives that would meet their actual needs, not just their buzzword bingo card."

A hint of a smile crept onto Robert's face. "Fair point. What's your proposed solution?"

"Liam and Noah are working on an architectural simplification proposal. I'm reviewing it with them when I'm in New York next week. We can't rebuild everything, but we can consolidate key services to reduce integration issues."

Approval warmed Robert's voice. "You've got Liam and Noah collaborating already? I'm impressed."

"They both want the project to succeed," Marcia said. "They just needed someone to bring them together."

She moved to the next slide, labelled "Process Issues."

"The requirements process is broken," she explained.

"GFP continuously changes scope without understanding the impact on timeline or quality. There's no formal change control, so the team absorbs these changes without pushing back."

"Elizabeth won't like hearing that," Robert warned.

"She already knows it," Marcia countered. "She's just never had anyone quantify the impact." She clicked to a graph showing how requirement changes correlated with missed deadlines. "This isn't about saying no to changes. It's about making the consequences visible so GFP can make informed decisions."

Robert studied the graph. "You're suggesting a more formal change control process?"

"Yes, but with transparency, not bureaucracy. Simple impact assessments for each change, clearly communicated to Elizabeth and Malcolm. They decide if the trade-off's worth it; we stop pretending we can absorb everything without consequences."

"And you think Elizabeth will accept this?"

Marcia's voice was confident. "Based on my experience with her, yes. She doesn't like surprises or false promises. She'd rather have hard truths than pleasant fiction."

Robert looked impressed. "You seem to have Elizabeth's measure. What about the people issues?"

The next slide showed a simple diagram of the team structure, with Seattle and New York represented as separate bubbles with minimal connection points.

"The geographical divide has become a cultural one," Marcia explained. "Seattle builds back-end services. New York builds customer-facing components. When integration issues arise, each side blames the other. There's no sense of shared ownership."

"That's been an ongoing challenge," Robert admitted. "Brett tried to manage it from Seattle, but the New York team always felt like second-class citizens."

"They still do," Marcia said. "That's why I'm going there next week. But beyond showing up in person, we need structured collaboration. Joint architecture sessions, cross-office pairings for critical features, and a unified delivery process instead of separate workflows."

"That sounds resource-intensive," Robert noted.

"Less expensive than rework and missed deadlines," Marcia countered. "The cost of disconnection is higher than the cost of collaboration."

Robert let the point settle, his gaze returning to the slide. "Valid point. What about the client relationship?"

The final slide showed a simple diagram of communication flows between Alpha and GFP, with multiple disconnected lines.

"Too many communication channels, no single source of truth," Marcia explained. "GFP gets different stories from different people. Brett tried to control all client communication himself, but he became a bottleneck. We need a structured approach that involves the right people at the right time."

"Such as?"

"Weekly status meetings with the full team and client stakeholders. Biweekly steering committee with executives. Daily check-ins between counterparts - Alpha QA with GFP QA, for example. Create transparency without overwhelming anyone."

Robert tapped his fingers on the table, processing the information. "This is comprehensive, Marcia. More thorough than I expected after just three days." He paused. "But a diagnosis isn't a cure. What's your actual recovery plan?"

Marcia clicked to a slide titled "90-Day Recovery Plan." It outlined three phases:

Phase 1 (Weeks 1-4): Stabilise
- Implement change control process
- Begin architectural simplification
- Establish cross-office collaboration structure
- Clarify roles and responsibilities

Phase 2 (Weeks 5-8): Accelerate
- Complete priority architectural improvements
- Implement automated testing for critical paths
- Cross-train team members
- Reset timeline expectations with GFP

Phase 3 (Weeks 9-12): Sustain
- Deliver major milestone (Core Banking Module)
- Document lessons learned
- Transfer knowledge across teams
- Establish long-term governance model

"The key insight," Marcia explained, "is that we can't fix everything at once. We need to Stabilise the patient before we can cure the disease. By focusing on the most critical issues first - change control, architecture, and team alignment - we create breathing room to address the rest."

Robert studied the plan, his expression thoughtful. "When do we deliver the first major milestone to GFP?"

"Week 10," Marcia said confidently. "Three months from now. That's realistic given our current velocity and the improvements we'll implement. We could promise earlier, but we'd be setting ourselves up to fail."

"Elizabeth wants it sooner. Malcolm too."

"I know," Marcia acknowledged. "But promising what we can't deliver will only damage their trust further. If we exceed expectations and deliver early, that's a win. If we set unrealistic expectations and miss them again, that's a catastrophe."

Marcia's structured vision transformed the conversation - what had seemed like a hopeless tangle now looked like a clear roadmap. She could see Robert's scepticism give way to confidence

Robert was silent for a moment, a smile tugging at the corner of hismouth. "You know, this is exactly why I put you in this role. Most managers would be scrambling to promise the moon right now."

"The moon is lovely," Marcia said, with a quick, quiet chuckle, "but hard to deliver on schedule."

Robert laughed, then glanced at his watch. "I've got five minutes before my board call. What do you need from me to make this work?"

"Two things," Marcia said without hesitation. "First, support with Elizabeth. I need you to back me up when I present this timeline, even if she pushes for something faster."

"Done," Robert didn't hesitate. "And second?"

"Resources for knowledge transfer between offices. I want to send Seattle developers to New York and bring New York developers here, at least for short periods. That will cost more than video calls, but it will pay dividends in team cohesion."

Robert evaluated the idea. "Approved, within reason. Work with finance to set a budget."

"Thank you."

"Don't thank me yet," Robert said, standing as his phone buzzed with a reminder. "The hard part starts Friday when you present this to Elizabeth and Malcolm. They're not going to be thrilled about a three-month timeline."

"I know," Marcia said, gathering her laptop. "But they'll respect the honesty and the clear plan."

"I hope you're right." Robert walked her to the door.

"One more thing, Marcia. What's your biggest concern? The thing that keeps you up at night about this project?"

Marcia thought through the question carefully. "Team engagement," she said finally. "We've got good people who've been beaten down by missed deadlines and blame. Rebuilding their confidence and sense of ownership is my biggest challenge."

Robert stroked his chin, clearly pleased with her answer. "Focus there, then. Systems and processes matter, but engaged people will find solutions to problems we haven't even identified yet."

As Marcia headed back to her office, she felt a surprising sense of calm. The meeting had gone better than expected. Robert's support was crucial, especially for the upcoming presentation to Elizabeth.

Her phone vibrated – Liam had sent an update: *Architectural proposal is progressing. Noah has good insights on API consistency.*

Marcia let the screen fade to black. The collaboration she'd nudged into motion was already bearing fruit. By bringing Liam and Noah together, she'd created the conditions for solutions to emerge naturally.

That, she realised, was the essence of what James had called 'The Power to Convene'. It wasn't just about putting meetings on calendars. It was about creating the right conversations between the right people - conversations that wouldn't happen otherwise.

For the first time since taking the role, Marcia felt confident in her approach. Not because she had all the answers, but because she was asking the right questions and bringing the right people together to find solutions.

That, perhaps, was what leadership was really about.

✧ ✧ ✧

The sky was already darkening as Marcia left Alpha's building that evening. Seattle's early winter sunset painted the clouds in shades of pink and purple, a stark contrast to the mounting grey she'd felt around the GFP project when she'd first stepped into her new role just days ago.

Her phone buzzed with a text from James: *How'd it go with Robert?*

Better than expected, she replied. *He approved the recovery plan approach and the cross-office travel budget.*

Told you he would, James texted back. *He didn't promote you to play it safe.*

Her step felt lighter as she walked to her car. James's confidence in her abilities continued to be a steadying force. As she drove home, she mentally rehearsed her presentation for Elizabeth and Malcolm on Friday. Robert's support was crucial, but ultimately, she needed to convince GFP that her plan was solid.

At home, Marcia kicked off her shoes and headed straight for her whiteboard. She'd added so many notes that she could barely find space for new insights. Taking a step back, she snapped a photo of the entire board before erasing half of it to make room for her New York preparation.

Her laptop chimed with an email notification. It was from Tessa:

Marcia,

I thought you might find this useful for your trip to New York. I've prepared a summary of all the requirement changes GFP has requested in the last three months, categorised by impact and originating stakeholder. The highlighted items came from NY-based GFP executives and might come up in your discussions there.

<GFP_requirement_changes_and_impact_Q4.xlsx>
Let me know if you need anything else before your trip.
Tessa

Attached was a meticulously organised spreadsheet - exactly the kind of data Marcia needed for her conversations in New York. She hadn't asked Tessa for this; the business analyst had taken the initiative on her own.

Marcia sent a quick reply:

Tessa,
This is incredibly helpful and exactly what I needed. Thank you for taking the initiative. Would you be available for a quick coffee tomorrow to discuss which of these changes had the biggest ripple effects? I'd like to highlight specific examples in my presentation to Elizabeth.
Marcia

Within minutes, Tessa had responded and they'd set up a 9:30 am coffee meeting.

As Marcia was about to close her laptop, another email arrived - this one from Liam:

Initial architecture proposal attached. Noah's input was valuable (surprisingly). We're focusing on authentication consolidation first, with API standardisation as phase two. Need 30 minutes tomorrow to walk through technical details before you head to NY.
-L

Marcia chuckled under her breath. The terse message was so typical of Liam's communication style – dry, efficient, faintly begrudging in its praise. The fact that Liam and Noah were collaborating without her direct involvement suggested the bridge-building was already working.

She checked her calendar for tomorrow and found a 30-minute gap at 2 pm. She quickly sent a meeting invitation to Liam, copying Noah so he could join virtually from New York.

Her calendar for tomorrow was now completely full, from her 8 am stand-up (which she'd instituted on her second day) through to a further check-in with Robert. In between were the remaining one-on-ones, follow up meetings, schedule planning, reviewing the budget forecast, and technical reviews.

As she prepared for bed, Marcia reflected on what she'd accomplished already. She hadn't solved all the project's problems - far from it - but she'd created movement where there had been stagnation. Liam and Noah were collaborating. The Seattle QA and development teams were talking directly rather than through tickets. Team members like Tessa were beginning to show initiative rather than waiting for direction.

All of this had started with a simple act: putting the right meetings on people's calendars and creating space for productive conversations.

✧   ✧   ✧

Thursday morning brought Seattle's typical winter rain, a steady drizzle that beaded on Marcia's umbrella as she walked from her car to Alpha's building. The lobby was busy with consultants grabbing coffee before heading to client sites, their Alpha-branded laptop bags a sign of the company's growth over the past few years.

"Morning, Marcia!" called a cheerful voice. It was Sarah from QA, waiting by the elevator with a cardboard tray of coffee cups. "Heading up to the stand-up?"

"Wouldn't miss it," Marcia said with a smile. "What's with

all the coffee?"

"Team morale booster," Sarah explained as they stepped into the elevator. "The QA team's been putting in extra hours to catch up on regression testing. Thought they could use a pick-me-up."

This was new. In their one-on-one, Sarah had described a team that felt undervalued and overwhelmed. Now she was taking steps to boost morale.

"That's thoughtful of you," Marcia said. "How's the testing going?"

"Better," Sarah admitted. "Since you facilitated that session with Liam, he's been more responsive to our bug reports. Not exactly warm and fuzzy, but at least he's replying same-day instead of making us wait."

The elevator doors opened on the eighth floor, where Marcia had arranged for the daily stand-up to take place in a large conference room. She'd deliberately chosen a neutral location rather than the development or QA areas, signalling that this was a team meeting, not one group's territory.

To her surprise, most of the team was already there, clustering around the room's whiteboard. Marcia couldn't help but smile as she watched Sarah cheerfully hand out coffees. It struck Marcia that a spark had reignited in the QA lead. Sarah's eyes were brighter, her posture more confident. The burnout was fading, replaced by a sense of purpose.

Liam stood in the centre, marker in hand, drawing diagrams as he explained something to a mixed group of developers and testers.

"...if we consolidate the authentication services here," he was saying, "we eliminate three integration points that have been causing headaches."

"Won't that affect the user profile features the New York team is building?" asked one of the developers.

"Already coordinated with Noah on that," Liam replied.

"He suggested a cleaner approach for profile data anyway. We're incorporating it into the proposal."

Marcia hung back, not wanting to interrupt the spontaneous collaboration. This was exactly the kind of cross-functional discussion the project needed - and it was happening without her having to facilitate it.

As she turned to set her coffee down, Lucas slipped past with a quick whisper. "Tried your tip in our QA sync yesterday - made everyone name one blocker. It worked."

Marcia's eyes brightened. "Great. Keep doing it."

At precisely 8:00 am, Marcia moved to the front of the room. "Good morning, everyone. Happy Thursday - let's make it a good one," she said lifting her coffee in a casual toast. "Before we start the stand-up, I want to acknowledge something I just observed: technical discussions happening across team boundaries. That's - *exactly* - the kind of collaboration we need more of."

She noticed Liam straightening slightly at the recognition, though his expression remained impassive.

"Now, let's go around the room for quick updates. Remember, this is about surface-level status and identifying blockers, not deep problem-solving. We'll schedule separate sessions for that."

For the next fifteen minutes, team members gave crisp updates. The format Marcia had introduced - what you accomplished yesterday, what you're working on today, and any blockers - kept the meeting focused. The New York team joined via video, with Noah coordinating their updates.

When it was Liam's turn, he surprised Marcia by specifically addressing a concern raised by the New York team. "Noah mentioned an issue with the customer profile API yesterday. I've reviewed it and have a fix ready to test. Should resolve the data inconsistencies you've been seeing."

On the video screen, Noah gave a small, appreciative

nod. "Thanks, Liam. That'll unblock Alisha's feature work."

After the meeting, as people filed out, Marcia approached Liam. "I noticed you specifically addressed New York's blocker. That kind of cross-office support is just what we need." She said with a smile and appreciative nod.

Liam shrugged, clearly uncomfortable with praise. "It was a simple fix. Made more sense for me to handle it than to explain it to someone else."

"Still, it made a difference," Marcia said. "Looking forward to our architecture review this afternoon."

Liam let out a short breath through his nose and headed towards his desk, the usual tension loosening a fraction. Recognition, it seemed, mattered even to those who claimed not to care about it.

Marcia lingered a moment in the empty conference room, absorbing what she'd just witnessed. Liam - who barely a week ago was openly bitter - had volunteered a fix for someone in another office. She hadn't expected to see walls between Seattle and New York start coming down so soon. *Maybe convening everyone really is that powerful*, she thought, a spark of hope lighting in her.

On her way to her coffee meeting with Tessa, Marcia's phone lit up – Noah texting: *The Seattle-NY dynamics are shifting already. Liam reached out to Alisha directly to discuss her feature needs. Never happened before.*

That's great to hear, Marcia replied. *How's the mood in the NY office about my visit?*

Curious and cautiously optimistic. Alan (NY director) wants to meet you first thing. I've arranged for the team to take you to lunch at our favourite deli.

Perfect. Looking forward to it.

Marcia slipped the phone into her bag, a quiet lift of optimism in her chest. The simple act of scheduling a trip to New York was already changing perceptions. The team there

the thoroughness of the analysis. Liam and Noah had clearly spent significant time collaborating on the document. More importantly, they'd found common ground in their technical assessment.

"What's the estimated effort to consolidate these services?" Marcia asked.

Liam glanced at Noah before answering. "Two weeks of focused development, plus one week of testing. Three senior developers - two from Seattle, one from New York."

"Plus, regression testing across dependent systems," Noah added. "Sarah's team would need to be heavily involved."

Marcia made a note. "And the benefits?"

Liam clicked to the next slide. "Thirty percent reduction in integration issues based on our bug analysis. Simplified deployment pipeline. Faster performance for user authentication. And it removes a major source of friction between the Seattle and New York teams."

"That friction being?" Marcia prompted, wanting to hear their perspective.

Noah answered. "Seattle owns two authentication services, New York owns one. When users experience login issues, everyone points fingers across offices. A unified service with shared ownership eliminates the blame game."

Marcia weighed it; the technical benefits were clear, but the team dynamics benefits might be even more valuable.

"I'm sold on the approach," she said. "Let's incorporate this into the recovery plan for Elizabeth. What would you need to get started immediately?"

Liam and Noah exchanged glances again, this silent communication surprising Marcia. They'd clearly developed some rapport during their collaboration.

"Three things," Liam said. "First, dedicated time for the developers involved - no other assignments for three weeks.

Second, a joint design session with both offices to finalise details. Third, clear communication to GFP about what we're doing and why."

"I can arrange the first two," Marcia said. "The third will be part of my presentation to Elizabeth on Friday. Any chance you could join that meeting, Liam? Having the technical perspective would be valuable."

Liam looked uncomfortable. "Client meetings aren't really my…"

"I think it's a good idea," Noah interrupted from the screen. "Elizabeth respects technical expertise. Having you explain the authentication issues would carry weight."

Liam's reluctance was visible, but after a moment he relented. "Fine. But I'll need to prep. Elizabeth asks pointed questions."

"That she does," Marcia agreed. "How about we do a dry run at the end of the day? James can play Elizabeth and ask the tough questions."

"Works for me," Liam said.

"One more thing," Noah added. "The New York team would like some visibility into how their components fit into this architectural shift. Could we schedule a joint session next week when you're here?"

"Absolutely," Marcia said, opening her calendar. "How about Wednesday morning? I'll be in the New York office, and we can include the Seattle team virtually."

The meeting wrapped up a few minutes later, with clear next steps for everyone. As Liam gathered his materials, Marcia noticed a subtle change in his demeanor. The perpetual tension in his shoulders had eased a little, and he seemed more engaged than in their previous interactions.

"This is good work, Liam," she said as he prepared to leave. "You and Noah make a strong team, despite being three thousand miles apart."

Liam paused. "He understands the technical challenges," he said simply. "And he's not afraid to speak his mind."

"Unlike most people around you?" Marcia suggested with a small smile.

Liam almost smiled back. "Most people either ignore my concerns or get defensive. Noah actually listens and then challenges me with real questions, not excuses."

After Liam left, Marcia remained in the conference room, reviewing her notes. The architectural proposal would be a cornerstone of her recovery plan for Elizabeth. It addressed a fundamental technical issue while also tackling team dynamics.

As she was about to leave, James appeared in the doorway. "How'd it go with the tech titans?"

"Surprisingly well," Marcia said. "They've developed a solid proposal for consolidating authentication services. Liam's even agreed to join the Elizabeth meeting on Friday."

James's eyebrows shot up. "Liam? In a client meeting? Colour me surprised."

"Noah suggested it, and Liam agreed. I think they've formed some mutual respect."

"The Power to Convene strikes again," James said with a cheeky grin, settling into a chair. "You put the right people together, and solutions emerge that neither would have developed alone."

Marcia closed her laptop. "It's more than just scheduling meetings, isn't it? It's about creating the right conversations between the right people."

"Exactly," James leaned back slightly, please by her phrasing. "Any manager can drop a meeting on the calendar. The real skill is knowing who needs to be in the room – and what questions will unlock progress."

"Speaking of questions," Marcia said, thoughtful now, "how should I approach Alan Prescott in New York? He's protective of his team, and my visit could be seen as Seattle swooping in to take control."

James turned this over in his mind. "Be transparent about your intentions. Acknowledge their concerns without making promises you can't keep. And find something concrete you can deliver while you're there - a decision, a resource, a clear next step."

"I've been thinking about that," Marcia said. "What if I propose a rotation program? Seattle developers spending time in New York and vice versa. It would build cross-office understanding and reduce the us-versus-them mentality."

"That could work," James agreed. "But be prepared for budget questions. Travel isn't cheap."

"Robert already approved the concept," Marcia said. "I'll work out the details with finance next week."

James looked impressed. "You've been busy. How's the presentation for Elizabeth coming along?"

"Getting there. I've got the framework and key points. Need to incorporate the authentication proposal and Tessa's analysis of requirement changes."

"That reminds me," James said, checking his watch. "Robert wanted an update on your preparation. He's free in about twenty minutes."

Marcia nodded. "I'll head to his office once I finalise these notes."

After James left, her thoughts turned to the authentication proposal. What struck her wasn't just the solution itself, but how Liam and Noah had found genuine common ground - collaborating because of a shared purpose.

Sometimes the best way to bridge personal or office divisions was to focus on a concrete problem that affected everyone. The authentication issues created headaches for both teams, giving them a shared enemy to unite against.

As she gathered her things, Marcia's phone buzzed with

an email notification. It was from Elizabeth:

Marcia,

In addition to your recovery plan, Malcolm and I would like to discuss GFP's upcoming quarterly business review. Our executive leadership is expecting updates on digital transformation progress. We need to align on messaging.

Also, please ensure your presentation addresses the authentication issues specifically. We've received numerous complaints from our regional managers about login problems.
Elizabeth

Marcia read the email twice, noting Elizabeth's specific mention of authentication issues. This was perfect timing - the very problem Liam and Noah were addressing was top of mind for the client.

She forwarded the email to Liam with a note:

This is why your involvement on Friday is crucial. Your authentication analysis addresses one of their key pain points.

His reply came back quickly:

Will prepare slides specifically addressing their concerns. Already analysing their error logs from last month.

Marcia paused over the screen, impressed by Liam's initiative. Their previous interactions had painted him as brilliant but difficult. Now she was seeing another side - someone who cared deeply about solving problems when he felt his expertise was valued.

On her way to Robert's office, Marcia checked in with Sarah about the QA implications of the authentication changes.

"We'll need comprehensive regression testing," Sarah confirmed. "But honestly, anything would be better than the current setup. My team spends at least 30% of their time troubleshooting authentication-related bugs."

"Liam mentioned you'd need to be heavily involved in the testing plan," Marcia said.

Sarah looked surprised. "He actually acknowledged QA's role? That's new."

"People rise to expectations," Marcia observed. "Treat people as valuable contributors, and they'll contribute more value."

"Management wisdom," Sarah said with a curious look. "Is that from a book or your own experience?"

"Both," Marcia admitted. "I've had good mentors."

As she continued to Robert's office, Marcia reflected on how much had changed in just four days. The team was starting to come together. Liam and Noah were collaborating. QA and development were communicating more effectively. A technical solution had emerged for one of their most pressing problems.

The Power to Convene was proving to be remarkably effective, especially when wielded with intention.

✧   ✧   ✧

Robert's assistant waved her in as she arrived. "He's ready for you," she said, then added with a raised eyebrow and just enough sarcasm to be noticeable, "Seems in a good mood today."

"Got it," Marcia said, hiding a smirk, heading into the CEO's office.

Robert was standing by his window, looking out at the rain-slicked streets of downtown Seattle. "Marcia," he said, turning as she entered. "Tell me some good news. I could use it after my board call."

"We've identified a solution to the authentication issues," Marcia said, getting straight to the point. "Liam and Noah have developed a proposal to consolidate the three separate services into one unified approach. It would address a major pain point for GFP and reduce cross-office friction."

Robert's expression brightened. "Now that *is* good news. Timeline?"

"Three weeks for implementation and testing. We'd need dedicated resources, but the impact would be significant."

"Done," Robert said without hesitation. "What else?"

For the next ten minutes, Marcia updated Robert on her preparation for the Elizabeth meeting and her planned approach for the New York visit. He asked pointed questions about resource allocation and client expectations, but seemed satisfied with her answers.

"You've accomplished more in a week than Brett did in his last month," Robert observed. "The team is responding well to your leadership style."

"It's early days," Marcia cautioned. "We still have a long way to go."

"True, but momentum matters." Robert returned to his desk. "One more thing before you go. I spoke with Elizabeth this morning. She's cautiously optimistic about your approach, but Malcolm remains sceptical."

"That tracks with what I've observed," Marcia said. "Elizabeth values honesty and clarity. Malcolm wants speed above all else."

"Your challenge tomorrow will be satisfying both of them," Robert said. "Elizabeth will appreciate the thorough analysis, but Malcolm needs to see immediate action."

Marcia pursed her lips in understanding. "That's why I'm bringing Liam. The authentication proposal is something we can implement immediately while continuing work on the broader recovery plan."

A flicker of doubt tightened in her chest. Winning over Elizabeth was one thing - but Malcolm's demand for speed left no room for missteps. What if her plan wasn't strong enough? What if she overestimated her ability to steer two powerful stakeholders toward a shared path? The fear was old, familiar - the quiet worry that she wasn't yet the leader everyone suddenly seemed to believe she was.

"Smart approach," Robert agreed. "Let me know how it goes."

As Marcia left Robert's office, her mind was already spinning with preparations for the meeting with Elizabeth and Malcolm. The authentication proposal provided a concrete starting point - a tangible solution to a pressing problem. But she needed more than that to build confidence in her overall recovery plan.

Back at her desk, she opened her presentation and added a slide specifically addressing Elizabeth's concerns about the quarterly business review. If GFP's executives needed to show progress, Marcia would give them something concrete to report - even if it was just the beginning of the turnaround.

Her calendar reminder showed one last meeting for the day - her prep session with Liam and James for the Elizabeth presentation. After that, she'd finalise her materials and get some rest. Tomorrow would be a critical test of her nascent leadership approach.

As she gathered her notes for the James meeting, Noah texted: *New York team is looking forward to your visit. Alan's still a bit wary, but he's agreed to join us for lunch on Tuesday.*

Perfect, Marcia replied. *Looking forward to meeting everyone in person.*

One meeting at a time, one conversation at a time, she was building bridges and creating momentum. The Power to needed to know they mattered - that their concerns were worth a cross-country flight.

At the coffee shop, Tessa was waiting with a spreadsheet open on her laptop. "I've highlighted the ten requirement changes that caused the most disruption," she said after they exchanged greetings. "Three of them came directly from Malcolm, which might be awkward for your presentation."

Marcia sipped her latte. "Better to be transparent than to tiptoe around it. Malcolm needs to understand the impact of these changes just like everyone else."

"A refreshing approach," Tessa said. "Brett would never call out anything from Malcolm directly."

"I'm not calling anyone out," Marcia clarified, her pitch slightly higher than intended. She went on in a more deliberate voice. "I'm highlighting patterns so we can improve the process together. This isn't about blame - it's about creating a system that works for everyone."

They spent the next twenty minutes reviewing the changes and their ripple effects. Marcia was impressed by Tessa's thoroughness and insight. She wasn't just tracking changes; she was analysing patterns and identifying root causes.

"You know," Marcia said as they wrapped up, "you have a real talent for process analysis. Have you ever considered moving into a more strategic role?"

Tessa looked startled. "Like what?"

"We could use someone to own the requirements and change-control process - someone who understands both the business and technical implications. It would be a new position, but I think Robert would approve it given our current challenges."

"You'd recommend me for that?" Tessa asked, clearly surprised. "I mean... I've made mistakes before," she admitted quietly. "Sometimes I still wonder if I'm ready for something bigger."

"I would - and you are," Marcia said. "Think about it. We can discuss more when I'm back from New York."

A cool breeze followed them down the block as they left the café, carrying the familiar sounds of downtown Seattle - traffic, footsteps, and the low murmur of early meetings spilling from nearby buildings.

The walk gave Marcia a moment to settle her thoughts before stepping back into the rhythm of the project. She reflected on the morning's interactions. The stand-up had created visibility across teams. The coffee with Tessa had laid groundwork for a potential process improvement and a team member's growth. Her trip to New York was already shifting perceptions before she even got on the plane.

A familiar tension stirred - knowing her decisions now shaped more than one team. But she also felt the steadiness she'd earned over the past few years: focus on the work, create clarity, build connection. The rest would follow.

None of these actions was particularly complex or time-consuming. But together, they were creating momentum - small ripples combining to form a wave of change.

Back at her desk, Marcia opened her presentation for Elizabeth and added a slide about the specific requirement changes Tessa had identified. Transparency might be uncomfortable in the short term, but it was essential for rebuilding trust.

Her phone buzzed with an email notification from Robert:

Due to a meeting conflict, can we push out the check-in on NY trip plans to later in the day, let me know what works.

Marcia added a placeholder meeting to her calendar, to remind herself to do this. As she did, she noticed how different her calendar looked from a week ago. Instead of inherited meetings with vague purposes, every slot was now purposeful - designed to bring specific people together for clear reasons.

The Power to Convene, was proving to be more profound than she'd initially realised. It was about orchestrating the right interactions at the right time to create momentum toward a shared goal.

And that momentum, however slight, was beginning to build.

"Blocked needs Owner and When."

✧ ✧ ✧

"Authentication services are the linchpin," Liam said, his cursor highlighting a complex diagram on the conference room screen. "Three separate systems that should be one."

Marcia took it in, watching as Liam walked through the architectural proposal he and Noah had developed. On the video screen, Noah sat in the New York office, occasionally adding context or clarification.

"The original design assumed each region would need different authentication requirements," Noah explained. "But in practice, GFP standardised their identity management globally last year."

"So we're maintaining three systems for a business requirement that no longer exists," Marcia summarised.

"Exactly," Liam said, a hint of approval in his voice. "It's creating sync issues, token validation problems, and unnecessary complexity."

The three of them had been reviewing the architectural proposal for twenty minutes, and Marcia was impressed by

Convene was proving to be the foundation for everything else she needed to accomplish.

Now she just needed to convince Elizabeth and Malcolm that her approach would deliver the results they desperately needed.

✧ ✧ ✧

Friday morning brought unexpected sunshine to Seattle, streaming through the conference room windows and creating pools of light on the polished table. Marcia arrived twenty minutes early to set up her presentation, connect her laptop, and review her notes one final time.

The end-of-day dry run with Liam on Thursday had gone well. James had played the role of Elizabeth with unsettling accuracy, peppering Liam with pointed questions about the authentication solution. To Marcia's relief, Liam had remained composed, explaining complex technical concepts clearly without condescension.

Now, as the actual meeting approached, Marcia arranged printouts of the presentation at each seat. She'd learned early in her career that some executives preferred paper they could write on, even in this digital age. Plus, her friend in sales always said they were a good backup in case the tech failed.

"Nervous?" James asked, appearing in the doorway with two coffees.

"Realistically concerned," Marcia replied with a wry smile, accepting one of the cups. "Elizabeth I can handle. Malcolm is the wild card."

"Malcolm responds to confidence," James advised, taking a seat. "He won't necessarily agree with you, but he'll respect you if you hold your ground on things you're certain about."

The door opened again, and Liam entered, looking

almost unrecognisable in a crisp button-down shirt instead of his usual tech company hoodie. His hair was combed, though it was already starting to rebel against the styling.

"Is this too formal?" he asked awkwardly, tugging at his collar.

"It's perfect," Marcia assured him. "Thanks for making the effort."

A corner of his mouth twitched; he immediately opened his laptop and began reviewing his slides, his focus narrowing to the task at hand.

At exactly 10:00 am, Elizabeth Parker strode into the room, followed by Malcolm Wright. Elizabeth looked as immaculate as ever in a tailored charcoal suit, her silver bob gleaming under the lights. Malcolm, with his British formality and perpetual expression of mild impatience, carried a leather portfolio embossed with the GFP logo.

"Good morning," Marcia greeted them, extending her hand. "Thank you both for making time for this presentation."

"We're eager to hear your assessment," Elizabeth said, her tone neutral but not unfriendly. "I see you've brought technical support."

Liam stood, extending his hand with only slight hesitation. "Liam Everett, Principal Architect. I'll be covering the authentication solution we've developed."

Malcolm raised an eyebrow. "The authentication issues have been particularly problematic for our regional managers. I hope you have more than analysis to offer."

"We do," Liam said simply, surprising Marcia with his restraint. The old Liam might have launched into a defensive explanation of how complex the problem was.

Robert arrived last, apologising for his slight delay. "Board call ran over. Let's get started."

Marcia took a deep breath and moved to the front of the

room. "As promised, I've spent this week conducting a thorough assessment of the GFP project. Today I'll present our findings and, more importantly, our recovery plan."

She clicked to her first slide: "GFP Digital Transformation: Recovery Plan."

"Before diving into solutions, I want to frame the current situation honestly." She showed the four-quadrant analysis from her meeting with Robert: Technical, Process, People, and Client. "The project faces challenges in each of these areas, all interconnected."

Elizabeth's chin dipped in a measured acknowledgement; Malcolm's expression remained impassive.

Marcia continued, "Rather than a single catastrophic issue, we're dealing with a series of compounding problems: architectural complexity, process breakdowns, team fragmentation, and communication gaps."

She clicked to the next slide, showing the graph Tessa had prepared of requirement changes and their impact on timelines.

"This analysis, prepared by our business analyst Tessa Tanaka, shows how requirement changes have impacted delivery dates." Marcia pointed to specific spikes in the graph. "When requirements shift but timelines don't, quality and team morale inevitably suffer."

Malcolm leaned forward. "Are you suggesting GFP is to blame for the delays?"

"Not at all," Marcia said evenly. "I'm highlighting a process issue that needs to be addressed by both Alpha and GFP. We need a more transparent approach to change management so that business decisions can be made with full awareness of their implications."

Malcolm's jaw tightened. "Impact analysis sounds like a polite way of saying slow down. We don't have that luxury."

Marcia didn't look away. "It's a way of saying *choose*

knowingly. If we trade time for scope, we'll do it with eyes open - and with your explicit sign-off."

She clicked to the next slide, showing a simple change control process. "This isn't about saying no to changes. It's about providing impact analysis so GFP can make informed decisions about trade-offs between features, quality, and timeline."

Elizabeth made a note on her printout. "This makes sense. We often don't understand the ripple effects of what seem like minor adjustments."

"Exactly," Marcia agreed. "Now, let's address the technical challenges, specifically the authentication issues you mentioned in your email, Elizabeth. For this, I'll hand over to Liam."

Liam stood and took Marcia's place at the front of the room. His initial stiffness faded as he began explaining the authentication problem.

"GFP's current implementation uses three separate authentication services," he explained, showing a diagram of the existing architecture. "This was designed when we thought each region would have different requirements, but since GFP standardised their identity management globally last year, this architecture now creates unnecessary complexity."

Malcolm interrupted. "What does this mean for our users in practical terms?"

"Inconsistent login experiences," Liam said promptly. "Session timeouts that make no sense. Regional managers having to log in multiple times when moving between systems. It's also a noticeably slower authentication process than industry standard."

Malcolm's expression eased a fraction; the direct answer seemed to satisfy him.

Liam continued, showing the proposed solution. "We've

developed a plan to consolidate these services into a unified authentication approach. This would resolve the issues regional managers are experiencing, simplify maintenance, and create a foundation for future features."

"Timeline?" Elizabeth asked.

"Three weeks," Liam said confidently. "Two weeks for development, one week for testing. We'd need three dedicated senior developers - two from Seattle, one from New York."

"Ok... faster than I expected," Elizabeth admitted.

"We're not rebuilding from scratch," Liam explained. "We're consolidating and standardising existing components. Noah in the New York office and I have already mapped out the technical approach."

Malcolm's eyebrows rose slightly at the mention of cross-office collaboration.

Marcia took over again. "This authentication solution represents our overall approach to recovery: identify high-impact issues, develop targeted solutions, and implement them with cross-office collaboration."

She clicked to the 90-Day Recovery Plan slide, walking Elizabeth and Malcolm through the three phases: Stabilise, Accelerate, and Sustain.

"The authentication work falls into Phase 1," she explained. "It delivers immediate value while we address the underlying process and team issues."

Malcolm interjected. "This all sounds logical, but there's an elephant in the room. When will we get back on schedule for the overall digital transformation? Our executives are presenting to shareholders next quarter."

He didn't wait for an answer. "I'm not asking for philosophy," Malcolm said. "I'm asking for a date we can defend to the Street."

Marcia had anticipated this question. "The Core Banking

Module can be delivered at the end of Week 10 with the quality standards GFP expects. That's March 21st."

Elizabeth made a brief note. "Uncomfortable truth beats a comfortable miss," she said. "Go on."

Malcolm frowned. "That's still two months behind our original timeline."

"It is," Marcia acknowledged. "And I could promise an earlier date to make this meeting more comfortable, but that wouldn't be honest or realistic given the current state of the project."

She clicked to a new slide showing a revised roadmap. "What I can offer is this: we'll deliver the authentication improvements in three weeks, giving your regional managers immediate relief from their biggest pain point. We'll then deliver incremental improvements every two weeks, prioritised by business impact."

Elizabeth studied the roadmap. "So rather than waiting three months for everything, we get continuous improvements along the way?"

"Exactly," Marcia confirmed. "Each delivery adds business value, and you can showcase progress to your executives throughout the quarter."

Robert, who had been quietly observing, spoke up. "This approach reflects a fundamental shift in how we're managing the project. Continuous delivery instead of big-bang releases. Transparent communication about trade-offs. Cross-office collaboration instead of siloed teams."

Malcolm tapped his pen on the table, considering. "The March date is problematic for our quarterly business review. Is there no way to accelerate the Core Banking Module?"

Marcia looked at Liam, who shook his head subtly.

"Not without compromising quality," Marcia said firmly. "And I believe that would be a mistake given the visibility and importance of this system."

Malcolm aligned his papers. "Compromise is relative. We can tolerate controlled risk."

Marcia shook her head. "Not on authentication or funds flow. Those are zero-failure domains."

The room went still. Malcolm and Elizabeth exchanged glances, having one of those wordless conversations that longtime colleagues develop.

"What if," Elizabeth said finally, "we adjusted the scope of the Core Banking Module to deliver the most critical features first? Could that give us something meaningful to demonstrate in February?"

Marcia paused, thinking. "Potentially, yes. If we worked together to prioritise features based on both business impact and technical dependencies, we could create a meaningful February milestone."

"I'd need to be involved in that prioritisation," Liam added. "Some features are more interconnected than others from a technical perspective."

"Of course," Elizabeth agreed. She turned to Malcolm. "This could work for the quarterly review. We showcase the authentication improvements and the highest-priority banking features, with a clear roadmap for the rest."

Malcolm leaned back slightly, conceding the point with a slow exhale. "It's not ideal, but it's pragmatic. And frankly, more credible than what we've been hearing for the past three months."

Marcia felt a wave of relief, though she kept her expression professional. "Then our next step would be a prioritisation workshop. I'd recommend including business stakeholders, technical leads from both offices, and the QA team to ensure we're making informed decisions."

"Make it happen," Elizabeth said decisively. "Monday, before you head to New York."

"I'll coordinate with your assistant this afternoon,"

Marcia promised.

The meeting continued for another twenty minutes as they discussed specific details of the recovery plan. When they reached the end of the presentation, Robert spoke up.

"Elizabeth, Malcolm - are we aligned on this approach?"

A faint, businesslike smile touched Elizabeth's mouth. "Yes. It's clear, realistic, and addresses our most pressing concerns. The authentication solution alone will make a significant difference to our field operations."

Malcolm was more measured. "I'm cautiously optimistic. The prioritisation workshop will be crucial - we need to ensure the February milestone delivers meaningful business value."

"Agreed," Marcia said. "I'll work with your team to prepare for that workshop, ensuring we have the right participants and information."

As the meeting concluded, Elizabeth lingered behind while Malcolm spoke with Robert near the door.

"That was characteristically honest," she said to Marcia. "Brett would not have given us that level of transparency."

"And would that have given you more confidence?" Marcia asked.

Elizabeth didn't hedge. "Not for a second. Which is why we were considering moving the project to another vendor."

The candid admission surprised Marcia. "And now?"

"Now we'll give your approach a chance," Elizabeth said. "The authentication solution is promising, and your overall plan makes sense. But Marcia,..." Her tone grew more serious. "we need to see continuous progress. No more prolonged silences followed by bad news."

"You'll get weekly updates from me personally," Marcia promised. "Transparent and honest, even when the news isn't what we'd all like to hear."

Elizabeth inclined her chin, satisfaction contained. "I'll

hold you to that." She turned to Liam, who was packing up his laptop. "Thank you for your clear explanation of the authentication issues. It's the first time I've truly understood what's been happening technically."

Liam looked momentarily startled at being directly addressed. "You're welcome. I'm, glad it was helpful." He stammered out.

As the room began to empty, Marcia stayed seated, feeling the tremor of adrenaline in her hands. She hadn't dazzled anyone or tried to force agreement; she'd just stayed steady. *There was power in that calm*, she realised - a different kind of authority she hadn't recognised before.

After Elizabeth and Malcolm left, Robert approached Marcia and Liam. "Well done, both of you. That was precisely what they needed to hear."

"The prioritisation workshop will be challenging," Marcia cautioned. "Malcolm will push hard for more features in the February milestone."

"Handle it the same way you handled today," Robert advised. "Be honest about trade-offs, but flexible where you can be." He checked his watch. "I need to get to another meeting. Keep me updated on the workshop plans."

After Robert left, Marcia turned to Liam. "Thank you for your support today. Your technical credibility made a real difference."

Liam shrugged, but Marcia could tell he was pleased. "It was just explaining the facts. But, it went better than I expected. Elizabeth actually listened."

"People usually do when they're given clear, understandable information without being talked down to," Marcia observed. "You struck the perfect balance."

As they walked back toward the development area, Liam asked, "Are you really going to let Malcolm dictate which features go into the February milestone?"

"Not dictate," Marcia clarified. "Influence, certainly. But we'll make it a collaborative decision, with technical feasibility given equal weight to business priorities. That's why I want you there."

Liam tilted his head, thinking. "I'll prepare a technical dependency map before the workshop. It'll help visualise which features can be easily separated and which ones are tightly coupled."

"Perfect," Marcia said. "Send me a draft when it's ready, and I'll incorporate it into the workshop materials."

As Liam returned to his desk, Marcia headed to her office to update James on the meeting's outcome. She found him waiting, a hopeful expression on his face.

"They went for it," she confirmed with a smile. "The authentication solution was our foot in the door, and the phased delivery approach sealed the deal."

"Fantastic," James said, genuine relief in his voice. "Robert texted me that it went well, but I wanted the details."

Marcia filled him in on the prioritisation workshop and the February milestone compromise. "It's a reasonable adjustment to our plan. And actually, having that interim milestone might help the team focus."

James gave a quick nod. "Smaller, more frequent *Liamies* are better for morale than one big, distant goal. Speaking of which, how did Liam do?"[1]

"Surprisingly well," Marcia said. "He was clear, respectful, and didn't get defensive when questioned. Elizabeth specifically thanked him afterward."

"Another success for the Power to Convene," James observed. "You brought Liam into a conversation he wouldn't normally have been part of, and everyone

---

[1] *Liamies* are regular doses of Liam's brilliance in smaller chunks.

benefited."

As James left, Marcia sat at her desk and updated her to-do list. She needed to:

1. Schedule the prioritisation workshop with Elizabeth's team
2. Brief Tessa and Sarah on the outcomes from today's meeting
3. Finalise plans for the New York trip
4. Update the team on the authentication solution approval

She sent quick messages to Tessa and Sarah, asking them to drop by that afternoon for updates. Then she crafted an email to the full team:

Hi Team,

I'm pleased to share that Elizabeth and Malcolm have approved our recovery plan approach, including the authentication service consolidation. Liam did an excellent job presenting the technical solution, and both GFP executives recognised the value it will deliver to their users.

Next steps:

- We'll schedule a prioritisation workshop for Monday next week to define a February milestone

- Authentication work will begin immediately, with dedicated resources as discussed

- I'll be visiting the New York office Tuesday-Wednesday to ensure alignment across locations

This is just the beginning of our recovery effort, but it's a positive start. Thank you all for your insights and collaboration this week.

Marcia

As she sent the email, a response from Noah arrived almost immediately:

Great news! The NY team is thrilled about the authentication solution getting approved. Alan wants to know if he should join the prioritisation workshop virtually or if you'd prefer to discuss when you're here next week.

Marcia weighed the options. Having Alan join virtually would ensure New York's voice was represented. But discussing it in person during her visit might help build the relationship with the New York director. She replied:

Both. Having him join virtually ensures New York's perspective is included from the start. Then we can dive deeper when I'm there next week.

Noah responded:

Perfect, I'll let him know.

Marcia leaned back in her chair, feeling a sense of accomplishment mixed with awareness of the challenges still ahead. The presentation had gone well - better than expected, honestly. But now came the hard part: delivering on the promises they'd made.

The authentication solution was relatively straightforward. The February deliverable would be more complex, requiring difficult trade-off decisions and cross-team coordination. And underlying it all were the team dynamics that needed to improve for sustainable success.

Still, they had momentum now. The Power to Convene had brought Liam and Noah together, creating a technical solution that opened the door with Elizabeth and Malcolm.

The prioritisation workshop would bring business and technical stakeholders into the same conversation, forcing transparent discussions about trade-offs that had previously been avoided.

The results weren't dramatic or instantaneous, but they were real and building upon each other.

Her phone chimed – Robert's message read: *Elizabeth just called. Very pleased with the meeting and specifically mentioned your integrity. Keep it up.*

She straightened, her conviction building. In a world where managers often tried to please everyone with unrealistic promises, the most powerful move was often the simplest: telling the truth - even when it wasn't what people wanted to hear.

That authenticity, combined with the Power to Convene, was proving to be a potent combination. The question now was whether it would be enough to turn around a project with deeply embedded challenges and deliver the February milestone everyone was now counting on.

As Friday was drawing to a close, and not knowing what to do next, she messaged a friend: *Emergency coffee meeting*

FIELD RULE: Calendar as a Decision Engine

- Mission first: Clearly state the objective of the meeting, e.g., Decide X by Y so Z can move.
- Small room, clear roles; FYI → async (meaning those who need to be informed don't need to attend and can receive a summary of the meeting).
- Cancel if no mission, owner, or pre-read.
- End early when done; log decisions.

Do this tomorrow: Add a meeting objective line to stand-up; cancel one ownerless meeting.

Chapter 3
The Power of Calculated Risk

Breakthroughs never come from playing it safe. The managers who change the game aren't reckless gamblers - they're architects of risk, bold enough to disrupt patterns and disciplined enough to protect the team while they do it.

✧ ✧ ✧

Push faster - inside guardrails you agree to beforehand.

✧ ✧ ✧

Saturday morning in Seattle unfolded in rare winter sunshine, its long shadows stretching through Marcia's favourite café, Emerald City Brew. The weekend scene was a scatter of students hunched over laptops and couples lingering over lattes. Marcia had arrived early to claim a corner table, spreading out her notes for the prioritisation workshop while she waited.

"I'd know that intense focus anywhere," came a familiar voice.

Marcia looked up to see Nelson Sidewell, an old friend from her college days who now ran a thriving innovation consultancy. His trademark red glasses and perpetually untamed curls made him instantly recognisable.

"Nelson!" Marcia stood for a quick hug. "Thanks for meeting me on such short notice."

"How could I resist? 'Emergency coffee meeting' has a certain dramatic flair." He settled into the chair across from her, setting down a house mug that read 'Organised Chaos' in playful lettering. "Though I expected more obvious panic given your text message."

Marcia smiled. "It's an internal panic. More dignified."

"Ah, the professional kind." Nelson nodded sagely. "So, what's this project crisis that couldn't wait until Monday?"

Marcia gave him a quick overview of the GFP project - the technical issues, team dynamics, and the newly promised February milestone that now loomed large in her mind.

"The authentication solution will work," she concluded. "I'm confident in that. But the February deliverable feels like trying to fit ten-pounds of features into a five-pound bag, even with careful prioritisation."

Nelson leaned back, studying her with the keen-eyed look that had made him a sought-after innovation consultant. "You're approaching this like a traditional project manager. Linear thinking. Sequential problem-solving." He stirred his coffee. "That's fine for stable environments, but terrible for rescue operations."

"What's the alternative?" Marcia asked. "We have constraints - time, resources, technical debt."

"Constraints are just boundaries," Nelson shrugged. "The question is how you operate within them." He pulled a napkin toward him and drew a simple graph with two axes labelled 'Risk' and 'Reward.'

"Most managers live here," he said, circling the bottom left quadrant. "Low risk, low reward. Safe decisions, incremental improvements, predictable outcomes." He tapped the top right quadrant. "But the interesting stuff happens up here. High risk, high reward."

Marcia frowned. "GFP doesn't need interesting right now. They need reliable."

"Do they?" Nelson challenged. "Or do they need results they haven't been able to get through conventional approaches? You said yourself - the traditional methods aren't working."

He was right, but Marcia wasn't convinced. "So, what are you suggesting? That I throw out the project management handbook?"

"Not throw it out. Set it aside temporarily." Nelson drew another diagram, this time with a wavy line moving upward through the high-risk, high-reward quadrant. "Innovation rarely follows a straight line. It zigs and zags, sometimes failing forward, but ultimately reaching heights that cautious approaches never could."

Marcia thought about the project - the fractured team, the technical complexities, the looming deadlines. "I can't afford failure right now, Nelson. The project's already struggling."

"I'm not talking about reckless gambling," Nelson clarified. "I'm talking about calculated chaos. Creating space for unexpected solutions by deliberately disrupting normal patterns."

He took a sip of his coffee. "Remember our senior design project? We were stuck for weeks using the standard approach, until Professor Harris forced us to swap roles for a day. You became the designer; I became the coder."

Marcia laughed. "That was a disaster."

"For about six hours," Nelson agreed. "And then?"

"And then we had a breakthrough," Marcia admitted. "Because we were asking different questions from our new perspectives."

"Exactly. Calculated chaos." Nelson tapped the high-risk, high-reward quadrant again. "The best managers know when to introduce controlled disruption to break through stuck patterns."

Marcia internalised the insight. The project was certainly stuck in dysfunctional patterns - Seattle versus New York, developers versus QA, technical priorities versus business demands.

"What might this look like for your project?" Nelson prompted.

Marcia hesitated. "Maybe... mixing up the usual teams? Pairing people who don't normally work together?"

"Good start," Nelson made a small go-on gesture. "What else?"

"Changing the work environment somehow. Or..." an idea began to form, "what if we approached the February target completely differently? Instead of traditional feature development, what if we did something like a focused innovation sprint?"

Nelson 's eyes lit up. "Now you're thinking. A time-boxed period where normal rules are suspended, teams are reconfigured, and everyone focuses on creative problem-solving rather than following standard processes."

"A hackathon," Marcia said, the concept becoming clearer. "A 48-hour event where we bring Seattle and New York together, physically and virtually, to tackle the February challenge in an intensive burst."

"With carefully designed constraints to focus creativity," Nelson added. "The best innovation happens not with total freedom, but with the right constraints that force creative thinking."

Marcia was warming to the idea, scribbling notes rapidly. "We could create cross-office, cross-functional teams. Mix developers, QA, business analysts. Give them clear goals but freedom in how they approach solutions."

"Will forty-eight hours be enough?" Nelson tilted his head, intrigued.

"Not to deliver an output, we'd need a little longer for that." Marcia updated her notes as the idea evolved. "Three-days might do it."

"And what might you discover?" Nelson asked.

"Hidden capabilities in team members. Unexpected solutions to technical problems. New ways of collaborating across offices." Marcia paused, seeing both the potential and the risks. "But it's a gamble. If it fails, we lose precious time we don't have."

Nelson shrugged. "Everything's a gamble. The question is whether you're being deliberate about your bets." He finished his coffee. "Traditional approaches have a predictable ceiling of success. They'll never deliver more than incremental improvement. Sometimes you need to play in the high-risk, high-reward space to achieve breakthrough results."

Marcia sat back, considering the implications. The idea was both exciting and terrifying. Elizabeth and Malcolm might embrace the innovative approach - or see it as a desperate Hail Mary.

"I'd need buy-in from the team," she said, thinking aloud. "Especially the key influencers like Liam and Noah. And Sarah in QA."

"Start there," Nelson suggested. "Float the concept with

your strongest team members first. Refine it based on their input. Then present it not as a wild experiment, but as a calculated strategy to achieve the February milestone."

They spent the next hour sketching out what the innovation sprint might look like - the team structures, the goals, the guardrails to ensure it didn't veer into truly chaotic territory.

As they wrapped up, Nelson said, "You know, Marcia, most managers would be looking for the safest path right now. The fact that you're willing to consider a higher-risk approach speaks volumes about your leadership instincts."

"Or my desperation," Marcia said with a self-deprecating smile.

"The best innovations often start from desperation," Nelson replied. "Just be intentional about the chaos you introduce. Make it calculated, not random. That's the difference between recklessness and strategic risk-taking."

After Nelson left, Marcia remained at the café, continuing to develop the concept. The innovation sprint was risky, certainly. But if it worked, it could not only deliver the February release but also transform how the team collaborated long-term.

"One goal. One risk budget. One rollback signal."

✧   ✧   ✧

Monday morning arrived with Seattle's familiar grey drizzle. Marcia had spent much of Sunday refining the innovation sprint concept, creating a structured proposal that balanced creative freedom with clear objectives.

As she stepped off the elevator at Alpha's offices, she spotted Liam by the coffee station, frowning at his phone.

"Morning, Liam," she said, pouring herself a cup. "How was your weekend?"

He looked up, his expression shifting from annoyance to neutral acknowledgment. "Productive. I mapped the technical dependencies for the February milestone features." He held up his phone. "Just sent it to you."

"Perfect timing," Marcia said. "I've been thinking about an alternative approach to the February work. I'd like your technical perspective before I float it more broadly."

Liam's eyebrows rose slightly. "What kind of alternative approach?"

"An innovation sprint," Marcia explained. "A three-day intensive event with cross-functional, cross-office teams tackling key features in a concentrated burst."

She expected immediate scepticism, but Liam just looked thoughtful. "Like a hackathon?"

"Similar, yes. But with more structure and specific business objectives."

Liam reflected for a moment. "Interesting. Standard processes haven't exactly been working for us." He glanced around the office. "Where were you thinking of discussing this?"

"I have a meeting room booked at 9:30 am. I was going to invite you, Sarah, and Noah on video call from New York. Just to explore the concept before taking it further."

Liam nodded. "I'll be there. I want to see how this works with my dependency map."

As Liam walked away, Marcia felt a small surge of optimism. She'd expected resistance to such an unconventional approach, especially from someone who valued technical precision. Instead, Liam seemed cautiously intrigued.

She sent quick messages to Sarah and Noah, then headed to her office to prepare for the discussion. The next few hours would determine whether her "calculated risk" strategy had any chance of success.

On her desk, she found a note from James: *Heard you were in the office Sunday. Everything okay? Call me when you get in.*

Marcia dialled his extension.

"You're working too many weekends," James said by way of greeting.

"Says the man who emailed me at 11 pm on Saturday," Marcia countered.

James chuckled. "Fair point. What's got you burning the midnight oil?"

"I'm considering a different approach for the February milestone," Marcia said. "Something more... unconventional."

"I'm listening."

"An innovation sprint. Bringing Seattle and New York together for three-days of intensive, cross-functional work on key features. Breaking the normal patterns to see if we can achieve breakthrough results."

There was a pause on the line. "That's certainly thinking outside the box," James said finally. "What prompted this?"

"A conversation with an old friend who specialises in innovation. And honestly, looking at the timeline and features, I'm not convinced traditional approaches will get us there."

"It's risky," James observed.

"Yes," Marcia agreed. "But potentially high-reward. I'm discussing it with key team members at 9:30 am to get their input before deciding whether to move forward."

"Sensible approach," James said. "Test the waters with your influencers first. Want me to sit in?"

Marcia thought for a moment. "No, I think they'll be more candid without an executive present. But I'll update you right after."

"Deal," James said. "And Marcia? I like that you're not just reaching for the standard playbook. This project needs creative thinking."

After hanging up, Marcia gathered her materials and headed to the meeting room. Her heart was beating a little faster than usual - this was a departure from her typically methodical approach. But as Nelson had pointed out, sometimes the highest rewards came from carefully calculated risks.

As she set up the room, Marcia thought about what she was really proposing: a deliberate disruption of established patterns to create space for new solutions. Encouraging calculated chaos, as Nelson had called it. Not random disorder, but strategic destabilisation of rigid thinking.

The question was whether her key team members would see it as brilliant or reckless. And beyond them, how would Elizabeth and Malcolm react? She was about to find out.

✧　✧　✧

"An innovation sprint?" Sarah repeated, leaning forward in her chair. "That sounds like a gamble."

The conference room felt smaller with the intensity of focus from the three people gathered around the table, plus Noah's attentive face on the video screen.

Marcia's stomach flipped at the word *gamble*. If this bold idea failed, they'd lose precious time they could hardly afford. She chewed her lip, looking around at the weary faces of her team. The conventional path wasn't working - that much was clear. *A controlled risk might be our best shot*, she thought, trying to convince herself as much as the others.

"Essentially, yes," Marcia confirmed, laying out the one-page concept document she'd prepared. "A three-day intensive effort where we reconfigure into cross-functional, cross-office teams specifically to tackle the February milestone features. It is a gamble," she conceded, her voice steady despite the flutter in her chest, "but doing nothing is a bigger one."

Liam studied the document, his expression unreadable. "This isn't how we typically work."

"That's precisely the point," Marcia said. "Our typical processes aren't getting us where we need to go, especially with the compressed timeline for February."

On the video screen, Noah stroked his beard thoughtfully. "I've participated in hackathons before, but never for production features. Usually, it's for prototypes or experiments."

"The principles are similar," Marcia explained, "but with more structure and specific business deliverables as the target. We'd create balanced teams mixing developers, QA, and business analysts from both offices."

Sarah tapped her pen against the table. "How would this work logistically? New York and Seattle are three hours apart."

"We'd schedule it for optimal overlap," Marcia said. "Start at 8 am Pacific, which is 11 am Eastern. Run until 8 pm Pacific, which is 11 pm Eastern on day one. Then repeat the next day. With a 5 pm Pacific finish on the final day."

"That's asking a lot of the New York team," Noah pointed out. "Especially those 11 pm finishes."

"We could compensate with time off afterward," Marcia suggested. "And maybe arrange hotel rooms near the office for New York team members who have long commutes."

Liam, who had been silently reviewing the concept, finally spoke. "I'm more concerned with the technical risks. Development at this pace often creates shortcuts that become technical debt later."

"Valid concern," Marcia acknowledged. "That's why I

want your input on guardrails - technical standards that can't be compromised even during the sprint."

She turned to a new slide showing a framework with three categories: "Must Have" (non-negotiable technical standards), "Should Have" (preferred approaches), and "Could Have" (optional enhancements).

"This is where your technical dependency map comes in, Liam. We need to ensure teams understand which corners absolutely cannot be cut."

"Understood. Who approves production changes?"

"You," Marcia said. "And you might use a feature flag approach to make things safer?"

Liam leaned back, considering. "I could develop a technical architecture checklist for each team. Minimum requirements to ensure we're not creating messes we'll have to clean up later."

"And we'd need strong QA involvement throughout," Sarah added, warming to the concept. "Not just at the end, but embedded in each team to test as features are developed."

Noah leaned closer to his camera. "What about the New York team's perspective? We've often felt decisions are made in Seattle without our input."

"That's another reason for this approach," Marcia said. "By creating truly integrated teams across offices, we break down those silos. And I'd want you to help lead this effort, Noah, ensuring New York's voice is represented."

Noah looked surprised. "Me? Not Alan?"

"Alan would be involved at a high level, but you have the technical credibility and collaborative skills to help make this work day-to-day."

A hint of a smile crossed Noah's face. "I'm flattered. And intrigued by the concept."

"How would we select the features to tackle?" Sarah

asked.

"That's where the prioritisation workshop comes in," Marcia explained. "We'd work with Elizabeth and Malcolm to identify the critical features for February, then map those to our sprint teams."

Liam, who had been scribbling notes, looked up. "What about team composition? How do we decide who works on what?"

"I'd want input from all of you on that," Marcia said. "We need balanced teams with complementary skills. No all-star teams and leftover teams."

"And leadership is comfortable with this?" Sarah asked sceptically. "It seems unconventional for Alpha."

"I'm discussing it with James and Robert after this meeting," Marcia admitted. "But I wanted your perspectives first. You're closer to the technical realities than they are."

The room fell silent as everyone considered the proposal. Liam was the first to speak.

"I was sceptical when you started explaining this," he said, surprising Marcia with his candour. "But looking at our current trajectory, I don't see how we deliver the February milestone otherwise. At least this approach acknowledges the reality that we need something different."

"The New York team would appreciate being true partners rather than just implementers," Noah added. "If we structure this carefully, it could address both the technical challenges and the collaboration issues we've been facing."

Sarah tapped the concept document. "QA is often the afterthought in rushed development. If we're truly integrated into the teams from the beginning, this could actually lead to better quality than our normal processes."

Marcia felt a surge of cautious optimism. "So, you're all provisionally on board?"

Three nods, including Noah's on the screen.

"With conditions," Liam clarified. "Technical standards can't be compromised. We need clear architectural guidelines for each team."

"And balanced teams with true cross-functional representation," Sarah added.

"And meaningful participation from New York, not just token involvement," Noah said.

"All reasonable conditions," Marcia agreed, making notes. "Let me draft a more detailed proposal incorporating your input. Then we can take it to James and Robert."

As they wrapped up the meeting, Liam lingered behind while Sarah headed back to her team and Noah signed off.

"This isn't how I expected you to approach the February deliverable," he said, gathering his notes.

"Too risky?" Marcia asked.

"Actually," Liam said, "I was going to say it shows you understand the situation better than I thought. Sometimes you need to introduce controlled chaos to break through entrenched problems. It's a principle we use in systems design - adding deliberate noise to overcome local maxima."

Marcia's brow furrowed, surprised by Liam's support. "That's exactly the concept. Calculated risk to achieve breakthrough results."

"The execution will be challenging," Liam warned as they walked out. "Not everyone embraces disruption to their routine."

"That's why I'm starting with you three," Marcia said. "If the strongest technical voices support it, others will follow."

As Liam headed back to his desk, Marcia felt a mix of excitement and apprehension. The concept had survived its first test with the key influencers. Now came the harder part - convincing James and Robert that intentionally disrupting the project's normal patterns was the right strategy.

She gathered her notes and headed toward James's office,

rehearsing her pitch. The February milestone represented not just a delivery commitment but a test of her leadership approach. Traditional methods had failed under Brett's management. Now she was proposing something radically different - creating space for innovation by encouraging calculated disruption of the status quo.

It was a gamble, certainly. But as she approached James's office, Marcia felt increasingly confident that it was a calculated risk worth taking. Sometimes the path to order requires a strategic dose of chaos first.

"Guardrails make speed safer."

✧ ✧ ✧

"An innovation sprint?" Robert Miller leaned back in his chair, eyebrows raised. The late morning light filtered through his office windows, casting dramatic shadows across the antique maps on his wall. "That's not typically how enterprise projects operate, Marcia."

James Anderson sat quietly in the corner, his expression thoughtful rather than dismissive.

"Traditional approaches haven't been working for this project," Marcia replied, standing her ground. "We've got fractured teams, technical complexities, and a tight deadline for February. Something has to change."

Robert drummed his fingers on his desk. "Walk me through the logistics again."

Marcia took a deep breath and outlined the concept - a three-day intensive effort with cross-functional, cross-office teams tackling the February milestone features. Teams would be deliberately mixed, pairing people who didn't normally work together, breaking down the Seattle-New York divide and the walls between development and QA.

"And your key technical people are on board with this?" Robert asked sceptically.

"Liam, Sarah, and Noah all support the concept," Marcia confirmed. "With appropriate guardrails, of course. Liam is creating technical architecture checklists to ensure we maintain standards."

Robert looked surprised. "Liam Everett is supporting something that disrupts his routine? Interesting."

"His exact words were that it shows I understand the situation better than he thought," Marcia said with a small smile. "He compared it to a systems design principle - adding deliberate noise to overcome local maxima."

Robert exchanged glances with James, who finally spoke up. "It's unconventional, but that might be exactly what this project needs. The GFP project has been stuck in dysfunctional patterns. Sometimes you need to shake things up to get unstuck."

Robert stood and walked to his window, looking out at the Seattle skyline. "What about Elizabeth and Malcolm? How will they react?"

"I think Elizabeth will be intrigued," Marcia said. "She's frustrated with the lack of progress and open to creative solutions. Malcolm might be more sceptical, but the focus on delivering the February milestone should appeal to him."

"And if it doesn't work?" Robert turned back to face her. "We'll have burned valuable time we don't have."

"We'll structure it to deliver incremental value," Marcia countered. "Even if we don't achieve everything we hope, we'll make more progress than continuing with the current approach. And we'll learn valuable lessons about cross-team collaboration that will benefit the project long-term."

Robert fell silent, weighing the proposal. "What resources do you need?"

Marcia felt a flutter of hope. That wasn't a no.

"Meeting space in both offices. Food and caffeine to fuel the teams. Some budget for New York hotel rooms since they'll be working late. And your public support - the team needs to know this isn't just a desperate experiment, but a strategic approach endorsed by leadership."

Robert steepled his fingers, considering. "James? Your thoughts?"

James leaned forward. "It's a calculated risk, but with high potential reward. The February release is critical for GFP's quarterly business review. If this helps us deliver, it's worth trying something different."

"And your technical team is on board," Robert mused, more to himself than to Marcia. "That's compelling."

He returned to his desk and sat down. "Alright, Marcia. You have my approval to move forward with the sprint. But I want daily updates during the event, and a clear assessment of what we achieved afterward."

"Absolutely," Marcia agreed, trying to keep the relief from her voice.

"One more thing," Robert added. "I want to be there for part of it. Not to micromanage, but to show my support. And I think Elizabeth and Malcolm should see it in action too."

"I'll coordinate with their schedules," Marcia promised. "Their presence would actually reinforce the importance of the effort."

As the meeting concluded and Marcia left with James, she let out a breath she hadn't realised she was holding.

"That went better than I expected," she admitted.

James smiled. "Robert values innovation more than you might think. He built Alpha on challenging industry norms. He just needed to see you had technical buy-in and a structured approach."

"Now comes the hard part," Marcia said. "Making it

actually work."

"When are you thinking of scheduling this?" James asked as they walked toward the elevator.

"Next week, after I return from New York," Marcia replied. "I want to use my trip to get the New York team fully on board and address any concerns directly."

"Smart," James said, approval quiet but clear. "Face-to-face will make a difference there."

Back in her office, Marcia immediately sent messages to Liam, Sarah, and Noah: *Robert approved the innovation sprint concept. Next step: detailed planning and team composition. Thank you for your support.*

Liam's response was typically brief: *Technical guardrails in progress. Will send draft tonight.*

Sarah was more enthusiastic: *Great news! Already thinking about QA integration strategy for the teams.*

Noah's reply came a few minutes later: *NY team will be excited. Alan might need convincing, but I'll start preparing the ground.*

Buoyed by their replies, she opened a new document to start mapping out the detailed plan. The initiative would need careful design to balance creative freedom with necessary structure.

Her phone vibrated - Tessa: *Heard about the innovation sprint from Sarah. I have some ideas about team composition based on working styles and skills. Can I share them with you?*

Absolutely, Marcia replied. *Stop by any time after 4 pm.*

The momentum was building. What had started as a weekend conversation with Nelson was transforming into a concrete plan with growing support. The concept of calculated risk - deliberate disruption of established patterns to create breakthrough solutions - was taking shape.

As Marcia finalised her planning, she thought about her upcoming New York trip. The sprint would only work if both offices fully embraced it. She needed to use her time in

New York to build genuine enthusiasm, not just reluctant compliance.

Her calendar alert reminded her the prioritisation workshop with Elizabeth and Malcolm was now 90-mintes away - the perfect opportunity to introduce the innovation sprint concept to GFP. If she could secure their support, the final piece would be in place.

Marcia leaned back in her chair, staring at the Seattle rain that had started falling again. The initiative was a calculated risk, pushing her team into the high-risk, high-reward quadrant of Nelson's graph. But sometimes, as he had reminded her, that's where the breakthrough results happened.

Outside her office, she could see the GFP project team going about their work, still in their separate groups - Seattle developers in one area, QA on another floor, the New York team a distant presence on video calls. Soon she would deliberately disrupt those patterns, reconfiguring them into combinations designed to spark creativity and collaboration.

It wouldn't be comfortable. Change rarely was. But as her mother used to say, "You can't steer a ship that isn't moving."

Marcia turned back to her planning document and began mapping out the next critical steps to make the innovation sprint a reality.

✧ ✧ ✧

Marcia paused outside the conference room, balancing her laptop and a binder of plans, and took one last calming breath. Through the door, she could see Malcolm's disapproving frown as he spoke with Elizabeth - not exactly a morale boost. Her palms were damp. *They might shoot this down in flames*, she thought, throat tight. But she also recalled the spark in her team's eyes when they discussed the sprint.

That enthusiasm was worth fighting for. Chin up, she pushed the door open, determined to sell this unconventional idea with every ounce of conviction she had.

"Let me get this straight," Malcolm said, his tone crisp and deliberate, the scepticism unmistakable. "You want to throw out conventional development approaches and run some sort of... hackathon... to deliver our February milestone?"

The room had grown tense. Elizabeth sat beside Malcolm, her expression more measured but clearly surprised. GFP's requirements lead and two product owners flanked them, exchanging uncertain glances.

Marcia stood her ground by the whiteboard. "Not throw out - adapt. The innovation sprint is a focused, structured approach designed specifically to overcome the challenges we're facing. It's not a free-for-all."

"It sounds experimental," Malcolm persisted. "Our quarterly business review isn't the place for experiments, Marcia."

"With respect, Malcolm," Liam said unexpectedly from the end of the table, "conventional approaches haven't been delivering results. We need to try something different."

All eyes turned to Liam, surprised by his intervention. He had a reputation for speaking up in client meetings and pushing back on management. At least on this occasion, his tone was more respectful.

Elizabeth leaned in. "Tell me more about the guardrails you mentioned. How do we ensure quality doesn't suffer?"

"Each team will have clear technical and quality standards they must meet," Marcia explained, grateful for the opening. "Liam has developed architecture guidelines, and Sarah will embed testers within each team from the beginning."

She clicked to the next slide showing the proposed team

structure. "We'll create balanced teams mixing Seattle and New York staff, developers, testers, and analysts. Each team will tackle specific features selected in today's workshop."

Elizabeth studied the diagram. "And this approach has worked for other projects?"

"Similar approaches have," Marcia confirmed. "Though we've tailored this specifically to our situation. The key is breaking down the silos that have been hindering progress."

Malcolm still looked unconvinced. "What makes you think three days of intensive work can accomplish what we haven't managed in months?"

Marcia's throat was dry. She knew proposing an innovation sprint was a gamble - if it failed, the project would lose precious time it couldn't spare, and *she* would lose the trust of everyone in the room. She felt all eyes on her, waiting for her to waver. Summoning her courage, Marcia squared her shoulders.

"Because we're changing the conditions," Marcia said, meeting Malcolm's gaze. "By reconfiguring teams, creating dedicated focus time without distractions, and bringing the right people together, " she inhaled, using the pause for effect. "We create opportunities for breakthroughs that don't happen in our regular workflow."

Elizabeth turned to Robert, who had been quietly observing. "What's your perspective on this approach, Robert?"

"I was sceptical initially," Robert admitted. "But after reviewing the detailed plan and hearing the technical team's support, I'm convinced it's worth pursuing. Sometimes unconventional challenges require unconventional solutions."

The room grew still as everyone considered the proposal. Malcolm tapped his pen against the table, clearly still hesitant.

"Here's what I propose," Marcia said, breaking the

silence. "Let's use today's workshop to identify and prioritise the features for February. Then we'll map those to the innovation sprint structure. You'll have complete visibility into the approach and can assess the risk-reward balance for yourselves."

Elizabeth inclined her chin, approval measured. "That's reasonable. I appreciate that you're thinking creatively, Marcia. The status quo clearly isn't working."

Malcolm sighed. "I still have reservations..." He exchanged a look with Elizabeth, then exhaled sharply. "Three days," he said, fingers drumming on the table. "Prove to me it isn't a waste."

Marcia had to resist the urge to break into a relieved smile. She gave a single, firm nod. "Three days is all I ask. We'll deliver." Her voice was calm, but inside she was buzzing with exhilaration. They had a chance.

As the meeting adjourned, Marcia allowed herself a quiet sigh. Gaining Malcolm's cautious approval felt like prying open a door that had been firmly shut - a risky plan was now officially in play, and it was on her shoulders to make it count.

✧ ✧ ✧

After a short recess, a wider group reconvened around the conference table, notebooks and coffee cups in hand, ready to tackle the next phase of discussion.

"Thank you," Marcia said. "Now, let's focus on what features are most critical for your quarterly business review."

The group worked through GFP's requirements for two hours, mapping business value against technical complexity. Liam provided crucial insights on interdependencies, while Tessa documented each decision and its rationale.

Sarah outlined three related defects in the core module

and proposed tracking them as a single core-stability work item. Elizabeth looked up. "Does that jeopardise February?"

"No," Sarah said. "Two days to fix, one day to re-test, in parallel with feature work. It removes the likeliest failure points in auth and funds flow. If we skip it, UAT could block."

Tessa logged the item and noted the re-test window.

By early afternoon, they had identified seven features as critical for February (including core stability and the continued authentication fix focus), with five more as 'stretch goals' if time permitted.

"This is a solid foundation," Elizabeth said as they prepared to break. "I'm still not entirely convinced about the innovation sprint approach, but I appreciate the clear prioritisation. It gives us something concrete to show leadership, regardless of how we get there."

"I'd like to observe part of this sprint," Malcolm added, surprising Marcia. "If we're going to take this unconventional approach, I want to see it firsthand."

"Of course," Marcia agreed quickly. "We'd welcome your participation. In fact, having business stakeholders available during the sprint helps teams make faster decisions when questions arise."

As the GFP team departed for a late lunch, Robert lingered behind with Marcia and Liam.

"That went better than I expected," Robert observed. "Elizabeth seems cautiously supportive."

"Malcolm less so," Marcia noted, "but he's willing to give it a chance."

Liam gathered his materials. "The feature prioritisation was valuable regardless. Now we have clear targets for the sprint."

"Speaking of which," Robert said, "when exactly are you planning to hold this?"

"Next Wednesday through Friday," Marcia replied. "That gives us time to prepare after my New York trip and still leaves buffer before the February release."

"Keep me updated on the detailed planning," Robert said. "This innovation sprint is unconventional for Alpha, but if it works, it could become a valuable tool for other challenging projects."

After Robert left to host the GFP lunch, Liam turned to Marcia. "Malcolm was sceptical, but that's his default state. The fact that he wants to observe the sprint is actually positive. He's curious despite himself."

Marcia's eyes crinkled. "I noticed that too. And thank you for speaking up. Having technical support made a difference."

"Just stating facts," Liam shrugged, though Marcia caught a hint of satisfaction in his expression. "Repeating the same play and expecting a different result isn't working," he added.

As Liam left, Marcia stayed behind to organise her notes from the workshop. The prioritisation had gone well, giving them clear targets for the sprint. But she could still sense the underlying scepticism, particularly from Malcolm.

As Sarah packed up, she paused beside Marcia. "Thanks for backing straight talk," she said quietly. "Honest, then specific worked - and I'm glad core stability made the list."

"It was good to call it out," Marcia said. "Now own the plan and run with it."

The New York trip now took on even greater importance. She needed to ensure both offices were fully aligned and prepared for the sprint. Any hesitation or resistance would undermine the intensive effort before it began.

Her phone pinged - Noah: *How did the prioritisation go? NY team eager for updates.*

Good progress, she replied. *Seven priority features identified for February. Malcolm and Elizabeth cautiously open to the innovation sprint. Will share details when I see you tomorrow.*

Airport pickup still on for 7.30 am? Noah asked.

Yes, thank you. Looking forward to meeting everyone in person.

Marcia gathered her materials and headed back to her office. Tomorrow she'd be in New York, working to bridge the geographical and cultural divide that had hindered the project. The innovation sprint concept had survived its first exposure to GFP leadership, but the real test would be in the execution.

As she walked through the Seattle office, Marcia could feel the subtle buzz of energy. Word about the initiative was spreading, creating a mixture of curiosity and apprehension. People were talking across team boundaries, speculating about how it would work and what teams they might join.

That alone was progress - conversations happening that wouldn't normally occur. The concept of calculated risk was already having an effect, disrupting patterns and creating new connections before the sprint even began.

A quiet confidence took root. The sprint was a gamble, certainly. But watching the early ripples of change move through the team, she felt increasingly confident that it was a calculated risk worth taking.

Tomorrow in New York, she would work to ensure that both sides of the project team were ready to embrace that creative disruption together. Now, she had to pack for the Delta red-eye.

✧　✧　✧

New York greeted Marcia with both biting wind and the promise of sunshine as she exited JFK's terminal. The city's energy hit her immediately - faster, louder, more intense than

Seattle's laid-back vibe.

"Marcia!" called a familiar voice. Noah waved from the curb, his Yankees cap pulled low against the cold. Beside him idled a black Lincoln Town Car, its hazard lights blinking in the pickup lane.

"Thanks for meeting me," she said, wheeling her carry-on toward him. "You didn't have to come all the way to the airport."

"Consider it proper New York hospitality," Noah said with a quick grin, taking her bag. "Besides, I figured you could use the travel time to get a download on the office dynamics before you arrive."

Once settled into the back seat of the car, Manhattan-bound traffic already crawling past the windows, Noah turned to her with a more serious expression. "So, this innovation sprint. The team's been talking about nothing else since yesterday."

"Good conversations or concerned ones?" Marcia asked.

"Both," Noah admitted. "Most of the developers are intrigued. They've felt stuck in the endless cycle of integration issues with Seattle. But Alan, he's worried this is Seattle imposing another process on us."

Marcia nodded, unsurprised. "That's exactly why I'm here - to make sure New York feels like an equal partner, not an afterthought."

"Smart move," Noah said. "Having you physically present makes a difference. Brett visited exactly once in eighteen months."

Noah's fingers tapped restlessly against his knee, betraying a worry he hadn't fully voiced.

"I'm still figuring out where the edges are," Noah admitted quietly. "Everyone here moves fast, and I just don't want to be the one who slows the team down."

Marcia looked over, surprised by the honesty. "You're

not slowing anyone down. You're helping us see what we've been missing."

The Town Car weaved through Queens traffic as Noah briefed her on key team members she'd meet today - Alisha, the front-end lead who'd been frustrated by constantly changing APIs; Miguel, their UX designer who felt their work was an afterthought; and several others who had grown increasingly disconnected from the Seattle team.

"What about Alan?" Marcia asked. "What's his main concern with the innovation sprint?"

Noah hesitated, thinking. "He's protective of the team. Worried they'll be blamed if it doesn't succeed. There's a history of Seattle dictating approaches, then pointing fingers when things go wrong."

"That's exactly what the sprint is designed to address," Marcia said. "By mixing the teams across offices, we eliminate the 'us versus them' dynamic. No more Seattle team or New York team - just feature teams with members from both locations."

"That's a significant change," Noah observed as the Manhattan skyline came into view. "You're essentially redrawing the organisational boundaries, even if temporarily."

"Sometimes boundaries need redrawing," Marcia said. "Especially when they've become barriers."

Forty minutes later, the car pulled up outside a glass-and-steel midtown building. Alpha's New York office occupied the fifteenth floor, with views of the Empire State Building to the south.

Marcia paused in the building's atrium, smoothing her blouse as her reflection looked back anxiously from the glass. James had warned her that Alan Prescott might view her presence as interference. She drew in a deep breath and reminded herself, *I'm here to listen and learn, not to impose.* Her stomach fluttered with nerves as she badged in, but she walked forward with purpose - determined to show the New York team she was on their side.

Entering the office with Noah, she immediately noticed the differences from Seattle. Where the Seattle office was spacious and somewhat casual, New York was compact, energetic, and slightly more formal. Desks were closer together, conversations were faster-paced, and most people were dressed a notch more professionally than their West Coast counterparts.

"Marcia!" A woman with curly hair and thick-rimmed tortoiseshell glasses approached with an extended hand. "I'm Alisha. We've spoken on video calls. Great to finally meet you in person."

More introductions followed as team members gathered around. Marcia noticed their curious expressions - they were assessing her, just as she was assessing them.

"Where's Alan?" she asked Noah quietly.

"Client meeting. He'll be back for lunch," Noah replied. "Which gives you time to connect with the team first."

Smart sequencing, Marcia thought. Building relationships with the team before facing their potentially sceptical leader.

Over the next two hours, Marcia met with key team members individually and in small groups. She asked questions and listened carefully, noting patterns in their concerns:

They felt decisions were made in Seattle without their input.
Their expertise wasn't valued equally with Seattle-based colleagues.
Communication was reactive rather than proactive.
They rarely received context for changes, just implementation requirements.

In Alisha's office, the front-end lead expressed her frustration bluntly. "I rebuild components weekly because Seattle changes APIs without warning. It's exhausting and demoralising."

"That's why integrating the teams during the innovation sprint is so crucial," Marcia explained. "When you're working directly with the Seattle developers on the same team, those communication gaps close naturally."

Alisha looked sceptical. "Three days won't change ingrained habits."

"Not completely," Marcia acknowledged. "But it can break the ice and establish new patterns. Think of it as a reset - creating space for different ways of working together."

By lunchtime, Marcia had spoken with most of the technical team. They were talented, passionate, and frustrated - exactly the combination that could benefit from the innovation sprint if properly engaged.

"Ready for lunch with Alan?" Noah asked, appearing at her temporary workspace.

"As ready as I'll be," Marcia replied, gathering her notes.

They walked two blocks to a deli that Noah described as "the team's second office." The warm, aromatic space was packed with midtown workers grabbing sandwiches, but a corner table had been reserved.

Alan Prescott was already waiting, a tall man in his fifties with neatly trimmed silver sideburns and a cautious expression. He stood as they approached.

"Marcia Hughes," he said, extending his hand. "Finally, Seattle sends someone who doesn't just dial in."

"I should have come sooner," Marcia acknowledged, taking a seat. "That's on me. On the last New York client visit, there wasn't time to come into the office."

Noah slid into the seat beside her, giving Alan a brief nod. "Thanks for making time, Alan."

Alan didn't smile, turning to Marcia. "We've heard that before. Seattle drops in, says the right things, and we're back to shipping hotfixes for decisions we didn't make."

"Fair," Marcia said, meeting his gaze. "I'm here to change *that* pattern - starting by listening."

He blinked once, recalibrating, then let out a slow breath. His fingers stopped drumming on the table; he set the menu aside. "Well, you're here now. Noah tells me you have some... innovative plans."

"I do," Marcia confirmed as they ordered sandwiches. "But before we get into that, I'd like your read on where things stand."

Noah added, "And if anything I've shared missed the mark, say so. Better we fix it here."

Alan studied her for a moment, as if deciding how frank to be.

"The New York team feels like second-class citizens," he said finally. "We get requirements without context, deadlines without input, and blame without authority. That's the blunt truth."

Marcia ran her thumb along the edge of the paper napkin in front of her, taking a moment before responding. "I appreciate the honesty. What I've heard from your team today confirms that."

"Then you understand why I'm sceptical about this innovation sprint," Alan continued. "It sounds like another Seattle initiative being imposed on us."

"That's exactly why I'm here," Marcia said. "This isn't Seattle's sprint or New York's sprint. It needs to be our sprint - planned and executed together with equal input from both offices."

Their sandwiches arrived, momentarily pausing the conversation.

"The concept has merit," Alan admitted after taking a

bite. "Breaking established patterns can yield breakthroughs. But the execution matters. How do you ensure true equality in the process?"

"Start with team composition," Marcia explained. "Equal representation from both offices on each feature team. Leadership roles distributed across locations. And I'll be very visible about valuing New York's expertise."

Noah leaned in. "And decision flow won't be one-way - joint design sessions and shared backlog ownership."

"What about after the sprint?" Alan pressed. "We go back to the same siloed structure?"

"Not if I can help it," Marcia said firmly. "The sprint is a catalyst, not a one-time event. It's designed to establish new collaborative patterns that continue afterward."

She outlined her longer-term plans: rotating team members between offices, regular joint architecture sessions, and shared accountability metrics that discouraged finger-pointing.

As they finished their sandwiches, Alan's expression had softened slightly.

"You've clearly thought this through," he acknowledged. "And I appreciate you coming in person to discuss it. That alone signals a different approach than what we're used to."

"So, you'll support the innovation sprint?" Marcia asked.

"Conditionally," Alan said. "I want New York team members in meaningful roles, not just participants. And I want to be involved in planning the team structures."

"Absolutely," Marcia agreed immediately. "In fact, I'd like you to co-lead the sprint planning with me. Equal partnership from the start."

Something shifted in Alan's demeanour - a subtle relaxation of his defensive posture.

"In that case," he said, offering his hand, "you have my support."

Back at the office, Marcia spent the afternoon in a conference room with Alan, Noah, and Alisha, mapping out the sprint structure. They video-conferenced with Liam and Sarah in Seattle, collaboratively designing team compositions and feature assignments.

By late afternoon, they had a draft plan that genuinely reflected both offices' perspectives. The innovation sprint was taking shape as a truly joint initiative.

As they wrapped up, Alan made an unexpected offer. "The team usually goes for drinks on Tuesdays at a place around the corner. It would mean a lot if you'd join us."

"I'd be honoured," Marcia replied.

✦   ✦   ✦

At a crowded Irish pub that evening, Marcia found herself surrounded by the New York team in a more relaxed setting. Conversations flowed more easily, with technical discussions intermixed with personal stories and office jokes.

"They didn't expect you to come," Noah said quietly, joining her at the bar while she waited for a drink. "Brett always had 'important calls' when social invitations came up."

"This is the important call," Marcia replied. "Understanding the team as people, not just resources."

As they rejoined the group, Marcia reflected on the day's progress. She'd come to New York hoping to build support for the innovation sprint. She would be leaving with something more valuable - the beginnings of genuine trust from the New York team.

Still, a small tension lingered. Trust was forming, but fragile - the kind that could evaporate with one misstep or assumption. She reminded herself to stay present, stay honest, and let the relationships strengthen through the work.

The sprint still faced significant challenges. But with both offices now genuinely engaged in the approach, they at least had a fighting chance at breakthrough results.

Marcia raised her glass as Alan proposed a toast to the combined team effort.

✧　✧　✧

The Wednesday workshop wrapped just after six, long enough for the Manhattan skyline to dissolve into a warm, glittering haze. Marcia packed her notebook, feeling the careful fatigue that comes from a day that demanded her full attention - but also rewarded it. The New York team had been sharper, more candid, and far more invested than she'd expected stepping into the week.

As she stepped into the elevator, Noah caught the door with a practiced hand.

"Good second day," he said, shifting his bag. "You got them talking more than I've seen in months."

"I'm impressed by the team," Marcia said. "Direct, technical, honest. They didn't hold back."

Noah gave a small, knowing smile. "That's the thing you should remember about this office. Seattle thinks New York is combative. We're not - we just say what we mean. What frustrates us isn't hard conversations. It's, being kept in the dark."

The elevator hummed softly as they descended.

Marcia tilted her head. "Meaning Brett?"

"Meaning everyone felt decisions were being made somewhere else," Noah said. "We stopped getting context. We stopped getting explanations. Eventually, people assumed the worst."

Marcia exhaled slowly. That lined up with everything she'd sensed today - the caution behind their questions, the hesitation before speaking openly, the sideways glances seeking confirmation that honesty was now allowed.

"Thank you," she said. "That's helpful."

"Just be straight with us," Noah replied as the elevator opened into the lobby. "Even if the news isn't good. That's all this office really asks."

Outside, the New York evening buzzed with life - sirens in the distance, taxis sliding through rain-polished streets, the smell of street food mingling with cold air. Marcia stepped out under the canopy, watching Noah merge into the crowd with a final wave.

She stood there for a moment, letting the city's restless energy settle around her.

Today had gone well - better than she'd dared hope. She pulled out her phone and typed a quick note:

If it's bad, say it's bad.
NY requires directness. No surprises.
Lead with truth, even when inconvenient.

Sliding the phone back into her coat pocket, Marcia felt the insight lock into place. New York didn't need reassurance - they needed a leader willing to be transparent, even when it was uncomfortable.

Tomorrow she'd fly back to Seattle.

Friday she'd face the team again.

But tonight, standing in the heartbeat of another city, she finally understood something crucial: Trust wasn't built by having all the answers. It was built by telling the truth early enough that people could help shape the path forward.

She turned toward her hotel, the wind cold on her face, but the clarity warm in her chest.

FIELD RULE: Controlled Chaos Pre-Brief (30 minutes)

- One goal; one risk budget; one rollback signal.
- Must / Should / Could on the wall.
- Name the rollback owner.
- Decide: Go / Test / No-Go; log decision id.

Examples:

For the authentication work, the team might set **one goal** (ship the updated flow), **one risk budget** (allow two schema adjustments), and **one rollback signal** (stop if the QA harness fails twice consecutively).

Must: Protect the core path. For the authentication work, the API must remain backward-compatible throughout the sprint.

Should: Reduce avoidable friction. Teams should use the provided contracts and guardrails before inventing alternatives.

Could: Explore optional improvements - small quality upgrades or UI refinements - only if the Musts and Shoulds are already satisfied.

Do this tomorrow: Run one pre-brief before any risky change.

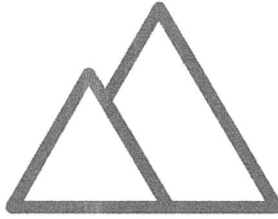

Chapter 4
The Power of Perspective

Good managers solve the problems they can see. Great managers step back until the invisible patterns reveal themselves. Perspective is the gift of distance - the ability to see not just the trees, but the hidden forest shaping them.

✧ ✧ ✧

Zoom until the work makes sense.

✧ ✧ ✧

The Friday after returning from New York, Marcia sat in her office staring at the whiteboard covered with plans for the innovation sprint. Coloured sticky notes formed a complex matrix of teams, features, and schedules. Her mind hummed with the quiet energy of anticipation - they were only three days away from the sprint, and every detail mattered.

A knock at her door broke her concentration. James stood there, looking uncharacteristically hesitant.

"Got a minute?" he asked. "Robert wanted me to check if you need anything for next week's sprint."

"Come in," Marcia said, gesturing to a chair. "I think we're in good shape logistically. Alan and I have finalised the team compositions. Liam and Noah have prepared the technical guardrails. Sarah's created quality checkpoints for each feature."

James inclined his head, uncertainty still in his eyes. "That's all good, but Robert's concerned about the bigger picture. You've put a lot of eggs in this innovation sprint basket."

"It's a calculated risk," Marcia acknowledged, "but a necessary one. Standard approaches weren't getting us anywhere."

"I agree," James said quickly. "But have you thought about what happens if the sprint doesn't deliver everything we hope? Malcolm's already sceptical."

Marcia got up and closed her office door. "To be honest, I've been wrestling with that question all week. The sprint won't solve everything - that's unrealistic. But if we can establish new patterns of collaboration and make meaningful progress on the February milestone, I'll consider it a success."

James seemed relieved by her candour. "That's exactly what I needed to hear. It's not about perfection; it's about breaking through the stalemate."

"Precisely," Marcia said. "But there is one thing I'm still struggling with. Even with all our planning, I feel like I'm missing something important - some pattern or connection that would make everything clearer."

James leaned forward, intrigued. "What kind of pattern?"

"I'm not sure," Marcia admitted. "The authentication issues, the Seattle-New York divide, the changing requirements - they're all symptoms of something deeper. I just can't quite see it yet."

James's eyes glinted with amusement. "Ah, you're looking for the invisible."

"The *invisible?*"

"It's what separates good managers from great ones," James explained. "Good managers solve the problems they can see. Great managers step back to find the patterns others miss - the invisible forces shaping everything else."

Marcia reflected on it. "Like Liam seeing that our architecture was too complex, not because any individual component was wrong, but because the overall pattern created unnecessary integration points?"

"Exactly," James nodded. "When you're too close to a situation, you see trees instead of the forest. Sometimes you need to step back - literally and figuratively - to see what's really happening."

He stood up and walked to the whiteboard. "May I?"

"Please," Marcia said, handing him a marker.

James drew a simple diagram of three concentric circles. "Most managers operate here," he said, pointing to the innermost circle. "Tactical, day-to-day issues. Some move to this middle ring - strategic planning, resource allocation. But the real insights come from stepping all the way out here," he tapped the outermost circle, "where you can see patterns that aren't visible from the inside."

"And how do I get to that outer circle?" Marcia asked.

"Physical distance often helps," James suggested. "Take a walk. Find a quiet space away from the office. Let your mind wander. And ask different questions - not 'how do we fix this problem?' but 'why does this pattern keep occurring?'"

Marcia stared at the concentric circles. Something about the visual resonated with her.

"It's not just about the sprint itself, is it?" she said slowly. "It's about what the sprint reveals - patterns of interaction, communication breakdowns, assumptions that need challenging."

"Now you're seeing it," James smiled. "The sprint is a means, not an end. It creates conditions where hidden patterns become visible."

Marcia studied James's three concentric circles and felt a subtle shift in her thinking. "Most managers operate here…," he'd said, pointing to the innermost circle of immediate tasks. And there she was, smack in that centre, firefighting everyday issues. *No wonder they kept missing the bigger picture.* "That's enlightening," she murmured, tapping the outer circle on the notepad where she'd copied the sketch. She realised James was nudging her to step back and look for patterns instead of drowning in details. It was a humbling insight - and exactly what she needed.

As James left, Marcia couldn't shake the feeling that she was on the edge of an important insight. She decided to take his advice literally. Grabbing her coat, she headed for the elevator.

"I'll be back in an hour," she told Tessa as they passed in the lobby. "Need some fresh air to think."

Outside, Seattle's winter chill cleared her head as she walked toward the waterfront. The city's pace felt slower than New York's frenetic energy but more deliberate than she'd previously noticed. Watching the ferries cross Puget Sound, Marcia let her mind drift, considering the project from different angles.

What were the patterns she was missing? What invisible forces were shaping the GFP project's challenges?

By the time she reached a bench overlooking the water, something was emerging in her mind - not a solution exactly, but a new perspective. The technical issues, team fragmentation, and requirement changes weren't separate problems. They were manifestations of the same underlying pattern: disconnection.

She unlocked her phone and pulled up the quarterly business review reports, scrolling between the Seattle and New York metrics. A footnote caught her eye: New York was counting client-reported issues, while Seattle counted all defects, including those found internally. No wonder New York's 'defects resolved' looked low - they were using a different definition.

Every time Seattle touted a technical efficiency - *backend response time improved by 20%* - New York's summary highlighted a disconnect - *end-users still frustrated with login process*. Both teams were working hard - just with different definitions and focus; they weren't speaking the same language. This was the disconnect Noah had been hinting at.

She took a screenshot and highlighted the mismatched points with her finger, heart quickening with a mix of alarm and excitement. *We've been aiming at different targets*, she thought, amazed at how obvious it seemed in hindsight.

Disconnection between business needs and technical realities. Disconnection between Seattle and New York. Disconnection between what GFP said they wanted and what they actually needed.

The innovation sprint wouldn't just deliver features - it would reconnect what had become disconnected. Force alignment where misalignment had become the norm. Create shared understanding where assumptions had prevailed.

Still holding her phone, she switched to her notes app and began typing rapidly, seeing connections she'd missed before:

Authentication issues stemmed from disconnected architectural decisions.
Seattle-NY divide reflected disconnected priorities and information flows.
Changing requirements came from disconnected understanding between business and technical needs.

As the pattern crystallised, Marcia felt a strange calm replace her anxiety. The innovation sprint wasn't a desperate gamble - it was exactly the right way to address the fundamental disconnection plaguing the project.

Walking back to the office with renewed clarity, Marcia realised this was what James had meant about seeing the invisible. Sometimes you needed to step back - physically and mentally - to recognise the patterns hiding in plain sight.

Back at her desk, Marcia added a new slide to her sprint kick-off presentation: 'Reconnecting the Disconnected'. This wasn't just about delivering features; it was about reestablishing the connections necessary for sustainable success.

The sprint was still a risk, but now it was an even more calculated one - addressing not just the visible symptoms but the invisible pattern beneath them. As Marcia refined her approach, she sensed this perspective shift would be crucial not just for the sprint's success, but for her growth as a leader.

A notification from Liam appeared: *Technical guardrails document complete. Something's still bothering me about the integration approach, but can't put my finger on it. Will keep thinking.*

Marcia tapped the notification away, amused by the timing. Perhaps Liam too was reaching for that outer circle of perspective, trying to see the invisible patterns that others missed.

✧ ✧ ✧

The evening sky had darkened by the time Marcia finally left the office. Most of the team had departed hours ago, but she'd stayed behind, refining the sprint plan with her newfound perspective on the project's disconnection patterns.

Her condo welcomed her with silence - a stark contrast to the mental noise she'd been navigating all day. She kicked off her shoes and heated up leftover Thai food, carrying it to her living room whiteboard. The board still displayed her original project assessment, now covered with sticky notes and arrows tracking her evolving understanding.

As she ate, Marcia stared at the board, letting her thoughts wander freely. The pattern of disconnection seemed even clearer now than during her waterfront epiphany. But something still nagged at her - a missing piece she couldn't quite identify.

Her phone buzzed with a text from Noah: *Just reviewed Liam's technical guardrails document. Solid framework. NY team has some questions about integration points, but nothing major. How are you feeling about Wednesday?*

Cautiously optimistic, she replied. *Had an insight today about the underlying patterns. Will explain on tomorrow's call.*

Patterns? Noah texted back.

It's about disconnection - across offices, between business and technical needs, within the architecture itself. The sprint isn't just about features; it's about reconnecting what's become disconnected.

Noah's response came after a thoughtful pause: *That resonates. Have you considered this might extend to GFP internally too? Elizabeth and Malcolm don't always seem aligned.*

Marcia sat up straighter. Noah had just added another dimension to her emerging pattern - one she hadn't fully considered. The disconnection didn't stop at Alpha's boundaries; it extended into GFP's organisation as well.

She grabbed a marker and added 'GFP internal alignment' to her whiteboard, drawing connections to the other elements. Elizabeth focused on long-term transformation while Malcolm prioritised immediate market response. Their competing priorities cascaded down through the project, creating contradictory demands.

You just expanded my pattern, she texted Noah. *Thank you.*

Happy to help, he replied. *That's the beauty of cross-office collaboration - different perspectives reveal what others miss.*

Marcia felt the idea click into place. Even this simple text exchange demonstrated the value of connecting different viewpoints - exactly what the innovation sprint aimed to achieve on a larger scale.

Energised by this new insight, she moved to her laptop and opened Elizabeth's latest email about the quarterly business review. Reading between the lines, she could see the tensions Noah had highlighted. Elizabeth emphasised comprehensive transformation while Malcolm's added comments focused exclusively on competitive market features.

This wasn't just about delivering a February milestone; it was about helping GFP resolve their own internal disconnection through the process.

A knock at her door interrupted her thoughts. She wasn't expecting anyone this late.

"Package delivery," called a voice.

Through the peephole, she saw a courier holding a small box. Signing for it, she was surprised to find Robert Miller's business card attached to the package.

Inside was a book titled "Systems Thinking for Business Transformation" with a handwritten note:

Marcia - James mentioned your search for patterns. This helped me see Alpha's growth challenges differently years ago. Might offer some perspective for GFP. - Robert

Intrigued, Marcia flipped through the book, stopping at a heavily highlighted chapter called "Finding Leverage Points in Complex Systems." One passage jumped out:

The most effective interventions target connection points between system elements, not the elements themselves. Change how parts connect, and you change the whole system's behaviour.

She carried the book to her whiteboard, looking at her disconnection pattern with fresh eyes. What if the innovation sprint wasn't just about delivering features or even building relationships? What if it was about redesigning the connections between all elements of the system - technical, human, and organisational?

This perspective made even Liam's architectural concerns clearer. The authentication issues weren't just technical problems; they were symptoms of disconnected decision-making processes. By consolidating the services, they weren't merely fixing a technical flaw but establishing a pattern of unified decisions that could extend beyond this specific issue.

Marcia started on a fresh section of her whiteboard and began mapping the system differently - not as separate problems to solve but as connection points to strengthen or redesign. Each innovation sprint team wasn't just building features; they were establishing new connection patterns that could persist after the sprint ended.

As midnight approached, Marcia had filled the board with a new framework. The innovation sprint now had an additional layer of purpose - creating conditions for reconnection at multiple levels:

1. Technical integration (API standardisation, authentication consolidation)
2. Team collaboration (cross-office, cross-functional teams)
3. Business-technical alignment (embedded stakeholders, rapid feedback)
4. GFP internal alignment (joint prioritisation, visible trade-offs)

By targeting these connection points simultaneously, they could change the system's behaviour more fundamentally than addressing each issue separately.

Exhausted but exhilarated, Marcia took photos of her whiteboard work and sent one to James with a message: *Found more invisible patterns. Thank you for pushing me to look deeper.*

His reply came moments later despite the late hour: *This is exactly what great leaders do - see the system beneath the symptoms. Get some sleep. You can share this perspective with the team on Monday.*

Marcia booked a Saturday morning court at the indoor tennis centre near Green Lake, already picturing the steady rhythm of serves and returns. Forty-five minutes of thwacking a ball across the net was her best way of shaking off the week. She confirmed the booking, then closed her laptop and felt the week's tension give way to a steadier energy.

As she set down her racquet bag by the door and got ready for bed, she realised her anxiety about the innovation sprint had transformed into something else: a sense of purposeful anticipation. Liam particularly might respond to this systems view - it aligned with his technical instincts about consolidation and simplification.

The sprint no longer felt like a gamble. It was a strategic intervention aimed squarely at the invisible patterns that had been holding the entire project back.

✧ ✧ ✧

"You're mapping the entire system," Liam said, a hint of surprise in his voice. He stood before Marcia's home-whiteboard propped up on her desk early Monday morning, coffee forgotten in his hand as he studied her late-night insights.

"I'm trying to," Marcia grinned, pleased he saw it. "After our conversation on Friday about the integration approach bothering you, I realised we needed to step back and see the bigger picture."

Liam moved closer to the board, examining the connection points she'd identified. He pointed to the technical integration section. "This explains why the authentication consolidation feels so important beyond just fixing a feature. It's establishing a pattern of unified architecture that affects everything downstream."

"Exactly," Marcia said, relieved that he understood. "It's not just about fixing authentication - it's about changing how we make architectural decisions."

Sarah entered Marcia's office, followed by Tessa. Marcia had called this impromptu meeting with her key team members before the day's regular stand-up.

"Sorry I'm late," Tessa said, then stopped when she saw the whiteboard. "Wow. That's comprehensive."

Marcia gestured for everyone to sit. "I had some insights over the weekend about what we're really trying to accomplish with the innovation sprint. It's bigger than just delivering features."

For the next fifteen minutes, she walked them through her perspective on the disconnection patterns plaguing the project - technical, organisational, and cross-company. She explained how the sprint could serve as a catalyst for reconnection at multiple levels simultaneously.

"So, we're not just building features," Sarah said slowly. "We're rebuilding connections."

"And creating new ones," Marcia added. "The sprint teams aren't random groupings - they're deliberately designed to establish connection points that should have existed all along."

Liam had barely spoken, his attention fixed on the whiteboard. Finally, he turned to Marcia. "This matches what's been bothering me about our approach. We've been treating symptoms individually instead of addressing the system they exist within."

"Exactly," Marcia said, encouraged by his understanding. "What do you think, Tessa?"

The business analyst tapped her stylus against her tablet thoughtfully. "It explains why requirement changes have been so disruptive. It's not just about the changes themselves - it's about how they flow through a disconnected system, creating amplified chaos at each broken connection point."

"And if we fix the connections -" Sarah began.

"Changes become manageable instead of destructive," Tessa finished.

Marcia felt a surge of excitement. They were getting it. "I'd like to incorporate this perspective into our sprint kick-off. Not the technical details, but the core insight about reconnection. I think it will help everyone understand why we're approaching this differently."

"It gives purpose beyond the deadline," Sarah said, conviction steady. "Makes it about building something sustainable, not just hitting a target."

Liam, who had returned to studying the whiteboard, spoke without turning around. "We should adjust the team compositions slightly. If connection points are our leverage, we need to ensure we have the right people at each critical junction."

"What are you thinking?" Marcia asked.

"Alisha from New York should lead the user profile team, not support it," Liam said decisively. "She understands the connection between front-end experience and back-end services better than anyone. And I should work directly with Noah on the API standardisation rather than overseeing it remotely."

Marcia blinked in surprise. Liam rarely volunteered for collaborative leadership roles. "That would mean traveling to New York during the sprint."

"Yes," he said simply. "Some connections need to be established in person."

The room fell silent as everyone processed this unexpected offer. Liam, who typically avoided travel and preferred working alone, was volunteering to fly across the country to collaborate in person.

"I think that's an excellent idea," Marcia said carefully. "If you're sure."

Liam agreed with a quiet confidence. "The system perspective makes it clear. Without that connection point strengthened, other efforts will be undermined."

As the meeting wrapped up and the team headed toward the daily stand-up, Marcia felt a shift in their collective energy. The system perspective had transformed their understanding of the sprint from a high-pressure deadline to an opportunity for meaningful reconstruction.

"Marcia," Liam said, lingering behind as the others left. "This systems view - it's something I've felt intuitively but struggled to articulate. Architecture is ultimately about connections, not just components."

"I'm glad it resonates," she replied. "I think it will help others see beyond their immediate tasks too."

"Just one thing," he added, hand on the doorframe. "When you share this with the broader team, emphasize that we're not just creating temporary connections for the sprint. We're establishing patterns that should continue afterward."

"I will," Marcia promised.

The daily stand-up had a different quality that morning. As team members shared updates and coordinated their day, Marcia noticed them naturally making connections between their work and others' - something that had been rare before. Word had already spread about her systems perspective, creating small ripples of changed behaviour.

James joined her as the stand-up dispersed. "I see your perspective shift is already having an effect," he observed. "Liam volunteering to go to New York? That's unprecedented."

"The power of seeing patterns," Marcia said, a spark of assurance in her tone. "When people understand the 'why' beneath their work, they make different choices."

"That's the essence of the power of perspective," James said, meeting her eyes with a steady look. "Speaking of which, Robert would like an update on your sprint preparations this afternoon. I think he's particularly interested in this systems approach you've developed."

"I'm ready whenever he is," Marcia said. "Though I should warn you - I might bring my whiteboard drawings."

James laughed. "Please do. Robert appreciates visual thinking."

As Marcia walked back to her office, she received a message from Noah with the subject line *Connection Patterns in New York*. He'd taken her insights and applied them specifically to the New York office dynamics, identifying additional connection points she'd missed from her Seattle vantage point.

This is brilliant, she replied. *Would you mind walking the NY team through this perspective before the sprint starts? It would help establish context.*

Already scheduled for this afternoon, Noah responded. *Alan was particularly interested. Said it puts words to what he's felt was missing in our project structure.*

By lunchtime, Marcia had received similar messages from three other team members, each adding their perspective to the connection patterns. The simple act of reframing their challenges had unleashed a wave of insights across the team.

In her meeting with Robert after lunch, she brought her laptop loaded with the diagrams she'd created overnight.

"James tells me you've had a breakthrough in how you're approaching the project," Robert said, gesturing for her to sit.

"I think so," Marcia said, opening her presentation. "I've been trying to see beyond the individual issues to the system they exist within."

As she walked Robert through her analysis of disconnection patterns and leverage points, she watched his expression shift from polite interest to engaged concentration.

"This isn't just about the GFP project, is it?" he said when she finished. "This is a framework that could apply to any complex project facing similar challenges."

"I suppose it could," Marcia acknowledged, somewhat surprised by his observation.

Robert leaned forward. "Marcia, what you've developed here is valuable beyond just fixing this immediate situation. It's an approach to diagnosing and addressing systemic issues that plague many enterprise projects."

He turned to the screen displaying her connection

pattern diagram. "With your permission, I'd like to share this framework more widely - not just with delivery managers, but with team leads and functional groups across the account. Their perspectives could add layers you might not see from within the sprint team. You'd still remain the owner of the framework, but this would give you richer input to validate and refine it."

"Of course," Marcia said, honoured by his recognition. "Though it's still evolving as the team adds their perspectives."

Robert folded his hands, approval evident. "That's the beauty of it. It's a living framework that improves with diverse input - embodying the very connection principle it describes."

As Marcia stepped into the hallway outside Robert's office, she spotted Tessa waiting with a stack of notes. They fell into step, entering the elevator together. Marcia was still turning over Robert's words when her phone buzzed with a new message from Liam: *Flight to NY booked for sprint.*

Marcia almost dropped her phone.

"Liam volunteering?" Tessa gasped, reading over her shoulder.

"I know," Marcia murmured, a smile tugging at her lips. It was unprecedented - the same Liam who once scoffed at cross-office visits was now eagerly jumping in. Marcia felt a surge of pride. She replied with a quick thumbs-up emoji and a *Thank you for going the extra mile.* She realised this wasn't just a travel plan. It was proof of a shift in perspective: Liam now saw the New York team's success as tied to his own. One of her toughest sceptics was becoming a true partner.

Another ping followed: *Alisha confirmed she'll lead the user profile team. System connections taking shape.*

Marcia tucked the phone away, her pulse still racing. The power of perspective wasn't just in the seeing - it was in how that seeing transformed action.

With this framework to guide them, Marcia felt increasingly confident that the sprint could deliver the breakthrough results they needed. Not because they would work harder, but because they would work differently - with a shared understanding of the system they were trying to change.

✧ ✧ ✧

"I didn't expect a field trip today," Marcia said as James led her into the elevator and pressed the button for the building's top floor.

"Sometimes you need literal perspective to reinforce metaphorical ones," James replied with a cryptic grin. "Besides, you've been staring at whiteboards for several days straight. A change of scenery will do you good."

It was late-afternoon Tuesday, just one day before the innovation sprint would begin. The past 48-hours had been a blur of preparation - finalising team compositions, setting up collaboration spaces in both offices, arranging for food deliveries, and briefing Elizabeth and Malcolm on what to expect.

The elevator doors opened to reveal a space Marcia had never visited before - the building's observation deck, normally reserved for corporate events. Floor-to-ceiling windows offered a stunning 360-degree view of Seattle, broken only by slender mullions. To the North stood the Space Needle, and in the clearest corner Mount Rainier shimmered faintly through the winter haze.

"Robert keeps this space for special occasions," James explained, leading her to the west-facing windows. "I thought it might help with your systems thinking."

Marcia approached the glass, taking in the sprawling city

below. From this height, Seattle's complexity became a comprehensible pattern - neighbourhoods flowing into each other, streets forming grids and arterials, the waterfront embracing downtown in a gentle curve.

"It's different from up here," she observed. "Individual buildings become part of a larger design."

"Exactly," James leaned slightly towards the glass, eyes following the geometry below. "Down at street level, you see the shop fronts and traffic lights. From here, you see how it all connects."

He handed her a small set of binoculars. "But the real power comes from being able to zoom in and out - seeing both the system and its components."

Marcia raised the binoculars, focusing on a busy intersection. She could see people crossing streets, cars waiting at lights, a delivery truck double-parked. Individual stories playing out within the larger urban system.

"That's what your connection patterns framework does," James continued. "It lets you zoom out to see the system while still understanding the detailed interactions within it."

Marcia lowered the binoculars, turning to face James. "Is that why you brought me up here? For a leadership metaphor?"

James laughed. "Partly. But also because I have news about tomorrow's sprint, and I thought you might need the calming influence of this view when you hear it."

Marcia's stomach tightened. "What's happened? Is Elizabeth backing out?"

"No, quite the opposite," James said. "Malcolm has invited GFP's CTO to observe part of the sprint. Apparently, your systems perspective caught his attention when Malcolm shared it. He wants to see this approach in action."

"Their CTO?" Marcia felt a wave of anxiety. "Xavier Delgado? He's notoriously critical of consulting firms.

Elizabeth once told me he believes most of them just 'repackage common sense at premium prices.'"

"The very same," James confirmed. "And yes, he's sceptical by nature. But Malcolm thinks your connection patterns framework might resonate with him. Xavier has been pushing for systems thinking within GFP for years."

Marcia turned back to the window, taking in the view as she processed this development. The CTO's presence raised the stakes considerably. If the sprint impressed him, it could elevate the entire project's profile within GFP. If it didn't...

"When will he be there?" she asked finally.

"Thursday afternoon - the sprint's middle stretch. Malcolm thinks that timing will show both the process and outcomes."

Marcia nodded slowly. "We should brief the teams. Liam especially needs to know - he'll be presenting the authentication solution."

"Already handled," James assured her. "And Liam was surprisingly unfazed. He said something about technical truth speaking for itself."

That sounded like Liam, Marcia thought with a small smile. His confidence in his technical solutions never wavered, regardless of the audience.

They stood in comfortable silence, watching a ferry cross Elliott Bay, its wake creating a perfect V in the water below.

"You know," James said finally, "most new leaders in your position would be panicking about now. Innovation sprint, high-profile client executives, cross-office collaboration challenges. Yet you seem remarkably centred."

"Trust me, there's plenty of internal panic," Marcia admitted. "But something's changed in the past few days. Since I started seeing the connection patterns, the individual challenges feel less overwhelming. They're just components in a system we're working to improve."

"That's the power of perspective," James's mouth curved in a small, approving grin. "When you can see both the forest and the trees - and the relationships between them - even complex situations become navigable."

Marcia gestured toward the cityscape. "From here, traffic jams just look like temporary bottlenecks in an otherwise functional system. I guess I'm trying to view our project challenges the same way."

"That's exactly right," James said. "And it's why I think Xavier's visit might be perfect timing. He'll either see a team in chaos or a team systematically rebuilding connections - and I'm betting on the latter."

As they began to leave the observation deck, Marcia took one last look at the city below. The patterns were clearer from this height - the way neighbourhoods connected through transit lines, how green spaces provided breathing room between dense areas, how the waterfront shaped the downtown core.

Back in the elevator, James handed her a folder. "One more thing - Robert asked me to give you this. It's feedback from the teams on your connection patterns framework."

Marcia opened the folder to find pages of notes, diagrams, and build-outs of her original concept - each from a different team member's perspective. Testing had added quality connection points. Development had detailed technical integration nodes. Even the project management office had contributed, mapping communication flows between stakeholders.

"Everyone's adding their expertise to the framework," she said, touched by their engagement.

"That's what makes it powerful," James said as the elevator doors opened, approval in his voice. "You provided the core insight, but their contributions are making it comprehensive. It's becoming a shared vision."

As Marcia walked back to her office, she felt a renewed sense of purpose. Tomorrow's innovation sprint would be challenging, Xavier's visit would add pressure, but the team was aligning around a common understanding of what they were really trying to accomplish.

Her phone screen blinked to life - Alan: *NY office setup complete. Teams already starting to mingle across functions. Your systems framework has people talking about connections they never considered before. See you tomorrow morning on the 8am PT video kick-off.*

Attached was a photo of the New York office with Alisha explaining something to a mixed group of developers and analysts, pointing to a whiteboard covered with connection diagrams similar to what Marcia had drawn days earlier.

The seed she'd planted was already growing, taking different forms as team members applied the perspective to their specific areas. Whether the sprint achieved all its technical goals or not, it had already succeeded in shifting how people understood their work and its relationship to the larger system.

As she walked past the development area, Marcia noticed Liam speaking with Sarah - an uncommon sight just two weeks ago. They were reviewing a diagram of testing touchpoints for the authentication solution, with Liam actually listening to Sarah's input rather than dismissing it.

Small changes, but significant ones. Connections forming where disconnection had been the norm.

Tomorrow would bring the innovation sprint with all its intensity and uncertainty. Xavier's visit would add high-level scrutiny to their approach. But with their new shared perspective, they were better equipped to navigate these challenges than ever before.

Marcia smiled as she returned to her office, ready for one

final review of the sprint plans. The power of perspective wasn't just about seeing differently - it was about helping others see differently too.

"Local wins must serve the whole."

✧ ✧ ✧

Marcia's condo was unusually quiet that evening. She'd expected to feel anxious on the night before the innovation sprint - perhaps pacing the floor, triple-checking documents, or making last-minute adjustments to team compositions. Instead, she found herself calmly sipping tea by the window, watching Seattle's lights flicker against the night sky.

Her whiteboard had been wiped clean. Not because she no longer needed it, but because the framework she'd created had moved beyond her private thinking space. It now existed in shared documents, team conversations, and collaborative plans. Her individual insight had become collective understanding.

She scrolled through her phone, reviewing final messages from the day. Everything was ready - meeting spaces configured in both offices, catering arranged, technical environments prepared, teams briefed. Liam's flight to New York had landed safely, with Noah sending a humorous photo of Liam looking slightly disoriented by the city's pace as they left JFK.

A text from James appeared: *Get some sleep. Tomorrow will be intense but worthwhile. The team is ready.*

I will. And thank you for taking me to the observation deck today. That perspective was exactly what I needed. She replied, appreciating the care and confidence.

Her phone rang - Elizabeth Parker. Unusual for her to

call this late.

"Elizabeth, hello," Marcia answered, trying to keep the surprise from her voice.

"Sorry for the late call," Elizabeth said, sounding slightly harried. "Just wanted to check in before tomorrow's sprint. Malcolm mentioned Xavier will be joining at some point."

"Yes, we're prepared for his visit," Marcia assured her. "I understand he's interested in the systems approach we're taking."

"That's part of why I'm calling," Elizabeth said. "Xavier is... particular. He's brilliant but can be dismissive if he thinks we're just applying buzzwords without substance."

Marcia kept her voice light. "I've heard about his reputation."

"I'm not worried about your substance," Elizabeth clarified quickly. "Your connection patterns framework is exactly the kind of thinking he appreciates. But I wanted to give you some context about what he's really looking for."

Marcia grabbed a notepad. "I'm listening."

"Xavier believes most digital transformation efforts fail because they focus on technology in isolation rather than the interconnected systems they exist within," Elizabeth explained. "Sound familiar?"

"Very," Marcia said, realizing how closely this aligned with her own recent insights.

"He's been pushing for more systemic approaches within GFP for years, often with resistance from more traditional executives. Including Malcolm, though he'd never admit it."

Marcia scribbled notes, piecing together another layer of the GFP dynamics. "So, Malcolm inviting Xavier - that's significant?"

"Extremely," Elizabeth confirmed. "It suggests your approach is penetrating even Malcolm's traditional mindset. And it gives Xavier an opportunity to demonstrate his systems philosophy in action."

"No pressure," Marcia said with a small laugh.

"Actually, I think it's positive pressure," Elizabeth replied. "Xavier could become your strongest advocate if he sees authentic systems thinking in your approach. And frankly, we need his support for the broader transformation roadmap."

After they hung up, Marcia added Elizabeth's insights to her notes. The sprint was taking on additional dimensions - not just delivering features or rebuilding team connections but potentially influencing GFP's internal approaches to transformation.

She turned back to the window, watching a ferry's lights cross the dark water for a time. Feeling sleepy, she set down her phone and prepared for bed, knowing tomorrow would demand all her energy and focus.

That night, Marcia dreamed of a river running wide beneath a pale sky. On one bank, teams of people gathered restlessly; on the far side, a city shimmered with possibility.

In the clearing nearby, Tessa worked quickly, weaving two strands of thread - one red, one blue - into a vast fabric. The cloth billowed upward until it formed the curved envelope of a hot-air balloon. Its basket rose with it, carrying Robert and James, who leaned over the edge and pointed out patterns in the landscape below, tracing invisible lines that only made sense from such a height.

On the river itself, two crossings unfolded at once: Liam edging carefully across a swaying wooden bridge. Beside him, Noah guided a small ferry, steadying its course as it pushed across the current, carrying others safely with him.

At the far bank stood Sarah, calm but firm, a gatekeeper at the landing. She examined each arrival - bridge-crosser or ferry passenger - letting them pass only once she was sure they carried what was needed. Behind her, the city seemed to draw closer, its streets aligning into patterns, as though the act of crossing itself was pulling the future into focus.

She watched the strange procession unfold, and felt a quiet certainty rise within her. Somehow, she knew this was the real work of innovation: each person contributing in their own way to bring the vision to life.

In the morning, she didn't remember the specifics of the dream, but the feeling remained: today she wouldn't just run a sprint - she would *hold the room*.

FIELD RULE: Change Your Altitude
(Street → Skyline → Systems)

- **Street (now)**: What's the user-visible problem right in front of us? User pain now; 1 real example.
- **Skyline (release, milestone)**: What outcome does this roll-up into, and which trade-offs are we making?
- **Systems (end-to-end, company level)**: How does this affect flow, cost, risk, or other teams?
- **Signal, not noise**: If debate stalls, **change altitude** - answer Street, then Skyline, then Systems.
- **Owner & When**: Capture the decision at the altitude where it belongs (log decision, Owner and When).

Do this tomorrow: Start every design huddle with: "Street in one sentence. Skyline in one metric. Systems in one risk."

Chapter 5
The Power of Presence

A manager's presence is like a lighthouse in a storm. The beam doesn't fix the waves, but it steadies every ship that sees it. Presence is power - not because you're everywhere, but because you choose to show up where it matters most.

✧ ✧ ✧

Steady is faster.

✧ ✧ ✧

"T-minus five minutes, Marcia."

Marcia stepped into the wide glass foyer on the ninth floor, as Robert's assistant gave the cue. The double doors to Conference Room A stood open, revealing a transformed space - tables pushed to the perimeter, collaboration spaces created with mobile whiteboards and stacks of sticky notes and marker caddies, and a large video wall dominating one end, showing the equally transformed New York office, and two team members from Chicago.

A tall, wheeled Momentum Board stood near the video wall at eye level, pre-labelled Today | Blocked | Cleared and waiting for its first card.

A second whiteboard carried the sprint guardrails:

Risk budget: 3 days - test environments only.
Must: keep customer data safe; no production changes without Liam's sign-off; every change behind a feature flag.
Should: achieve stable cross-site sync and show one integrated demo daily.
Could: experiment with cross-region cache if time allows.

This floor, usually home to executive briefings and quarterly strategy reviews, now buzzed with a different kind of energy. Coffee cups in hand, an unusual hum of cross-functional conversation filling the air. QA analysts chatted with developers. Business specialists discussed speculative requirements with technical architects. Even the elusive Chicago database team had emerged from the depths, caught in the sprint's gravity.

For a moment, the scale of what she was about to lead hit her all at once. These weren't just tasks or deliverables - these were people looking to her to reset months of fractured trust. What if she couldn't hold the room? What if the approach that had worked in small groups collapsed under the weight of three offices watching her at once? A flicker of fear tightened in her chest before she forced herself to breathe, steady and deliberate. She had rebuilt momentum before - now she had to believe she could do it on a larger stage.

Marcia paused at the entrance, taking in the scene. This was a visible sign that their approach was already working - people who rarely interacted were connecting naturally, drawn together by shared purpose and the deliberate disruption of normal patterns.

"Quite the turnout," James said, appearing beside her. "New York looks just as engaged."

On the video wall, Marcia could see the New York team assembling. Liam stood somewhat awkwardly near Noah, his Seattle hoodie making him instantly recognisable among the more formally dressed New York staff. Alisha was arranging people into their cross-functional groups, her tortoiseshell glasses catching the light as she moved energetically through the room.

"It's really happening," Marcia said, a mix of excitement and apprehension in her voice.

"Indeed it is," James said, his voice low and reassuring. "Ready to kick things off?"

Taking a deep breath, Marcia stepped into the room. Conversations quieted as she made her way to the front, faces turning toward her expectantly. She felt a flutter of nervousness in her stomach - not just about the sprint itself, but about how she needed to set the tone for these crucial three-days.

"Good morning, everyone," she began, her voice stronger than she expected. "I see Seattle is ready, and..." she turned to the video wall, "New York and Chicago as well. Welcome to our innovation sprint."

The room fell completely silent, all eyes focused on her. Marcia sensed something beyond mere attention - anticipation, perhaps even hope. These were people who had been stuck in frustrating patterns, eager for something different.

"Before we dive into features and technical details, I want to share why we're approaching this differently," she continued. "This isn't just about meeting a deadline or checking boxes for the February milestone. It's about reconnecting what's become disconnected."

She gestured to a large visualisation of her connection patterns framework displayed on the wall.

"Earlier this week, many of you have contributed to this evolving framework. You've identified broken connections - between offices, between functions, between technical components. In these three-days, we're not just building features. We're deliberately reestablishing those connections."

Marcia moved away from the podium, stepping closer to the teams.

"Each innovation squad has technical goals, yes. But you also have connection goals - specific relationships and communication patterns you're establishing that should continue long after this sprint ends."

She noticed heads nodding, particularly among those who had helped refine the framework.

"The teams weren't formed randomly," she explained. "You're with people whose perspectives complement yours - whose knowledge fills gaps in your own. Together, you see a more complete picture than any of you could individually."

On the video wall, she could see the New York team leaning forward, fully engaged. Liam stood with arms crossed but was listening intently.

"We have challenging technical goals," Marcia acknowledged. "The February milestone matters. But how we get there matters too. The connections you build during this sprint will serve us long after these specific features are delivered."

She swept a hand to take everyone in. "Now, some practicalities. Each team has a designated space. Food will arrive throughout the day - please take breaks when you need them. Your team leads have detailed objectives and technical guardrails. I'll be circulating between teams, as will Sarah from QA and Tessa from business analysis."

Glancing at the New York screen, she added, "Alan and I co-led the sprint planning, and he'll be coordinating in New York alongside Noah, ensuring teams have what they need. Liam is providing technical guidance across both locations. Alisha is leading the user profile team with members from both offices."

She paused, then added with intentional emphasis: "Elizabeth and Malcolm will visit this afternoon. GFP's CTO Xavier Delgado will join us on Thursday. They're not here to evaluate individuals - they're here to observe our approach. Stay focused on your work, not on impressing executives."

This earned a few knowing smiles - the pressure of client observation was something everyone understood.

"Any questions before we break into teams?"

A developer raised his hand. "What's our definition of success for the sprint?"

Marcia appreciated the directness. "Three things. First, meaningful progress on the February milestone features. Second, established connections between previously siloed functions and offices. Third, insights about how we should work going forward. We're not expecting perfection - we're creating momentum and direction."

As the teams dispersed to their designated areas, Marcia felt a subtle shift in her own energy. The nervousness had transformed into focused presence. This moment required more than just careful planning - it demanded leadership presence that inspired confidence and maintained direction amid the controlled chaos they were creating.

Marcia cupped her hands lightly in front of her as the clusters of engineers and analysts dove into their tasks. "How do you feel?" James whispered at her side, scanning the buzzing room.

"Honestly? A little apprehensive," Marcia admitted under her breath. Dozens of rapid conversations in both Seattle and New York were already flying, and she felt an urge to hover over each one. "I just want to keep everyone moving in the same direction."

James gave her an encouraging nod. "You set the stage. They know you're here if they need you."

Marcia straightened her shoulders, the slight knot in her stomach easing. He was right - this wasn't about directing every detail, it was about being present and attentive. "Alright," she smiled, mostly to herself. "Let's see what they can do."

She moved between the forming teams, checking in briefly with each. The authentication group was already sketching architecture diagrams. The user experience team was mapping customer journeys. The integration team had developers from both offices huddled around a shared code repository.

On the video wall, she could see Noah guiding the New York contingent with similar energy. Liam had already found his counterparts and was deep in technical discussion, his earlier awkwardness replaced by intense focus.

James appeared at her side again, arms crossed, a hint of pride in his eyes. "They're off and running," he observed. After a pause he added, "You know, I've been managing teams for decades, but watching you handle this taught me a few things."

Marcia blinked, startled. "Me? Teach *you*?"

"Absolutely," James dipped his head, approval quiet

rather than showy. "The way you got Liam and Noah to collaborate - I wasn't sure that was even possible. Reminded this old dog he still has a few tricks left to learn."

Marcia exhaled, the tension she'd been carrying easing into a shaky laugh of relief and disbelief. "Feels like we've just jumped off a cliff and are building our parachute on the way down."

James laughed. "That's exactly how innovation should feel. Scary, exhilarating - and worth the leap when everything's on the line."

Across the room, Marcia noticed one team seemingly stalled already, with uncomfortable silence and uncertain glances. She excused herself and headed their way, recognising that different teams would need different kinds of support. Some would thrive with autonomy; others would need more active guidance to establish productive patterns.

As she approached the struggling team, Marcia consciously adjusted her demeanour - projecting calm confidence rather than concerned supervision. This wasn't about swooping in to solve their problem but creating space for them to find their way forward.

"How's it going here?" she asked, pulling up a chair to join their circle rather than standing over them.

"We're stuck on where to start," admitted one developer. "The API standardisation is tangled with the user profile features, which depend on the authentication work..."

Marcia nodded. "Complex interdependencies. What if we map them visually to find the critical path?"

She grabbed a whiteboard marker and started drawing as team members contributed points. Within minutes, the energy had shifted from paralysis to engagement. She wasn't solving their technical challenge - she was modelling how to approach it systematically.

"I think you've got this now," she said after the team had

identified a clear starting point. As she stood to leave, she noticed they continued the conversation with renewed momentum, no longer looking to her for direction.

Moving through the room, Marcia realised that her role during the sprint wasn't what she had initially imagined. She wasn't the technical expert or even the primary decision-maker. Her value was in her presence - how she moved between teams, asked questions, removed obstacles, and maintained focus on both the technical goals and the connection patterns they were establishing.

Three hours into the sprint, teams had settled into productive rhythms. The room buzzed with focused energy - markers squeaking on whiteboards, keyboards clicking, occasional bursts of conversation or debate. On the video wall, the New York office mirrored this productive hum, with Liam now visibly engaged in a technical discussion with Seattle counterparts.

What struck Marcia most was how the energy differed from their normal work environment. There was an intensity but also a fluidity - people moving between conversations naturally, contributing where needed rather than staying in prescribed lanes. The artificial boundaries they'd established to create 'calculated chaos' were paradoxically leading to more organic collaboration than their normal structured processes.

Checking her phone, a banner from Elizabeth slid in: *We'll be arriving in an hour. Malcolm is bringing an additional executive - our Head of Digital Banking. No pressure, but the stakes just got higher.*

Marcia took a deep breath. The innovation sprint was underway, gaining momentum with each passing hour. The teams were embracing both the technical challenges and the connection opportunities. Now they would face their first major test - client executives observing their unconventional approach in action.

As she composed a quick reply to Elizabeth, Marcia reminded herself that the power of presence wasn't just about being physically there. It was about how she carried herself, the confidence she projected, and the deliberate attention she brought to each interaction. The next few hours would test that skill more than any since she'd taken on the Delivery Manager role.

"Calm is the quickest way to speed."

✧ ✧ ✧

"They're here," Tessa whispered, appearing at Marcia's side as she observed the authentication team's progress. "Elizabeth, Malcolm, and someone I don't recognise - probably the Head of Digital Banking."

Marcia habitually smoothing her blazer, eyes on the team. "How's the energy in the room?"

"People noticed, but they're staying focused," Tessa reported. "Your reminder about not performing for executives seems to have stuck."

"Good. Let's keep it that way." Marcia took a deep breath and headed toward the entrance where James was already greeting the visitors.

Elizabeth Parker radiated composed authority in a tailored navy suit, impeccable as always. Malcolm stood beside her, every detail crisp - from his Windsor knot to his mirror-shined shoes. The third visitor - a women in her forties - wore her thick black hair twisted into a low chignon, not a strand out of place. Her watchful gaze surveyed the room with undisguised curiosity.

"Marcia," Elizabeth motioned with her hand. "This is

Sophia Patel, our Head of Digital Banking. She's ultimately responsible for the products we're building."

Marcia offered a respectfully firm handshake. "Welcome. We're in full sprint mode, as you can see."

"Fascinating approach," Sophia said, her gaze still taking in the transformed workspace. "Elizabeth's been telling me about your connection patterns framework. I'm eager to see it in action."

"We'd be happy to show you around," Marcia offered. "The teams are deeply focused, so we'll observe without disrupting their flow."

Malcolm checked his watch. "We have forty-five minutes before our next meeting. Perhaps a quick tour and then a status update?"

"Perfect," Marcia agreed, gesturing toward the nearest team space. "Let's start with the authentication solution, then move to user profiles and API standardisation."

As they approached the authentication team, Marcia noticed a subtle shift in the room's energy. Voices lowered slightly, postures straightened. Despite her earlier reminder, the presence of executives created an inevitable ripple effect. Her challenge was to minimize its impact on the teams' momentum.

"This group is consolidating the three separate authentication services into a unified approach," she explained as they observed from a respectful distance. "Liam and his counterparts in New York identified this as a critical integration point."

On the large screen, they could see Liam engaged in intense discussion with Noah and the New York technical team, completely oblivious to the executive visit in Seattle.

"He seems passionate," Malcolm observed.

"Liam is our principal architect," Marcia explained. "He's visiting New York right now - he volunteered to work directly with that team to strengthen the cross-office connection."

Elizabeth's eyebrows rose slightly. "Liam volunteered?" She lowered her voice, "Brett always described him as... challenging to engage."

"People respond to being valued," Marcia said simply. "Liam's insights are central to our connection patterns framework."

They moved to the user profile team, where Alisha was leading a hybrid group split between Seattle and New York. Digital design sketches were projected on screens while developers discussed implementation approaches.

"This is one of our most integrated teams," Marcia explained. "Front-end and back-end developers working together rather than in sequence, with business analysts and UX designers embedded directly. Alisha from New York is leading this effort."

"The UI mock-ups look promising," Sophia commented, studying the screens. "Much more intuitive than our current approach."

"That's a direct result of the cross-functional team," Marcia noted. "When designers work alongside developers in real-time, we avoid the handoff problems that typically create friction."

As they continued the tour, Marcia maintained a calm, confident presence despite her heightened awareness of the executives' scrutiny. She answered questions directly, highlighted team achievements without overpromising, and consistently emphasised the connection patterns underlying their approach.

"What I find most impressive," Sophia said as they completed the circuit, "is not just the technical work but the energy in the room. These teams seem genuinely engaged."

"They are," Marcia confirmed. "People thrive when

artificial barriers are removed, and they can see how their work connects to the bigger picture."

They settled in a small conference room for the status update, where Marcia shared an overview of progress against the February milestone features.

"We're on track with the authentication consolidation," she reported. "The user profile features are progressing well. The API standardisation has uncovered some unexpected complexity, but the team has identified a path forward."

Malcolm leaned forward. "And you believe all this will be completed by Friday evening?"

"We'll make significant progress on all fronts," Marcia said carefully. "Some features will be complete, others will have clear implementation paths with the major obstacles removed. But the sprint's value goes beyond feature completion - it's establishing connection patterns that make future work more effective."

Malcolm seemed about to press further when Sophia spoke up.

"The connection patterns concept is fascinating," she said. "It aligns with what Xavier has been advocating - viewing our transformation as an interconnected system rather than as isolated technology projects."

Elizabeth's expression brightened in agreement. "That's why Xavier is so interested in tomorrow's visit. He sees this approach as validation of his perspective."

Marcia sensed an opportunity to understand the GFP dynamics better. "How does your organisation typically approach these transformations? I'd be interested in understanding where our framework might complement your methods."

The question opened a revealing discussion. Sophia described their traditional project-by-project approach, while Elizabeth outlined Xavier's push for more systemic thinking.

Malcolm, surprisingly, acknowledged that their conventional methods had limitations when dealing with complex interconnected systems.

"That's precisely what drew me to your innovation sprint concept," he admitted. "Initially I was sceptical, but seeing how your teams are working today - it's clearly different from our typical consultant engagements."

As the discussion continued, Marcia realised she was witnessing a microcosm of GFP's internal transformation debate played out in this small conference room. The innovation sprint wasn't just delivering technical features; it was providing GFP executives with a tangible example of an alternative approach to complex challenges.

When it was time for them to leave, Sophia stayed behind.

"I appreciate what you're doing here, Marcia," she said quietly. "GFP needs this kind of thinking. We've been stuck in outdated patterns, and it's holding us back in the market."

"Change is never easy," Marcia acknowledged. "Especially in established organisations."

"No, but sometimes it takes an outside perspective to break through entrenched thinking," Sophia said, reaching into her bag and handing Marcia a business card. "In case you need anything before tomorrow. I'll be back with Xavier - I think you'll find him a strong ally for your approach."

Marcia slipped the card into her notebook exhaling quietly, remaining steady.

✧ ✧ ✧

After the executives departed, Marcia returned to the main sprint room, checking in with teams and addressing questions that had accumulated during her absence. The energy remained high, with visible progress on whiteboards and screens throughout the space.

James joined her as she reviewed a technical diagram with the API standardisation team.

"That went well," he said when they stepped away. "Especially with Sophia. She's a key influencer at GFP."

"I noticed," Marcia replied. "She seems to understand what we're trying to accomplish beyond just the technical deliverables."

"Your presence during that visit was perfect," James observed. "Confident without being defensive, knowledgeable without dominating. You've really grown into this role."

Marcia felt a small surge of pride at his words. "I'm learning that leadership presence isn't about having all the answers - it's about asking the right questions and creating space for others to contribute."

"Exactly," James nodded approvingly. "And speaking of space, I should let you get back to your teams. They draw confidence from your presence on the floor."

As James departed, Marcia checked the time - nearly 4 pm. The teams had been working intensely for eight hours, with another four to go before the day's wrap-up. She could see signs of fatigue beginning to appear - slower movements, more coffee runs, occasional frustrated sighs.

This was when her presence mattered most. Not to push harder or demand more, but to provide the steady, grounding energy that would help teams navigate the inevitable mid-sprint slump.

She deliberately walked the floor with unhurried confidence, pausing at each team not to check progress but to offer support. A word of encouragement here, a clarifying question there, occasionally redirecting a team that had gone down a rabbit hole. Her manner was calm and assured, creating a sense that everything was proceeding exactly as it should.

A shout went up from the integration table. "Sign-in just broke - people can't get past login."

Voices tightened. Two teams converged. "It worked an hour ago." "Not with the Chicago update." "Roll back the settings?"

Marcia stepped into the cluster without raising her voice. "Sixty seconds. Eyes on me." The room stilled. "We'll get signal, not noise - one thread at a time."

Marcia thought: *Street: sign-in failing. Skyline: keep sprint progress green.*

"What changed in the last hour?"

From New York, Liam answered over the video link. "We added a small, required context field to the sign-in message."

"And our test script is still sending the old payload," Noah said.

Marcia noticed herself thinking in parallel to acting. *Change altitude. Systems: auth $\rightarrow$ profile only. Don't widen.* Her thoughts ran a beat ahead of her words.

Hands hovered over keyboards. "Don't touch the system yet," Marcia said, palm out, gentle but final. "We don't widen the blast radius."

She pulled a fresh card and wrote:

Sign-in: message mismatch

"Test exactly one end-to-end flow, nothing extra," Marcia said. "Just the web app signing in and loading the profile."

"Sarah, you're observer. Facts, not theories. Call what you see," Marcia directed calmly.

"Timer, ten minutes," she looked to Lucas. "In pairs: Noah fixes the test, Alisha reviews; Priya with Chicago on sign-in." Marcia said. The same Priya who'd wrestled with FreshWorks database chaos - now the platform lead people turned to when things were on fire.

Marcia added. "Liam watches logs. Everyone else, hold."

Keys tapped. A minute later, Liam called, "Found it - missing field rejected."

"On it," simply from Noah, and a minute later "Ok to release?"

"Approved," from Liam.

"Fix pushed," Noah said. "Trying again."

Sarah watched the board, exhaling when she saw it. "200 from sign-in... 200 from profile. Green." She drew a long breath in.

A soft wave of relief moved across both rooms. Someone started to clap; Marcia shook her head, smiling. "Save it for *Cleared*." She paused. Then she slid the card across, to relieved applause.

The tension unwound; the steady buzz returned as the teams resumed work.

On the video wall, Noah steadied the New York room, while Liam remained deeply engaged with the technical teams, seemingly immune to fatigue. Alisha was leading an energising design review, her animated gestures visible even through the video feed.

A little later, Liam crossed to New York's Momentum Board and slid 'DB index fix' into *Cleared*, drawing a quiet ripple of approval from both rooms.

Marcia raised a hand to the camera; Liam gave a two-finger salute in acknowledgement.

"Be the metronome, not the megaphone."

✧ ✧ ✧

As evening approached, food arrived - a welcome break that reinvigorated the teams. Marcia used this opportunity to check in with Sarah, who had been circulating between teams all day.

"Quality hasn't been sacrificed despite the pace," Sarah reported. "Actually, having QA embedded in the teams from the start is producing better code than our normal process. Issues are being caught and fixed immediately rather than weeks later."

"Another connection point strengthened," Marcia noted.

By 8 pm, teams began their day-one wrap-ups, documenting progress and identifying goals for tomorrow. Marcia gathered everyone for a brief all-hands session.

"You've accomplished incredible things today," she told the combined Seattle-New York-Chicago team. "The progress is evident not just in the technical solutions but in how you're working together. Tomorrow brings fresh challenges - including Xavier's visit. Thanks for your hard work today, and let's continue this momentum tomorrow."

As teams departed for well-earned rest, Marcia remained behind with Tessa and Sarah, consolidating notes and preparing for tomorrow. The authentication solution was nearly complete, exceeding expectations. The user profile features were on track. The API standardisation had uncovered complex issues but was progressing toward viable solutions.

More importantly, the connection patterns were visibly strengthening. People who had never collaborated were now working closely together and functioning as integrated teams across offices. Cross-functional groups were making decisions faster and with better outcomes than their siloed predecessors.

"We should document these emerging patterns," Marcia suggested as they wrapped up their review. "Not just what we delivered, but how the handoffs and trust made it possible."

She paused at the door and sent a quick Slack DM to Liam: *Great work today. One thought for tomorrow - you don't need to jump on every fix. Sometimes being there, calm and visible, is enough. The team takes the cue. Give it a try?*

The reply came a minute later: *Counterintuitive... but I'll try.*

That's the point, she typed back. *I'll be looking for calm, not heroics.*

As Marcia finally headed home after a fourteen-hour day, she felt a quiet confidence. Like a practiced speaker - or an experienced driver - she was starting to think about the destination while she spoke and moved. This ability was growing stronger with practice.

The power of her presence today hadn't come from commanding attention or dominating conversations - it had come from steady, authentic leadership that created space for others to shine.

That, she was beginning to understand, was the true power of presence - not demanding the spotlight but illuminating the path for others.

✧ ✧ ✧

Morning light streamed through the windows as Marcia arrived at the office early, hoping for a few moments of quiet before day two of the innovation sprint began. To her surprise, several teams were already there - the authentication group huddled around Liam's empty desk in Seattle while he connected virtually from New York; the user profile team reviewing yesterday's progress with fresh eyes.

A brief database hiccup stalled the integration tests in New York. On the video wall, Liam didn't grab a chair or a keyboard; he listened, asked two questions, and let his engineers work. Ten minutes later the bay was humming again. He caught the camera, gave the smallest nod - message received.

"Couldn't stay away either?" Tessa asked, appearing with two coffee cups and handing one to Marcia.

"There's something magnetic about this energy," Marcia admitted, gratefully accepting the coffee. "How early did people start arriving?"

"Some never really left," Tessa said. "The API team stayed until midnight working through the security issue. Everyone kept saying the same thing - when everything started going sideways, you were just... steady."

Marcia smiled faintly. "I figured at least one of us should stay calm."

As they walked, the words lingered in her mind. James's voice came back to her from one of their recent discussions about the hidden powers - *Presence isn't about charisma; it's about calm when others lose theirs.*

Tessa followed her into the workspace. "They were back by 7 am this morning," she added.

Marcia felt a mixture of pride and concern. "We need to make sure they pace themselves. Xavier's visit is at 2 pm - we need everyone sharp for that."

"Speaking of which," Tessa lowered her voice, "there's a rumour that Xavier isn't just observing. Apparently, he's evaluating this approach for potential adoption across GFP's entire digital portfolio."

"Where did you hear that?"

"Sarah overheard Malcolm telling Elizabeth yesterday. The stakes might be higher than we realised."

Marcia sipped her coffee, considering this new

information.

By 7:55 am, the room was again buzzing with focused energy. The video wall showed the New York office equally engaged, with Liam now visibly more comfortable among his East Coast colleagues.

"Day two kick-off in five minutes," Marcia announced, moving through the room. "Quick status updates, then back to the sprint."

The teams gathered, faces showing a mix of determination and fatigue. Marcia took in the room, sensing they needed something more than just progress reports this morning.

"Before we dive into updates," she began, "I want to acknowledge something. What you accomplished yesterday was remarkable - not just the technical progress, but the way you're working together. I've seen people collaborating who have never exchanged more than an email before. I've watched Seattle, New York, and Chicago function as one unified team rather than separate offices."

The room quieted, everyone's attention focused on her words.

"Today brings Xavier's visit, which some might see as additional pressure. I see it differently. It's an opportunity to demonstrate not just what we're building, but how we're building it."

She made eye contact with team members around the room and on the video screen. "Now, let's hear those updates so we can get back to the incredible work you're doing."

The status reports were concise but encouraging. The authentication consolidation was nearly complete, with Liam and Noah leading final integration tests. The user profile features were on track, with Alisha's team solving a particularly thorny UX challenge. The API standardisation had overcome yesterday's obstacles and was making steady progress.

"Excellent work all around," Marcia concluded. "You know your priorities for today. Xavier arrives at 2 pm, but don't let that distract you. Focus on your teams and your deliverables."

As teams dispersed, James approached with a concerned expression. "We might have a problem with the authentication solution. Liam just messaged me that they've hit an unexpected issue with the legacy integration."

"How serious?" Marcia asked.

"Potentially critical. The consolidated approach works perfectly in the test environment but fails when connecting to GFP's production authentication infrastructure. Liam says it's a fundamental architecture issue that was hidden until now."

This was exactly the kind of last-minute crisis that could derail the sprint - especially with Xavier's visit just hours away. The authentication consolidation was meant to be their most visible success story.

"Where is Liam now?" Marcia asked.

"Still in New York, working with Noah and their security team. He says they need access to GFP's security architecture documentation to diagnose the root cause."

Marcia checked her watch. "Do we have channels to request that documentation quickly?"

"Elizabeth might be our best bet," James suggested. "But she's in meetings all morning."

"I'll try Sophia," Marcia decided. "She seemed to understand what we're trying to accomplish."

Stepping into a quiet room, Marcia called Sophia directly, explaining the situation without minimising its seriousness but also without panic.

"I understand completely," Sophia said. "This is exactly the kind of issue that our siloed approach typically takes weeks to resolve. Let me connect you directly with our security architecture team. They can get Liam what he needs within the hour."

"That would be tremendously helpful," Marcia said, relieved by Sophia's responsiveness.

"And Marcia?" Sophia added before hanging up. "This is a perfect example of the connection patterns you're establishing. In our normal process, this request would go through three layers of management before reaching the right team."

After arranging the documentation access for Liam, Marcia returned to the sprint floor. Rather than immediately checking on the authentication crisis, she deliberately continued her regular rounds with the other teams, maintaining the steady presence they'd come to expect from her.

When she finally connected with Liam via video call in a side room, she found him intensely focused but not panicked.

"It's a classic case of security architecture designed in isolation," he explained, sharing his screen to show diagrams. "GFP's production environment uses a nested authentication model that isn't documented in their specifications. Our consolidated approach works technically but conflicts with their security boundaries."

"Can we solve it today?" Marcia asked directly.

Liam paused, scratching the back of his already dishevelled hair. "With the documentation Sophia provided, yes. We need to modify our approach to respect their security domains while still providing the unified experience. It's complex but doable."

"What resources do you need?"

"I've already pulled in two security specialists from the New York office. We'll need Sarah to help adjust the testing protocols once we implement the changes."

"You'll have her," Marcia promised. "Anything else?"

Liam hesitated, uncharacteristically uncertain. "This issue will be visible during Xavier's visit. The solution will be elegant once implemented, but the interim state is... messy."

Marcia understood his concern. Liam prided himself on technical excellence, and showing work in progress went against his nature.

"This is actually perfect," she said confidently. "It demonstrates exactly what the innovation sprint is designed to do - surface hidden issues and solve them collaboratively instead of discovering them weeks later when they'd be much more costly to fix."

Liam looked surprised by this perspective. "You want us to highlight the problem rather than minimise it?"

"Not highlight, but not hide either," Marcia clarified. "Show the issue, explain the root cause in the disconnected architecture, and demonstrate how your cross-office team is implementing the solution. It's a powerful example of the connection patterns in action."

A ghost of a smile appeared on Liam's face. "That's... a different way of looking at it. I can work with that approach."

As midday approached, Marcia sensed an uptick in tension throughout the room. Teams were making final pushes on their deliverables, aware of the approaching executive visit. The authentication team was particularly focused, with Liam coordinating efforts across both offices with unexpected leadership skill.

"He's different," Sarah observed, joining Marcia as she watched the video feed of Liam directing the New York security specialists. "More collaborative, less dictatorial. Even the way he explains technical concepts has changed - he's actually making sure people understand rather than just talking over them."

"Sometimes people just need the right conditions to show different aspects of themselves," Marcia replied. "The sprint is creating space for growth we might not see in our normal environment."

At 1:30 pm, Marcia gathered the team leads for a quick alignment before Xavier's arrival. The atmosphere was focused but not anxious - a testament to how far they'd come in just a day and a half.

Liam joined virtually, looking remarkably composed despite the authentication crisis. "We've implemented a workaround for the security domain issue and are testing it now. The permanent fix will require changes to GFP's infrastructure configuration, but we can demonstrate the concept today."

"Perfect," Marcia said, her tone approving. "That's exactly the kind of real-world problem-solving Xavier should see."

But as Marcia looked around the room - Seattle in front of her, New York and Chicago on the video wall behind - she felt how thing the moment was. One wrong word, one defensive comment, and the fragile trust between the three offices could snap back into old patterns.

For a moment, no one spoke. The hum of HVAC, the faint tapping of someone typing on the call in New York, even the hovering pointer on the shared screen seemed to underline the tension.

This was the first time all three offices would align live under her leadership. If it went poorly, the sprint could fracture along the same battle lines she'd inherited.

Marcia drew a slow breath, letting the silence settle before stepping into it.

"Remember, we're not putting on a performance," she reminded them. "Xavier wants to see authentic work in progress, including the challenges. Be honest about where things stand, but also highlight the new connections that are making progress possible."

As the call quieted again, Marcia felt a surprising steadiness rise within her.

"Leadership begins the moment you stop proving yourself and start improving the system," she said.

This was the moment to embody that truth.

Just before 2 pm, the elevator doors opened to reveal Xavier Delgado - a tall man with silver-streaked dark hair and piercing eyes that gave him a quiet intensity and immediately drew attention. Sophia accompanied him, along with Elizabeth and Malcolm.

As Marcia greeted them, she noted Xavier's observant gaze taking in the transformed workspace - the cross-functional teams, the connection pattern visualisations, the video wall showing equally engaged activity in New York.

"Dr. Delgado, welcome to our innovation sprint," Marcia said, extending her hand. "We're in the middle of day two, with teams making significant progress on our February milestone features."

"Please, call me Xavier," he said, his handshake firm but not dominating. "And I'd prefer to observe the teams in their natural state rather than receive a curated tour, if that's acceptable."

"Of course," Marcia agreed, appreciating his directness. "Feel free to observe any team, ask questions, and see how we're working. I'll accompany you to provide context, but I won't filter or manage the interactions."

"Excellent," Xavier said, clearly pleased. "Sophia tells me you've developed a framework around connection patterns. I'd be interested in seeing that in action."

"We have the perfect opportunity," Marcia said, guiding him toward the authentication team. "This group encountered a significant integration challenge this morning

- one that highlights exactly how disconnected systems create hidden problems."

As they approached, Liam's face appeared on a nearby screen, ready for the discussion. Marcia noticed he'd taken time to straighten his appearance despite the technical crisis - a small but significant sign of his growing comfort with client interaction.

"Xavier, this is Liam Everett, our principal architect who's currently working from our New York office," Marcia introduced them. "Liam, Xavier is interested in hearing about the security domain challenge you discovered."

Without missing a beat, Liam launched into a clear, accessible explanation of the issue - how GFP's undocumented security architecture had created an integration obstacle, how the cross-office team had diagnosed it, and how they were implementing both short-term and long-term solutions.

Xavier listened intently, occasionally asking precise technical questions that Liam answered with obvious expertise. What struck Marcia most was how Liam highlighted the collaborative process rather than just the technical solution - something the old Liam would never have emphasised.

"This is fascinating," Xavier said when Liam finished. "You've uncovered a systemic issue in our security architecture that's been causing integration problems across multiple projects. And you found it within hours rather than weeks because you had the right people connected in real-time."

"Exactly," Liam confirmed. "In a traditional process, this would have been discovered much later, requiring extensive rework. Because we had cross-functional, cross-office teams working together, we identified it early and developed solutions quickly."

Xavier turned to Marcia, genuine interest in his expression. "This connection patterns framework - it's not just a conceptual model, is it? It's a practical approach to addressing complex system integration."

"That's right," Marcia said. "It started as a way to understand our project challenges but evolved into a methodology for identifying and strengthening critical connections - both technical and human."

For the next hour, Xavier moved between teams, observing their work and asking thoughtful questions. Unlike many executives who focused solely on deliverables, he paid equal attention to how teams were working - their communication patterns, decision-making processes, and cross-functional integration.

When they finally gathered in a small conference room for a debrief, Xavier's expression was contemplative.

"I've been advocating for systems thinking at GFP for years," he said. "But it's remained largely theoretical. What you've demonstrated here is systems thinking in action - a practical approach to addressing complexity through deliberate connection-building."

Elizabeth and Malcolm exchanged glances, clearly pleased with Xavier's reaction.

"The innovation sprint format itself is interesting," Xavier continued, "but what truly matters is the underlying mindset shift - seeing our transformation as an interconnected system rather than isolated projects."

He turned to Marcia directly. "Your teams have accomplished more meaningful integration in two days than we typically achieve in weeks. And you've uncovered systemic issues that would have caused significant problems later. That's the real value here."

"Thank you," Marcia said. "The teams deserve the credit - they've embraced the connection patterns approach and made it their own."

Elizabeth met her gaze squarley. "True - but someone had to create the space for that. You were visible without being intrusive. Steady, confident, enabling rather than controlling. That's surprisingly rare."

Xavier offered a quiet smile. "And hard to teach. Most managers either disappear or dominate. You balanced it well."

After the executives departed, promising to return for tomorrow's final readout, Marcia found herself momentarily alone in the conference room. Xavier's observations about her leadership style had struck a chord - particularly his comment about "enabling rather than controlling."

She realised that the power of her presence during the sprint hadn't come from asserting authority or dominating conversations. It had come from creating the conditions where others could do their best work - removing obstacles, providing clarity, gentle coaching, and maintaining confidence when challenges arose.

As she returned to the sprint floor, Marcia saw the teams had gained renewed energy from Xavier's visit. Far from disrupting their flow, his genuine interest and insightful questions had validated their approach and boosted their confidence.

Liam appeared on a nearby screen, waiting to speak with her.

"That went well," he said when she approached. "Xavier grasped the technical concepts quickly."

"He did," Marcia agreed. "But what impressed him most was the collaboration - how you're working across offices to solve complex problems in real-time."

Liam's brows lifted a fraction. "I've been thinking about that. This approach - breaking down boundaries between specialties and locations - it's more effective than I expected.

The solutions we're developing are more robust because they incorporate diverse perspectives from the start."

Coming from Liam, this acknowledgment of collaborative value was remarkable. The same person who had once dismissed meetings as "time that could be spent coding" was now recognising the power of intentional connection.

As day two of the sprint continued into late afternoon, Marcia maintained her calm, steady presence throughout the floor. The energy remained high despite the long hours - fuelled by visible progress and the growing recognition that they were part of something significant - and perhaps a little caffeine.

Marcia had discovered that sometimes the strongest leadership came not from being the loudest voice in the room but from creating space for other voices to be heard.

The patterns they were establishing would continue long after the whiteboards were erased and the teams returned to their normal configurations. That, Marcia realised, was the true measure of their success.

"Leadership begins the moment you stop proving yourself and start improving the system."

✦ ✦ ✦

As evening settled over Seattle, the sprint entered its final stretch. The ninth floor glowed with the soft halo of overhead lights as teams pushed toward their closing objectives. Outside the windows, Seattle's skyline shimmered against the darkening sky, a stark contrast to the focused energy within.

Marcia moved between teams, her presence now a

familiar touchstone in the controlled chaos of the sprint. She noticed how people straightened slightly when she approached - not from fear or intimidation, but from a desire to share their progress. She had become, without consciously planning it, the gravitational centre around which the sprint orbited.

"Authentication fix is holding," reported a developer as Marcia paused at their station. "Liam's workaround is elegant - it respects GFP's security boundaries while still delivering the unified experience we promised."

"Excellent," Marcia nodded. "How's the documentation coming along?"

"That's the best part," the developer grinned. "Liam and Noah are creating a joint architecture document that both offices will maintain going forward. No more Seattle versus New York ownership disputes."

Another connection point strengthened, Marcia thought with satisfaction. A permanent change emerging from their temporary sprint structure.

A message notification from Elizabeth popped up: *Xavier can't stop talking about what he saw today. He's suggesting we extend the connection patterns approach to other projects. This could be a significant turning point for both our companies.*

Marcia tucked her phone away and kept moving, momentum building. On the video wall, the New York office showed similar energy despite the later hour in their time zone. Liam was visible in the background, huddled with a mixed group of Seattle and New York team members, his usual territorial boundaries seemingly forgotten in the collaborative flow. A moment later, he unmuted and cleared his throat quietly, not quite getting the order right.

Across the wall of screens, Alisha's face filled one pane; she lifted a hand, excitedly beckoning Marcia closer. A member of the cross-office user profile team shared their screen, and the room shifted as all attention was drawn to the wall displays. For a moment, no one spoke. The login flow pulsed on the shared screen, a blinking pointer waiting for someone to take the first step.

Marcia felt the weight of it: weeks of frustration, three offices that still learning how to trust each other, and a solution that had broken more than it fixed just forty-eight hours earlier. This wasn't just a demo - it was a test of whether the new connection patterns were real or accidental.

Priya adjusted her headset. Alan leaned closer to his mic in New York.

Marcia stepped forward, grounding her voice. "All right, team. Walk us through what we have."

"You've got to see this," the New York front-end lead said, gesturing to the screen. "Login is 43% faster. And with the authentication and profile updates together, the customer experience feels completely different."

"That's remarkable," Marcia said, genuinely impressed. "How did you achieve such significant improvements?"

Alisha leaned in, her voice quick with enthusiasm. "Previously, login was bouncing between three different services and making redundant calls to the database. Now the authentication and profile steps run in parallel, and we've fixed the caching, so nothing repeats unnecessarily. With QA testing in real time, we spotted these inefficiencies as we designed instead of after deployment."

"Excellence is never solo - it's always an intersection," Marcia said, recognising the collaboration.

As Marcia was about to go on, a sharp exchange of voices erupted. Sarah, and Noah on another pane of the video wall, were talking over each other, frustration mounting over a miscommunicated requirement.

Marcia stepped closer to the display and raised a hand toward the camera. "Hold on," she said evenly, her tone calm but firm enough to cut through. "Sarah, I hear you saying the data isn't coming through correctly. Noah, you're saying the schema was updated this morning, right?" She looked to each in turn, giving them space to answer.

Both fell quiet, breathing, finally acknowledging each other's points with nods. In a few guided sentences, Marcia helped untangle the misunderstanding - it turned out both sides were right once they shared their information. The tension dissipated as quickly as it had flared.

"Thanks, Marcia," Sarah said sheepishly.

Noah managed a small grin from New York. They were already refocusing on a solution together.

Marcia hadn't solved the technical issue herself, but by being present and attentive - even across offices - she'd kept the collaboration on track. She stepped back with a quiet sense of accomplishment as the team continued, crisis averted.

The room gradually settled back into its rhythm: markers squeaked on whiteboards, keyboards rattled, voices softened into steady problem-solving. Marcia lingered a few moments longer, watching the buzz settle into something steadier – something earned. When she returned to Alisha, the login speed improvements were still flashing across the screen, tangible proof of what cross-office collaboration could achieve.

"Excellence is never solo - it's always an intersection."

✧ ✧ ✧

As 8 pm approached, Marcia gathered the team leads for a final check-in before they broke for the day.

"Where do we stand for tomorrow's final push?" she

asked the group gathered in a small conference room, with New York joining virtually.

"Authentication solution is solid," Noah reported from New York, with Liam nodding beside him. "We've documented both the immediate fix and the recommended changes to GFP's security architecture."

"User profiles are exceeding targets," Alisha added. "We'll spend tomorrow morning on final polishing and integration testing."

"API standardisation is back on track," said Carlos, the integration lead. "We've established patterns that both offices will follow going forward. No more inconsistent interfaces." He added, "Studies have shown that well connected teams do better at building well connected interfaces, and I think that is what we are seeing here."

"Excellent progress across the board," Marcia summarised. "Tomorrow, we focus on final integration, documentation, and preparing for the closing presentation. Get some rest tonight - we need everyone sharp for the final day."

As the meeting disbanded, James appeared at her side. "Robert stopped by earlier while you were with the user profile team. He's impressed with what he's seeing."

"This has exceeded even my optimistic expectations," Marcia admitted. "It's not just the technical solutions - it's the collaboration patterns taking root. Despite a few rough edges, people are already building stronger connections across the teams."

"That's the real success," James agreed. "The February milestone features matter, but the lasting impact will be in how these teams continue to work together after the sprint ends."

"Speaking of which," Marcia said, "we should start planning for the transition back to normal operations. I don't want to lose the momentum we've built."

"Already thinking ahead," James said with a subtle grin. "That's why Robert promoted you so quickly."

After James left, Marcia took a moment alone in the conference room, reviewing her notes from the day. Xavier's visit had been a pivotal moment - his recognition of the connection patterns approach as a systems thinking methodology had elevated their work from a project-specific tactic to a potentially transformative strategy for both Alpha and GFP.

A soft chime from her phone interrupted Marcia's thoughts.

Liam. Video calling, not messaging.

She answered. "Hey - everything okay?"

"Yeah," Liam said, his voice quiet but steady. "Are you somewhere you can talk for a few minutes?"

Marcia glanced around the empty conference room. "I'm good. What's up? Everything okay with the authentication solution?"

"The solution is solid," Liam confirmed. "It's something else." He paused, seeming to gather his thoughts. "I've been offered a job at GFP."

Marcia blinked in surprise. "When did this happen?"

"After Xavier left today. He called me privately about leading a new architecture team focused on systems integration. Apparently, my work on the authentication solution impressed him."

This was unexpected - and potentially complicated. Liam was crucial to Alpha's technical strategy.

"How do you feel about the offer?" Marcia asked carefully.

Liam ran a hand through his hair, a now-familiar gesture when he was processing complex thoughts. "A week ago, I would have jumped at it. More money, prestigious position, chance to build something from scratch."

"And now?"

"Now I'm not so sure," he admitted. "This sprint has shown me something I didn't expect at Alpha. The connection patterns approach - it's changing how we work in ways I thought weren't possible. There's potential here I hadn't seen before."

Marcia sat back, studying him. "What are you asking me, Liam?"

"I'm not sure," he said with uncharacteristic uncertainty. "Maybe whether there's a path for me at Alpha to do the kind of systems architecture work Xavier is offering. Or maybe just your perspective on which opportunity has more potential."

This was a critical moment - not just for Liam's career but for the future of the connection patterns approach they were building. Marcia chose her words carefully.

"I can't tell you which path to take," she began. "But I can tell you that what we've started here has significant potential. The connection patterns framework could transform how Alpha approaches complex projects - and you've been instrumental in developing it."

She leaned forward slightly. "What I can promise is that if you stay, you'll have the opportunity to shape that transformation. The technical architecture work will be there, but with the added dimension of systems thinking across human and technical connections."

Liam drew a slow breath, considering his words. "I told Xavier I needed time to think about it. I'll give him my answer after the sprint wraps up."

After the call, Marcia sat alone, contemplating the conversation. Liam's potential departure would be a significant loss, but she wouldn't resort to desperate promises or emotional appeals, it wasn't her place to anyway.

His decision needed to be based on where he saw the most meaningful opportunity, not obligation or guilt.

Robert's text previewed on her screen: *Tomorrow's final presentation moved up to 2 pm. GFP CEO joining Xavier, Elizabeth, and Malcolm. No pressure.*

Marcia smiled wryly at the "no pressure" comment. The stakes continued to rise, but somehow, she felt equal to the challenge. The sprint had demonstrated what was possible when the right connections were established - both technically and among people.

As she finally headed home after a sixteen-hour day, Marcia reflected on how her relationship with the team had evolved. Her presence had shifted from that of a new manager trying to establish authority to a leader who created conditions for others to succeed. The team now looked to her not for micro-direction but for the steady confidence and clarity she provided.

Tomorrow was a high-profile final presentation at the sprint's conclusion. Liam faced a career-defining decision. The future of the connection patterns approach hung in the balance. Yet despite these pressures, Marcia felt a sense of calm readiness.

The power of presence wasn't about having all the answers or controlling every outcome. It was about bringing your full, authentic self to each moment and creating space for others to do the same. Through the crucible of the innovation sprint, she had discovered this truth not as an abstract concept but as a lived experience.

✧ ✧ ✧

"Good morning, everyone," Marcia called out as the teams assembled for the final day kick-off. "We've accomplished incredible things in just two days. Today we bring it all together."

The room buzzed with a different energy than previous mornings - a blend of exhaustion, anticipation, and pride. People moved with the focused intensity of those who could see the finish line ahead. On the video wall, the New York team mirrored this energy, Noah and Alisha organising their groups while team members cycled through testing scenarios.

"The schedule has changed slightly," Marcia announced, commanding immediate attention. "Our final presentation has moved up to 2 pm, and GFP's CEO will be joining Xavier, Elizabeth, and Malcolm."

A ripple of reactions moved through the room - raised eyebrows, straightened postures, a few anxious glances exchanged.

"This isn't cause for panic," Marcia continued, her voice steady and confident. "It's validation that what we're doing matters. The CEO's presence tells us our approach has gained attention at the highest levels."

She surveyed the room, making eye contact with key team members. "We'll spend the morning on final integration and testing. At noon, team leads will gather to prepare for the presentation. Remember - we're showcasing not just what we built but how we built it. The connection patterns are as important as the technical solutions."

Teams dispersed to their workspaces and Marcia resumed her rounds. After about an hour, she checked her messages.

Liam had just pinged her: *GFP auth integration complete. Long-term architecture recommendations documented. Got a few minutes to talk?*

She stepped into a quieter breakout space and hit the call icon. Liam picked up almost instantly, video off, voice calm.

"Morning," he said. "Or afternoon for me, I guess."

"Morning here," Marcia replied. "Thanks for the update. I saw the doc come through - it's excellent work."

"Glad it holds up. The team over here's running smooth. It's weirdly… optimistic in the room."

Marcia let a note of optimism into her voice. "I've been seeing the same on this end. There's a kind of flow happening that wasn't there before."

There was a short pause before Liam spoke again. "I'm still processing our conversation from last night."

"And?" she prompted gently.

"I want to see if this collaborative energy holds through delivery," he said. "Whether it's just sprint adrenaline or the start of something lasting."

"A fair distinction," Marcia said. "That's exactly what today will show us."

"Yeah," Liam murmured. "It's not just about whether we can build things differently - it's whether we can be different."

Marcia felt the weight of that statement. His choice wasn't just about career - it was about belief in the system they were co-creating.

"Whatever you decide, I appreciate the thought you're giving it," she said.

"I'll check in after the wrap-up session," he said. "And Marcia... thanks. For not trying to sell me. Just helping me see clearly."

As she moved back to the conference room to check on other teams, Marcia reflected on Liam's position. His career decision mirrored the broader question they all faced: was the connection patterns approach a temporary experiment or the beginning of a fundamental shift in how they worked?

The morning progressed with intense focus as teams integrated their components and ran final tests. The user profile team celebrated a successful end-to-end test that showed the dramatic improvements in login speed and error reduction. The API standardisation group completed their documentation, creating a blueprint for future development across both offices.

Sarah approached Marcia as she observed the integration testing. "We've caught, fixed, and *avoided* more issues in these three days than we typically address in three weeks," she reported. "Having QA embedded in the development process from the start makes all the difference."

"Another connection pattern worth preserving," Marcia noted. "We should document this approach for our standard processes going forward."

As noon approached, Marcia gathered the team leads in a conference room to prepare for the presentation. The energy was focused but confident - they had delivered on their promises and established new patterns that were already showing value.

"We have four key audiences this afternoon," Marcia explained. "Elizabeth understands our approach and is already supportive. Malcolm is convinced by results and will be looking for concrete deliverables. Xavier is focused on the systemic implications of our connection patterns framework. And the CEO will be evaluating whether this approach could transform GFP's overall digital strategy."

She turned to the whiteboard, sketching out a simple presentation structure. "We'll start with tangible results - the authentication solution, user profile improvements, and API standardisation. Then we'll zoom out to show how the connection patterns made these results possible. Finally, we'll outline how these patterns can be sustained beyond the sprint."

"Who's presenting what?" Alisha asked from the video screen, the New York team leads gathered around her.

"We'll share the stage," Marcia said. "Liam will lead the

authentication section, joining virtually. Alisha, you'll cover the user experience improvements. Carlos, you'll handle the API standardisation. I'll introduce and conclude, focusing on the connection patterns framework."

As they fine-tuned the presentation flow, Marcia noticed Liam's quiet confidence. Whatever uncertainty he felt about his career decision wasn't affecting his commitment to the sprint's success.

At 1:30 pm, the executive visitors began arriving. Elizabeth and Malcolm came first, followed shortly by Xavier. At precisely 1:45 pm, the room quieted as the GFP CEO stepped in. Diana Thompson's reputation preceded her - the leader who had taken more than one sluggish enterprise and forced it to rediscover its edge. She moved with unhurried confidence, her dark suit sharply cut, her gaze alert and measuring. Without raising her voice, she brought a temporary hush to the space, the kind of presence that made people sit straighter and listen harder.

Marcia greeted them warmly but professionally, guiding them to seats prepared at the front of the open presentation area. Around them, teams resumed working, creating a living demonstration of the innovation sprint in action.

As the clock edged toward two, the room gradually quieted. Marcia stepped to the centre of the presentation space, gesturing to the large screen behind her. "Welcome to the final day of our innovation sprint," she began. "What you're seeing around you represents a fundamentally different approach to complex challenges - one that focuses on reconnecting what had become disconnected across offices, functions, and technologies."

She pointed to the connection patterns diagram on display. "A week ago, we identified critical disconnection points in the GFP project. Instead of addressing symptoms individually, we targeted the underlying system through deliberate connection-building."

By the time she finished her introduction, the scheduled presentation time had arrived. The teams set aside their work and gathered close, ready to present. What followed unfolded with practiced fluidity: Liam explained the authentication solution with unexpected polish, demonstrating both the technical elegance and the cross-office collaboration that made it possible. Alisha showcased the user experience improvements, highlighting how direct collaboration between front-end and back-end teams had eliminated traditional handoff problems.

As Carlos concluded the API standardisation overview, Marcia stepped forward again to bring the narrative together.

"The technical solutions you've seen are impressive in isolation," she said. "But their real value comes from the connection patterns that made them possible - patterns that will continue to yield benefits long after this sprint concludes."

She displayed a simple visualisation showing how teamwork patterns had evolved over the three days, with collaboration networks growing increasingly dense and cross-functional.

"This isn't just about delivering the February milestone," Marcia emphasised. "It's about establishing sustainable connections that transform how we approach complex challenges going forward."

Throughout the presentation, Diana Thompson had remained thoughtfully silent, her expression revealing nothing. Now she leaned forward slightly, her attention fully engaged.

"Marcia," Diana said as the presentation wrapped, "your connection patterns framework reminds me of complex adaptive systems theory. Are you familiar with it?"

"Yes," Marcia replied, a little surprised by the academic

reference. "It draws on several strands of systems thinking, including that one."

Diana's eyes warmed with approval. "Most consultants claim to address complexity while actually oversimplifying it. Your approach acknowledges the interconnected nature of technical and human systems. That's commendable." She let her gaze move across the room before continuing. "Now - would someone show me how this integration actually works in practice, please?"

Liam leaned toward the screen, guiding her through the authentication demo. His explanation was steady, assured. Marcia watched as he handled both the technical detail and the executive attention with a fluency that hadn't been there a week ago.

"The elegant part," Liam explained, "is how we respected GFP's existing security boundaries while still creating a unified user experience. Rather than fighting the system's constraints, we designed with them."

Diana studied the solution, asking precise questions that revealed her technical depth. "And this approach could extend to other integration challenges?"

"Absolutely," Liam confirmed. "The pattern we've established here applies to any complex system integration. We've documented both the specific solution and the repeatable pattern for future use."

As the executives continued exploring the sprint outputs, Marcia circulated among the teams, acknowledging their contributions with encouraging words and gestures. Her presence was calm and assured - the steadying influence that had guided them through the intensive three-day effort.

Finally, the executives gathered for a closing conversation with Marcia and the team leads.

"This has been illuminating," Diana said. "Xavier was right to bring this to my attention. The connection patterns approach offers a potential framework for our broader digital transformation strategy."

She turned directly to Marcia. "I'd like to explore how we might apply this methodology more extensively across our relationship with Alpha. Perhaps a workshop with my leadership team to introduce the concepts?"

"We'd be delighted to facilitate that," Marcia replied, careful not to overcommit but recognising the significant opportunity.

"Excellent," Diana's voice held crisp approval. "Elizabeth will coordinate the details." She glanced at her watch. "I need to depart for another meeting, but I'm impressed with what I've seen today. Thank you all for your innovative approach to our challenges."

After the executives departed, a palpable sense of accomplishment spread through the room. Teams continued their work with renewed energy, knowing their efforts had succeeded at the highest levels.

James approached Marcia with an uncharacteristically broad smile. "Diana rarely stays for more than fifteen minutes at vendor presentations. She was here for nearly an hour. That's unprecedented."

"The teams deserved that recognition," Marcia said. "They've accomplished something extraordinary."

"You created the conditions for it to happen," James pointed out. "Your leadership presence throughout this sprint has been remarkable. People responded to that as much as to the structured approach."

As the afternoon progressed, teams completed their final documentation and integration tests. The February milestone features were not only on track but exceeding expectations in quality and performance. More importantly, the connection patterns established during the sprint had created sustainable improvements in how teams collaborated.

✧ ✧ ✧

At 5 pm, Marcia gathered everyone for a closing celebration. Pizza and beverages appeared, creating a festive atmosphere as all three offices connected via the video wall.

"Before we celebrate," Marcia said, gaining everyone's attention, "I want to acknowledge what we've truly accomplished here. Yes, we made significant progress on the February release priority features. Yes, we impressed GFP's executives, including the CEO. But most importantly, we transformed how we work together."

She gestured around the room and to the video screen showing the New York and Chicago team. "Three days ago, we were separated by geography, function, and process. Today, we're a unified team with shared understanding and purpose."

Her gaze found Liam on the video wall, standing near the back of the NY team with his arms crossed but a hint of a smile on his face. "Some people ask whether innovation comes from individual brilliance or collaborative effort. What we've demonstrated is that the most powerful innovations emerge when individual excellence connects within a well-designed system."

Amid the laughter and paper plates loaded with pizza, Noah lifted his soda can in a toast. "Can we all agree this felt pretty different from our usual crunch time?" he asked the room. Heads nodded and a few cheerful "Hear, hear" responses rang out.

"Different good or different bad?" Marcia teased, though her face was flush with pride.

"Good, of course," Noah grinned. He gestured toward Marcia on the screen. "I've never had a manager pull up a chair next to us and stay until the job's done - not just to monitor, but to help and listen. That kept us going, even over a video link."

Marcia felt her cheeks warm. "I just walked the floor and asked a few questions," she protested lightly.

Sarah shook her head, raising her slice of pizza in emphasis. "It's true. You being here with us made a huge difference. We didn't want to let you down - or each other."

Marcia's throat tightened with grateful emotion. She lifted her own drink. "To this team," she said earnestly. "You all proved what happens when we trust each other and work side by side." They clinked cups and bottles, a cheer rippling through the group. For a moment, Marcia blinked away the start of happy tears. There was something new in the room now - real camaraderie and confidence, built over three days of doing the hard work together.

She remembered how much she'd put on the line suggesting this wild sprint - and now she felt it had paid off.

Yet beneath the glow of the success, fatigue tugged at her. A quiet thought surfaced: what if she wasn't able to keep delivering at this level? What if this step upward was more than she could sustain?

As the celebration wound down and people drifted off into the night, Marcia felt a deep sense of satisfaction in her steady leadership so far - guiding without controlling and inspiring without dictating.

✧　✧　✧

About thirty minutes after Marcia arrived home, Liam video called. "I've made my decision," he said quietly.

Marcia raised an eyebrow questioningly.

"I'm staying with Alpha," he said. "What we've built here has more potential than I realised. The connection patterns strategy - it's more than just a project methodology. It could transform how we address complex systems integration across all our work."

"I'm glad to hear it," Marcia said sincerely. "Your expertise is crucial to taking this forward."

"I do have one condition," Liam added, his expression serious. "I want to lead a new architecture team focused on connection patterns implementation. Not just for GFP but across Alpha's client portfolio."

Marcia smiled. "I think Robert would be very receptive to that proposal. We should discuss it with him next week."

As the call ended, the screen faded to black and Marcia set her phone down on the kitchen counter. The apartment was quiet, the last of the day's adrenaline finally giving way to stillness. She glanced out at the city lights reflecting off the rain-slicked streets, letting the moment settle.

What had started as a scramble to rescue a failing project had become something far more meaningful. The power of presence wasn't just a leadership trait - it was a catalyst. And now, from scattered teams and siloed systems, something new had taken root: connection. Not just in theory, but in practice. And maybe - just maybe - it was only the beginning.

Marcia wondered if they could sustain the sprint's momentum.

FIELD RULE: Presence Under Fire
(10-Minute Reset)

- Still the room: eyes on the lead; forbid changes.
- Get signal: Facts first; what changed recently?
- One narrow path: state *one* recent change and *one* failing path; assign observer to narrate facts only.
- Timebox & pair: name pairs, set 10 minutes, then confirm next visible step.

Do this tomorrow: Use the 10-minute reset in your next incident.

You're halfway there.

If Marcia's journey has sparked reflection in your own role -
if you've highlighted a line, nodded at a scene, or felt seen
in a moment of doubt - would you consider leaving a short
review?

Even a sentence or two makes a big difference. It helps
others discover the book - and reminds me that the story is
landing where it matters most: with people like you.

To leave a review

💬 Head to your Amazon Orders page → find this book →
and select "Write a Product Review"

With gratitude,

Stephen J. McIntyre

Chapter 6
The Power of Process

Chaos is exhausting. What teams crave isn't more rules - it's clarity. The right process doesn't chain people; it frees them, like a hidden map that turns confusion into a game everyone knows how to win.

✧ ✧ ✧

Habits that survive bad days.

✧ ✧ ✧

Monday morning, the energy from the sprint still lingered. Marcia had barely settled at her desk when an email from Elizabeth flashed:

Subject: Quick request - click-through and CSV export?

Could we make the Q3 summary report clickable to the underlying transactions and add a "download CSV"? Should be straightforward

Instead of forwarding it, she pulled business analyst and tech leads into a ten-minute huddle. "Let's run this through our change-control checklist," she said, opening the template Tessa had drafted. Together they assessed the impact: the new report would add two weeks of work and jeopardise other deliverables.

Marcia drafted the reply with the numbers in view:

Elizabeth,
Adding drill-through and CSV means a new detail endpoint, row-level access checks, export audit logging, and performance work. The effort is ~2 weeks and bumps the payroll APIs integration, which would push testing into the release window.

Proposal: keep the current Q3 scope; schedule drill-through/CSV for Sprint 14 with a safe buffer. Happy to jump on a call if helpful.

Elizabeth answered before lunch:

Understood - let's keep Q3 as-is and slot drill-through/CSV into Sprint 14. Thanks for laying out the trade-offs.

It was a small procedural shift - analysing before acting - but it sent a clear message. In the office, word spread that 'Marcia won't let them move the goalposts without calling it out.' For the first time since Brett left, the team felt a sense of order returning.

✧　✧　✧

Following the innovation sprint, Alpha Consulting's Seattle

office had returned to its normal configuration. The temporary collaboration spaces in Conference Room A were gone, tables back in their usual positions, and the large video wall now quiet and black, rather than showing the New York team. Yet something had fundamentally changed.

Marcia noticed it immediately as she walked through the development area on level eight. People who had rarely acknowledged each other before now paused to discuss issues face-to-face. A QA analyst who had come up from level seven sat beside a developer, pointing at code on his screen rather than filing a formal defect report. She even saw faces from the normally isolated database team appearing more frequently on video calls, inviting conversation rather than reinforcing isolation.

A quiet satisfaction settled. These small changes were evidence that the connection patterns established during the sprint were beginning to take root in their day-to-day operations.

Sitting at her desk, as Marcia mapped the procedural fixes they needed, one snag kept appearing: requirements changes were coming from everywhere with no single place to land. She jotted a note to herself beside the workflow:

Central changelog → impact analysis → visible to all.
Talk to Tessa when we set up the cross-office metrics.

A little while later, James joined her at the coffee station. "Not bad for three days' work," he said.

"The real test will be whether it lasts," Marcia replied, pouring herself a cup. "Patterns can revert quickly once the pressure's off."

"True," James lifted his mug in a small salute. "But some connections, once formed, are hard to break. Have you seen your inbox this morning?"

Marcia winced. "I have, but I'm still catching up after the sprint."

"There's one from Diana you'll want to read. GFP's CEO doesn't email consultants directly very often."

Back in her office, Marcia found a new message near the top of her unread pile:

Marcia,

The innovation sprint exceeded my expectations, not just in technical deliverables but in demonstrating a fundamentally different approach to complex challenges. I'd like to explore extending the connection patterns methodology across our entire digital portfolio.

I've asked Elizabeth to coordinate a workshop with my leadership team next month. We see potential for this approach to transform not just the February milestone but our broader digital transformation strategy.

Diana Thompson CEO, Global Financial Partners
CC: James Anderson, Elizabeth Parker

Marcia read the message twice, processing its significance. Diana wasn't known for easy praise or impulsive decisions. Her interest in the connection patterns approach represented a potential shift in GFP's entire relationship with Alpha.

As she was contemplating a response, her office door opened. Liam stood there, looking more relaxed than she'd ever seen him, though his hair was still characteristically dishevelled.

"I spoke with Robert this morning," he said directly. "Thanks for setting up the meeting. I talked him through the architecture team idea, focused on connection patterns implementation."

"And?" Marcia prompted, gesturing for him to sit.

"He approved it," Liam said, the corner of his mouth and slight squint of an eye revealing a smile. "Said the innovation sprint results were 'compelling evidence' that the approach deserves dedicated resources."

"That's excellent news," Marcia said sincerely. "What's your vision for the team?"

Liam leaned forward, his usual reticence giving way to genuine enthusiasm. "A cross-functional group developing architectural patterns that support connection points across technical and human systems. Not just for GFP but as a foundation for all Alpha's enterprise integration work."

As Liam outlined his plans, Marcia noticed something she'd never seen in him before - a focus not just on technical excellence but on how technology enabled human collaboration. The sprint had changed him, just as it had changed the broader team dynamics.

James appeared in her doorway, knocking lightly. "Robert wants to see the three of us. Apparently, Diana called him directly after the sprint."

"That's unusual," Marcia said, rising from her desk.

"So is having the GFP CEO attend a consultant's innovation sprint," James replied, amusement threading his voice. "You've broken several precedents in the last week."

As the trio walked to Robert's office, Marcia reflected on how the sprint's success had created new possibilities.

Robert was standing by his window when they entered, the afternoon sun reflecting off the Sound behind him. "Congratulations," he said, turning to face them. "Diana just offered Alpha an expanded role in GFP's digital transformation. She specifically cited the connection patterns approach as the difference-maker."

"That's excellent news," Marcia said, taking a seat at the small meeting table in Robert's office.

"It's more than that," Robert continued, joining them. "It's validation of an approach that could differentiate Alpha in a crowded consulting market. The innovation sprint demonstrated that by focusing on connections rather than just components, we can deliver results that others can't."

He slid a folder across the table to Marcia. "I've reviewed the metrics from the sprint compared to our normal development process. The differences are striking - higher quality, faster delivery, greater stakeholder satisfaction."

Marcia opened the folder, scanning the detailed analysis. "Quality defect rate... down 60%?" she muttered, hardly believing it.

Liam, seated beside Marcia, scanned the figures with disbelief. "Honestly, I didn't expect the numbers to look that good either," he admitted, his tone more impressed than doubtful.

Marcia broke into a smile, looking up at him. "It's one thing to feel the project turning around - but seeing it quantified like this is incredible."

Liam allowed himself the smallest grin in return. He tapped one line on the report. "Consistent cross-office code reviews and shared dashboards... turns out those 'process things' actually worked."

"Our past selves would be stunned," Marcia chuckled. Only a month ago, Marcia knew, she and Liam might have rolled their eyes at such a rigid approach. Now the results spoke for themselves.

James added quietly, "And it wasn't just the numbers. The room felt different each day - more focus, more trust."

"So, what's next?" Marcia asked, looking up from the report.

Robert tapped his pen once, thoughtful. "That's what I

wanted to discuss with you. The GFP February milestone is important, but the implications of what you've developed go far beyond one project. I'd like to explore how we can standardise and scale this approach across Alpha's entire portfolio."

As Robert outlined his vision, Marcia recognised that the sprint had created an inflection point for Alpha's future direction.

✧　✧　✧

"It's the little things that make the difference," Marcia said, standing before the GFP project team in their first post-sprint status meeting. "The innovation sprint gave us momentum but maintaining that momentum comes down to daily discipline in how we operate."

The conference room was packed, with the New York team joining virtually on the wall screen. Everyone looked both energised and exhausted - the aftermath of three intense days followed by a weekend that hadn't been quite long enough for full recovery.

"Over the next two weeks, we'll be formalising some of the connection patterns that worked so well during the sprint," she continued, clicking to the next slide. "I'm giving it a working name for now - S.T.E.A.D.Y. - and we'll refine it as we learn."

1. **S** - Daily cross-functional Stand-ups
2. **T** - Cross-office Triage (prioritise bugs/defects)
3. **E** - Embedded QA in development teams
4. **A** - Async metrics dashboards with shared definitions
5. **D** - Clear ownership and Decision logging
6. **Y** - Yes/No gates; cross-office requirements review

"None of these are revolutionary on their own," Marcia acknowledged. "But together, they create a system where information flows freely, problems surface early, and solutions emerge faster."

"One more standard," Marcia said, gesturing to the wall. "The Momentum Board lives on." She'd replaced the mobile stand with a permanent board beside the dashboards: Today | Blocked | Cleared.

"Rule of three: every stand-up names our Today items, each Blocked has an owner, and we celebrate at least one Cleared before day's end."

A few people laughed at the *celebrate* line, and an easy murmur of assent moved through the room. Rituals make speed feel safe.

Marcia noticed Liam nodding slightly from his seat in the corner. Since returning from New York, he'd been unusually engaged in these process-focused discussions - a departure from his typical impatience with anything that wasn't purely technical.

"Questions?" Marcia asked as she concluded the overview.

A developer raised his hand. "The embedded QA approach worked great during the sprint, but do we have enough QA resources to maintain that full-time?"

"Good question," Marcia said, gesturing to Sarah who stood up from her seat.

"We're reorganising the QA team to make this sustainable," Sarah explained. "Instead of centralised testing at the end of development cycles, we'll have QA specialists embedded with specific feature teams. It actually requires fewer hours overall because we catch issues earlier."

The questions continued for several minutes, ranging from practical logistics to concerns about maintaining the cross-office connections that had formed during the sprint.

Marcia addressed each one directly, emphasising that these changes weren't optional experiments but their new standard operating model.

"One last thing before we break," Marcia said as the meeting drew to a close. "Elizabeth Parker will be sitting in on three stand-ups each week, starting tomorrow. Having direct client involvement was a key success factor during the sprint, and she's committed to maintaining that connection."

She glanced around to gauge the reaction. In the past, that kind of news would have drawn nervous looks or a sudden silence. This time, a few team members actually smiled.

"Let's show her how our new process keeps us on track," Tessa said, with a determined little nod.

Marcia felt a swell of pride at Tessa's sentiment. The fact that the team was eager - rather than anxious - to have an executive see their workflow was a testament to the steady rhythm and confidence they'd built. Instead of scrambling to put on a good face, they would simply show the solid work they were now doing every day.

"Rituals beat heroics."

✧　✧　✧

As the team dispersed, Tessa approached Marcia near the front of the conference room, opening her laptop to show a detailed metrics dashboard. "I've set up real-time tracking for our new operational patterns," she explained. "Green indicates where we're maintaining sprint-level performance, amber shows areas of concern, and red flags immediate attention needed."

Marcia studied the dashboard, impressed by Tessa's

initiative. Most of the indicators shone green, with just a few amber flags around cross-office collaboration - understandable now that the video wall was gone.

"This is excellent, Tessa," Marcia said. "The dashboard creates great visibility. Can you share access with all the team leads? I want everyone monitoring these connection points, not just management."

"Already done," Tessa confirmed with a smile. "And I've scheduled a weekly review to identify patterns and recommend adjustments."

Marcia voice warmed, recognising Tessa's potential. "You've really pulled the pieces together, Tessa. The consistency across teams - that's your fingerprint."

Tessa hesitated at the doorway. "I just organised what everyone was already doing," she said modestly. "It's nothing major."

"It's more than you think," Marcia replied, leaning back slightly. "You have a way of bringing order without dampening creativity. That's leadership, whether you call it that or not."

Tessa's eyes widened. "Leadership?"

"That dashboard isn't just a report; it's a bridge," Marcia said. "I'd like you to coordinate the cross-office metrics work. You've earned the trust of both business and dev, and you're good at defusing tension. I'll back you - and I'll be in it with you."

Tessa chewed her lip. "I'm not sure I'm ready to manage anyone."

Tessa hesitated. "I don't say this often," she murmured, keeping her voice low, "but sometimes I still worry I'm repeating mistakes from earlier in my career." She gave a tight, self-conscious smile. "I'm working on trusting myself again."

"You won't be doing it alone," Marcia said, voice calm

and assured. "We'll start together. You focus on clarity and flow; I'll clear the friction. You've got this."

"One more thing," Marcia said. "We also need a requirements changelog feeding that dashboard - simple, consistent, visible. One queue, impact noted on each request, and everyone can see it."

Tessa's brows lifted, already thinking. "So… the log becomes the source of truth for scope changes, and the dashboard shows the ripple effects."

"Exactly," Marcia said. "Design it so both business and dev can contribute - and no one's surprised."

"Alright… I can do that. I already have a few ideas for improving the dashboard layout," Tessa replied.

"Good. Bring them to the next check-in," Marcia said, genuinely pleased.

Tessa gave a small, thoughtful smile and stepped toward the door.

Marcia watched her go, feeling a quiet fulfilment that came from seeing growth she'd helped spark. For the first time in weeks, she wasn't just managing a project - she was passing on what others had once given her.

At the doorway, James had been leaning against the frame, watching the exchange with pride.

"You're systematising the magic," he observed as he joined her. "Making the exceptional into the expected."

"That's the challenge, isn't it?" Marcia replied, gathering her materials. "The sprint created breakthrough moments, but sustainable excellence comes from daily discipline in small things."

"Robert's impressed," James said as they walked toward her office. "He mentioned that Diana called him again yesterday. Apparently, she's already briefed GFP's board on the connection patterns approach."

"That's moving quickly," Marcia commented, surprised

by the rapid escalation to board level.

"They're feeling market pressure. Their competitors launched a new mobile banking platform last week that's getting rave reviews. The board is eager for anything that accelerates their digital transformation."

In her office, Marcia found an email from Liam with the subject line *Authentication Service Metrics*. Opening it revealed a detailed analysis showing ongoing improvement metrics since implementing the consolidated approach.

Attached was a brief note:

Small changes, big impact. The security architecture modifications we identified during the sprint created efficiencies beyond the authentication process itself. I've highlighted downstream improvements in the attached diagram.
-L

The diagram showed how the authentication consolidation had created a ripple effect throughout GFP's technical ecosystem - simplifying integration points, reducing data transfer overhead, and eliminating redundant security checks. What had begun as a targeted fix for a specific problem had generated system-wide improvements.

Marcia forwarded Liam's analysis to Elizabeth adding:

Early results from the authentication consolidation. The improvements extend beyond the immediate login experience to enhance overall system performance. Another example of how small, targeted changes can deliver outsized benefits.

Elizabeth's reply came surprisingly quickly:

This is exactly what Xavier was talking about. He's presenting the connection patterns approach to our technology steering committee next week. Would you and Liam be available to demonstrate the authentication improvements?

Before Marcia could respond, her phone rang. It was Malcolm Wright, GFP's CIO - unexpected, since he typically communicated through Elizabeth.

"Marcia," he said when she answered, his voice carrying the clipped precision of someone speaking from London. "I've just reviewed the authentication metrics - quite remarkable results. Well done, truly."

"Thank you, Malcolm. Liam's team deserves the credit for the implementation."

"Yes, well, that's partly why I'm calling. The board is particularly interested in how we might apply similar approaches to our European operations. Authentication has been troublesome with our recent acquisitions."

Marcia chose her words carefully. "The connection patterns approach could probably help integrate those acquisitions more seamlessly. It's designed to identify and strengthen critical junction points in complex systems."

"Precisely," Malcolm agreed. "I'd like to discuss expanding Alpha's scope to include our European integration challenges. Elizabeth mentioned you might be visiting the London office next month?"

"That's still tentative," Marcia said, surprised that a casual conversation with Elizabeth had apparently become part of GFP's planning. "But I could certainly make it work if needed."

After finishing the call with Malcolm, Marcia sat back in her chair, processing the implications.

A knock at her door made her jump. It was Carlos, the API integration lead, looking concerned.

"We've hit a snag with the standardisation rollout," he said, getting straight to the point. "Some of the legacy systems are resisting the new protocols. We can force it, but it might delay the February milestone."

Marcia gestured for him to sit. "Tell me more about it."

As Carlos detailed the technical challenges, Marcia recognised another opportunity to apply connection patterns thinking. Rather than forcing standardisation across all systems immediately, they needed to establish bridge patterns that allowed legacy and modern components to communicate effectively while gradually transitioning to the new standards.

"Let's adjust our approach," she suggested, sketching a diagram on her whiteboard. "Instead of wholesale replacement, let's create adapter patterns here, here, and here - allowing the legacy systems to maintain their internal protocols while presenting standardised interfaces to the rest of the ecosystem."

Carlos studied the diagram, tracing the lines with his eyes. "That could work. It's more elegant than forcing conformity, and probably more sustainable long-term."

"Sometimes the best way to change a system is to work with its natural tendencies rather than against them," Marcia observed. "Please document this approach as another connection pattern for Liam's architecture team."

After Carlos left, Marcia updated her project plan, adjusting timelines to accommodate the more nuanced API standardisation approach. The February target remained achievable, though with less buffer than she'd hoped.

✧ ✧ ✧

As evening approached, Marcia took a final walk through the office before heading home. The development area was lively - not the frantic pace of the innovation sprint, but a steady, sustainable rhythm that felt both productive and balanced.

Near Liam's desk, she noticed something new: a whiteboard covered with architectural diagrams labelled "Connection Patterns Library" in his precise handwriting. Each pattern showed a different approach to integrating systems, with annotations about when to apply each one.

Liam was building a repeatable framework from what they'd learned - transforming specific solutions into systematic approaches. It was exactly the kind of operational excellence that turned individual successes into scalable methodologies.

As Marcia headed home, she reflected on how their focus had evolved. The sprint had created breakthrough moments through deliberate disruption. Now they were building sustainability through disciplined attention to daily operations - systematising what worked, refining what didn't, and continuously strengthening connection points throughout the system.

The February milestone would be their first major test of whether this approach could deliver consistently.

✧ ✧ ✧

Two weeks after the innovation sprint, Elizabeth Parker strode into Alpha's Seattle office for the weekly status review. She looked different somehow - more relaxed, confident. Gone was the perpetual concerned frown Marcia had grown accustomed to during the project's troubled early days.

"The authentication improvements have been transformative," Elizabeth announced as she settled into the conference room chair. "Customer complaints about login issues have dropped away since implementation. Our call centre can hardly believe the difference."

Marcia let out a quiet, satisfied breath. "The technical changes were important, but I think the operational improvements are the real game-changer. The cross-functional teams are catching issues before they reach production."

"That's exactly what I wanted to discuss today," Elizabeth said, pulling out her tablet. "Xavier's been analysing your connection patterns approach, and he's identified something interesting. It's not just the big architectural changes making the difference - it's the cumulative impact of dozens of small operational improvements."

She pulled up a detailed graph showing defect rates over time. "See this sharp drop after the sprint? We expected that. But look at how the trend continues downward week over week. Each small process improvement compounds on the previous ones."

"Here's the summary," Elizabeth said. "Xavier's analysis, side by side." The screen switched to *Before* → *After* - same team, same scope, different operating rhythm.

Before	After
Login speed	
410 ms	**234 ms**
What it means: How fast the sign-in feels to a user.	
How to measure: Median time from "Sign in" click to profile/home screen.	
Bugs caught before release	
65%	**85%**
What it means: Quality built in, not patched later.	
How to measure: % of defects found before release.	
Time from idea to live	
21 median days	**13 median days**
What is means: How quickly we turn decisions into value.	
How to measure: Median days from decision recorded to feature live.	
After-hours interruptions	
0.9 pages per week	**0.3 pages per week**
What it means: Nights and weekends disturbed by production issues.	
How to measure: Number of urgent callouts outside business hours per week.	

Marcia studied the table with satisfaction. This was

precisely what she'd hoped to see - evidence that excellence in small tasks consistently led to bigger wins over time.

"We've been making systematic improvements in how we work," she explained, walking Elizabeth through their approach. "Daily stand-ups that actually solve problems instead of just reporting status. Checklists for code reviews that prevent common errors. Automated quality gates that catch issues immediately."

"None of those sound revolutionary," Elizabeth observed.

"That's the point," Marcia said, unruffled. "Revolution is flashy but often temporary. Evolution through consistent small improvements creates lasting change. We're building quality into the process rather than inspecting it at the end."

They looked up as Sarah entered with a folder of reports. "Right on time for the quality review," Marcia said, motioning for her to join them.

"The embedded QA approach continues to show impressive results," Sarah reported, displaying a chart showing steadily decreasing defect leakage. "By having QA involved from the beginning of feature development, we're preventing issues rather than just finding them later."

"What about the cross-office dynamics?" Elizabeth asked. "That was a major challenge before the sprint."

"We've instituted several small but crucial changes there," Sarah explained. "Synchronised stand-ups three times weekly. Paired testing between Seattle and New York. Shared quality dashboards that both teams monitor. These connection points prevent the silos from reforming."

After reviewing the technical progress and updated timelines, Elizabeth appeared genuinely impressed. "The February milestone is looking not just achievable but exceeding expectations. Malcolm will be pleased."

"Speaking of Malcolm," Marcia said, "he mentioned

expanding our scope to include European integration challenges. Has there been any development on that front?"

"The board approved initial exploration yesterday," Elizabeth confirmed. "They want a proposal for applying the connection patterns approach to our European acquisitions by the end of February. I hope you're prepared for more international travel."

After Elizabeth left, Marcia found Liam in the development area, reviewing code with a junior developer - something he would have delegated before the innovation sprint.

"Got a minute?" she asked.

"Yeah." Liam wrapped up with the junior developer before joining her.

"The architecture team is making good progress," he said as they walked toward her office. "We've documented twelve core connection patterns so far, with implementation templates for each."

"That's impressive," Marcia said, genuinely pleased with his initiative. "But I'm actually here about something else. How would you feel about London in March?"

"London?" Liam looked surprised. "What for?"

"GFP wants to extend the connection patterns approach to their European operations. They've had challenges integrating recent acquisitions, particularly around authentication and customer data systems."

Liam thought it over, reflexively running a hand through his hair. "The security architecture will be more complex with European privacy regulations. But the underlying connection patterns should still apply."

"So, you're interested?" Marcia asked.

"I wouldn't have been before," Liam admitted. "But seeing how the cross-office collaboration with New York improved our solutions... yes, I'm interested. The European technical teams will have perspectives we need to incorporate."

This was yet another sign of Liam's evolution. The small changes in how they worked had created ripple effects in individual behaviours as well as team dynamics.

Later that afternoon, Marcia joined Tessa for a walk-through of the February release features. The user experience demonstration showed remarkable polish, with seamless workflows across what had previously been fragmented systems.

"The integration feels natural," Marcia observed as Tessa demonstrated the customer journey. "You can't tell where one system ends and another begins."

"That's by design," Tessa explained. "We've been obsessive about the transition points. Every handoff between systems is meticulously crafted to feel invisible to the user."

It was another example of how attention to small details created outsized impacts. By focusing on the connection points between systems rather than just the systems themselves, they'd created an experience that felt cohesive despite the complex technology underneath.

"I've been thinking about my role in all this," Tessa said as they finished the review. "You mentioned the possibility of a new position focused on requirements and change control."

"I did," Marcia confirmed. "Have you given it some thought?"

"I have," Tessa nodded. "I'd like to propose a slight variation - focusing on connection points between business needs and technical implementation. Like a translator who ensures nothing gets lost in translation."

"A Business Connection Architect," Marcia suggested. "I like it. Draft a job description and we'll discuss it with Robert next week."

As evening approached, Marcia sat in her office reviewing the day's progress. The February milestone was firmly on track, with quality metrics continuing to improve week on week.

The requirements changelog was now pinned in every team room and linked from the project portal. New requests landed in one queue with a visible impact note. No more surprises. Simple, consistent, visible had stuck.

Metric definitions were standardised across offices, too. The dashboard labels now matched on both coasts, so Seattle and New York were measuring the same things in the same way.

The small operational changes they'd implemented were becoming standard practice, with teams internalising them as 'just how we work' rather than special initiatives.

James appeared, looking pleased. "Robert asked me to check if you're free for dinner tonight. Apparently, GFP's board approved an expanded scope for Alpha. He wants to discuss next steps."

"I'll make myself available," Marcia said, closing her laptop. "Any hints about what he has in mind?"

"Just that it involves formalising the connection patterns approach as an Alpha methodology," James replied. "The GFP success has caught attention throughout the company. Other delivery managers are asking how they can apply similar approaches to their troubled projects."

As they walked out together, Marcia reflected on how far they'd come. The GFP project had transformed from a potential failure into a showcase for a new way of working. The innovation sprint had provided the catalyst, but it was the daily discipline of operational excellence that had sustained and built upon those initial breakthroughs.

"You know what strikes me most about all this?" she said

to James as they waited for the elevator.

"What's that?"

"The biggest wins came from the smallest changes. Not grand reorganisations or massive technology overhauls, but dozens of small improvements in how people work together day to day."

"The power of process." James's tone was warm but matter-of-fact. "Excellence in small tasks compounds over time to create remarkable outcomes. It's less glamorous than the innovation initiative, but ultimately more transformative."

The elevator doors opened, revealing Robert waiting in the lobby. His expression was energised, already launching into ideas before they'd even greeted him properly.

"I'm thinking we formalise the connection patterns approach into a proper Alpha methodology," he said as they walked toward his car. "Not just for the GFP project but as a framework for all our complex integration work."

"I'd like to involve Liam's architecture team in that," Marcia suggested. "They've already documented twelve core patterns with implementation templates."

"Perfect," Robert said with an approving smile. "And we'll need to establish training programs, certification standards, the works. This could become Alpha's signature approach."

As they drove to dinner, Marcia felt a quiet sense of pride. The troubled project she'd inherited had become the launching pad for something much larger.

The power of process had proven itself again - excellence in small things consistently leading to big wins.

✧ ✧ ✧

The glass-walled boardroom on level ten buzzed with energy

as Marcia arranged her presentation materials. Today was the final review before the February milestone delivery - a moment that had once seemed impossibly distant when she'd first inherited the troubled GFP project.

Outside the windows, Seattle's winter sky had cleared briefly, letting afternoon sunlight stream across the table where her leadership team gathered. Sarah arranged her quality metrics. Tessa organised the user acceptance results. Carlos reviewed his integration reports. And Liam, surprisingly prompt for once, had his architecture documentation neatly prepared.

"Everyone ready?" Marcia asked, checking the time. In five minutes, Robert would arrive with Elizabeth, Malcolm, and possibly Xavier from GFP.

"All set," Tessa confirmed. "User acceptance testing cleared final approval yesterday with zero critical defects."

"And the changelog held," Tessa added. "Every change request went through impact analysis in a single queue. The dashboard picked up the deltas across offices - no surprises."

Marcia caught the confidence in her voice; the process was hers now.

"Authentication metrics continue to improve," Liam added. "Login success rates now at 99%, up from 96% before our consolidation."

Sarah looked up from her tablet. "QA certification complete across all components. We've never delivered this level of quality, especially not with an accelerated timeline."

The door opened, and Robert entered, followed by Elizabeth and Malcolm. Xavier wasn't with them, but Diana was - an unexpected addition that sent a ripple of straightened postures around the table.

"Hope you don't mind my joining," Diana said, settling into a chair. "I wanted to see the final results firsthand before our board presentation next week."

"We're honoured to have you," Marcia said smoothly, adjusting mentally to the CEO's presence. "We're just about to review the February milestone deliverables and the operational improvements that made them possible."

As Marcia launched into the presentation, she noticed Diana paying particular attention to the process metrics - the small, systematic changes that had accumulated into substantial improvements.

"These daily stand-ups," Diana interrupted, pointing to a slide showing communication patterns. "You mentioned they're structured differently than typical status meetings. Can you elaborate?"

"Certainly," Marcia replied. "Instead of the standard 'what I did yesterday, what I'm doing today' format, we restructured them to focus on connection points between teams. Each person highlights where their work intersects with others and identifies any potential integration challenges."

"This single change reduced coordination issues significantly," Tessa added, pulling up a supporting graph. "Problems surface earlier when people explicitly focus on how their work connects to others."

Diana skimmed the graph, satisfied. "Small change, big impact. Continue."

Marcia moved through the presentation methodically, highlighting how each operational improvement had contributed to the overall success. The checklist for code reviews that had eliminated common errors. The automated quality gates that caught issues immediately. The cross-office pairing that kept Seattle and New York aligned.

When Liam presented the authentication solution, he focused not just on the technical elegance but on the operational discipline that ensured consistent implementation.

"The architecture pattern itself is solid," he explained, "but it's the daily practices that maintain its integrity. Each change goes through a connection impact analysis that prevents unintended consequences."

As the presentation concluded, Diana leaned forward, her expression thoughtful. "What strikes me most is the sustainability of your approach. The innovation sprint created breakthrough moments, but these operational practices ensure consistent excellence over time."

"That's precisely our philosophy," Marcia confirmed. "Revolutionary moments create possibilities, but evolutionary practices deliver reliable results day after day."

Robert spoke up for the first time. "We're formalising this approach as a methodology for Alpha. The working title is 'Connection-Driven Delivery' - a systematic framework for complex integration projects."

Diana turned to Elizabeth and Malcolm. "I want this approach extended across our entire relationship with Alpha. The February milestone results speak for themselves."

After the executives departed, the team remained in the conference room, a shared sense of accomplishment settling over them.

"We did it," Sarah said simply, stating what everyone was thinking. "Not just the technical deliverables but the operational transformation."

"It wasn't one big thing," Tessa reflected. "It was a hundred small things done consistently well."

Liam rubbed his jaw, considering. "I've always focused on architectural elegance, but this project taught me that operational discipline matters just as much. The best architecture fails without consistent execution."

The room began to shift as people stood, closed laptops, and gathered their things. She joined a quiet side conversation as people lingered a little before returning to their desks.

While still on the tenth floor, Marcia detoured to find James at his desk, reviewing a tablet. He glanced up and smiled. "Word travels fast. Robert's already mentioned the readout - said Diana stayed through the entire technical section. That doesn't happen often."

"The results made it easy to present," Marcia said, still holding her notes. "Every metric exceeds targets, and the team owns the practices that got them there."

"Robert's already talking about applying the approach to other struggling accounts," James said, setting the tablet aside. "You've built a repeatable model - and people are noticing."

"The technical problems vary, sure, but the connection patterns and operational rhythms? Those transfer," Marcia said, her tone steady but animated.

A few minutes later, back in her office, Marcia took a moment alone to update her latest project journal. She'd maintained this private record since her first leadership role, documenting lessons learned, and insights gained.

Today's entry focused on the power of process:

GFP Feb Milestone Wrap-Up
It wasn't one big win that turned this project around. It was dozens of small things, done right and done consistently.
* *Stand-ups that mattered.*
* *Code reviews that caught real issues.*
* *Cross-office work that broke the silos.*
The innovation sprint gave us momentum, but process is what made it stick.
This is the real playbook:
Small things. Done well. Every day.
That's what creates lasting change.

As Marcia finished her journal entry, there was a knock at her door. It was Liam, looking somewhat hesitant despite his recent confidence.

"Do you have a minute?" he asked. "There's something I'd like to discuss before the London planning begins."

"Of course," Marcia replied, gesturing to a chair. "What's on your mind?"

"I've been thinking about the architecture team we're forming," he said, settling across from her. "It needs to evolve beyond just technical patterns. The connection points between technology and operations are where the real power lies."

"I agree completely," Marcia said, intrigued by this evolution in his thinking. "What are you proposing?"

"A more integrated approach," Liam explained, his enthusiasm growing. "Not just documenting technical patterns but mapping how they intersect with operational practices, team structures, and business processes."

As Liam outlined his vision, Marcia recognised the next evolution of their approach taking shape. The operational excellence they'd established was becoming the foundation for deeper transformations.

✧ ✧ ✧

The morning after the celebration, the project room felt different - calmer, steadier, as if the frantic momentum of the February milestone had finally exhaled. The sprint had delivered, yes, but Marcia knew the real test came afterward: sustaining the gains, cleaning up the rough edges, and stabilising the platform for what came next.

She stood at the whiteboard as the core leads gathered around: Priya from backend services, Daniel from data flows, Carlos from customer operations, and a handful of others who had quietly stepped up throughout the sprint.

"Before we shift focus to the European rollout," Marcia began, "we need a clear plan for how GFP work continues without losing momentum. The milestone may be complete, but sustain-and-recover is still very much alive."

Priya nodded. "We've drafted a stabilisation backlog - bug clusters, performance trims, a few security patches. Nothing we can't handle. We just need clear ownership lines."

"Exactly," Marcia said. "Each of you will lead a vertical: Priya on platform and backend stability, Daniel on payments, data and reporting, Carlos on customer-impact items. I'll still be here for decisions that require broader context or executive input, but you don't need me for day-to-day calls."

Carlos smiled. "So we escalate only when the recovery plan hits something hairy?"

"Right," Marcia replied. "If something threatens our service levels, regulatory posture, or cross-team alignment - bring it to me. Otherwise, you've got full authority to execute."

James entered a moment later, carrying a stack of laminated cards.

"Perfect timing," Marcia said. "James is going to run a short workshop on RACI-Lite."

He grinned. "I promise - it's less painful than it sounds. In fact, it'll help you all figure out exactly who's Responsible, who's Accountable, and where Marcia needs to stay Informed while she focuses on Europe."

Daniel leaned forward. "So for the sustain work, I'm Responsible... who's Accountable?"

"You are," James said. "RACI-Lite keeps it simple. Each major outcome has one clear A. If a decision crosses teams, you bring Marcia in. Otherwise, you own it."

Marcia watched the leads absorb this with a mixture of

pride and relief. They were ready - more ready than they realised.

"These next few weeks," she said, "will show whether the systems we built during the milestone can stand on their own. I have absolute confidence they can."

Priya raised a hand. "And Europe? When do we start shaping that?"

"Today," Marcia said, a small thrill of anticipation running through her. "But only because all of you have proven the GFP work is in safe hands."

The group dispersed into smaller huddles, sketching workflows and responsibilities across the whiteboards. For the first time since taking over the project, Marcia felt the strange sensation of leadership becoming lighter - not because there was less to do, but because there were more people ready to carry it with her.

✧ ✧ ✧

"Small things, done consistently, create excellence," Marcia said, pointing to the whiteboard where she'd mapped out their approach for GFP's European expansion. "That's what transformed the February milestone from a potential disaster into a showcase success."

The planning room was packed with both familiar faces and new team members who would support the European integration. Robert sat at the back, observing rather than leading - a sign of his confidence in Marcia's approach.

"For Europe, we'll face additional challenges," she continued. "Different regulatory environments, recently acquired companies with their own systems, and teams spread across multiple countries. But the core principle remains the same: excellence emerges from disciplined attention to the connection points."

Liam stood beside her, looking more comfortable in front of the group than anyone would have imagined possible a month ago.

"We've identified fifteen critical connection patterns for the European integration," he explained, bringing up a diagram on the screen. "Each addresses a specific integration challenge, but the underlying structure is consistent - identify the connection point, establish clear protocols, and implement verification practices."

"What's different from our usual approach?" asked a senior developer who'd recently joined from another project.

"Everything and nothing," Marcia answered, taking the question in her stride. "The technical aspects aren't revolutionary - we're applying industry best practices. What's different is our relentless focus on how things connect rather than the components themselves."

She clicked to a slide showing the results from the February milestone, with before-and-after metrics that told a compelling story. Login success rates improved from 96% to 99%. Customer satisfaction with the digital experience improved by 35%. Development velocity increased by 40%, while defect rates dropped by 60%.

"These results didn't come from a single breakthrough innovation," Marcia emphasised. "They came from dozens of small operational improvements that compound over time."

As the meeting continued, Marcia noticed how the team interacted differently than they had just weeks ago. Questions were more specific, focused on connection points rather than isolated components. People naturally referenced how their work intersected with others'. Even the language had shifted, with phrases like "integration impact" and "connection verification" becoming part of everyday conversation.

✧ ✧ ✧

After the planning session, Marcia found James waiting in her office, reviewing a document with the Alpha logo prominently displayed.

"The first draft of the Connection-Driven Delivery methodology," he explained, handing her the document as she entered. "Robert wants to publish it as Alpha's formal approach to complex integration projects."

Marcia flipped through the pages, recognising much of what they'd developed over the past weeks – the connection patterns framework, the operational practices that supported it, the metrics that verified its effectiveness.

"It's more comprehensive than I expected," she observed.

"Robert had the documentation team work with Liam's architecture group," James explained. "They've formalised what began as your intuitive approach into a systematic methodology."

"Does it capture the essence?" Marcia asked, settling behind her desk.

"See for yourself," James replied, pointing to a section titled 'Operational Excellence: Small Tasks, Big Wins.'

Marcia read the opening paragraph:

Success in complex integration projects doesn't come from grand gestures or revolutionary technologies alone. It emerges from disciplined attention to small operational details that systematically strengthen connection points throughout the system. Excellence in these small tasks, performed consistently over time, compounds into substantial results that isolated breakthrough moments rarely achieve.

"That captures it perfectly," Her voice warmed with satisfaction. "The power of process, made explicit."

"Robert wants you to lead a training session for all Alpha delivery managers next month," James added. "The GFP success has created significant interest throughout the company."

Before Marcia could respond, her phone buzzed with an email from Elizabeth:

Hi Marcia,

London office confirmed for your visit on March 14th. Key stakeholders from all three European acquisitions will attend. Diana has briefed them on the connection patterns approach, and they're eager to see how it applies to their integration challenges. Xavier will join virtually to provide continuity from the February milestone success.

Elizabeth

"Looks like the European expansion is moving quickly," Marcia commented, showing James the message.

"No surprise," he replied. "Success creates momentum. The February milestone results made believers out of sceptics."

Marcia walked through the development area later in the afternoon, observing the teams in action. The broader collaboration had become their standard way of working.

Near Liam's desk, the Connection Patterns Library whiteboard had expanded to cover an entire wall, filled with neatly drawn diagrams, bullet points, and colour-coded sticky notes - practically a knowledge mural documenting their best practices and lessons. A small group gathered around it, discussing how to apply specific patterns to the European regulatory environment.

"The GDPR compliance requirements actually align well

with our authentication model," Liam was explaining, pointing to a diagram. "We just need to extend the consent management pattern to handle country-specific variations."

Marcia stopped to watch, unable to suppress a smile. She remembered how in the project's early days, Liam would groan at the idea of any extra documentation. Now he was co-curating this ever-growing library of process refinements.

Liam caught her looking and approached with a chuckle. "We might need a bigger board," he said.

"I remember when you couldn't stand sticking notes on a wall," Marcia teased.

Liam shrugged, but he was clearly pleased. "What can I say? Seeing all this in one place... it actually helps."

She exhaled softly and met his eyes. "It really does. And it's not just paper up there - it's everything we've learned." She felt a warm pride seeing a once-reluctant teammate now leading the charge on continuous improvement.

Still carrying that sense of pride, Marcia left the dev floor behind. As evening approached, Marcia gathered with Robert and James in the small conference room they'd begun calling the 'war room' during the sprint. Now it functioned as a planning centre for their expanding work with GFP.

"The European expansion proposal is solid," Robert observed, reviewing the materials they'd prepared. "But I'm more impressed with how you've systematised the approach."

"That wasn't always the goal," Marcia conceded. "Revolutions create moments of possibility, but evolutions deliver consistent results over time."

"Well, this particular evolution has caught the attention of our competitors," Robert revealed. "Two other consulting firms have reached out about our 'innovative approach to complex integration.' Apparently, Diana mentioned it at an industry conference last week."

"Should we be concerned?" Marcia asked.

Robert shook his head. "Quite the opposite. It positions Alpha as a thought leader in enterprise integration. The Connection-Driven Delivery methodology could become our signature approach in the market."

Marcia leaned back slightly, absorbing the weight of Robert's words. The conversation had shifted - from reflection to momentum, from lessons learned to what came next. They spoke for a few minutes longer, aligning on next steps and priorities for the coming week.

As she prepared to leave for the day, Liam appeared in her doorway, laptop in hand.

"Final preparations for London," he explained. "I've mapped the critical connection points for each acquisition, with preliminary integration patterns for each."

"You're taking this European trip seriously," Marcia observed with a touch of humour. The Liam she'd first met wouldn't have prepared so thoroughly for it.

"The connection patterns approach works," he said simply. "I've seen the results. Plus, I feel like my contribution to pushing the approach forward is being appreciated. Now I want to see how it scales across different environments and regulatory frameworks."

His matter-of-fact acknowledgment of the approach's effectiveness, and of his personal transformation, reflected how far they'd come.

As Marcia walked to her car that evening, she reflected on the journey so far. They now stood at the threshold of applying this approach at an even larger scale, with the European expansion representing both a new challenge and an opportunity for refinement.

Small tasks, done with consistent excellence, had indeed led to the biggest wins of all.

✧ ✧ ✧

A few days later, the first real snag since the February milestone appeared.

"This phase should have been completed last week," Malcolm said over the conference line, his voice clipped. "What happened to the API usage report feature? GFP's operations team says it's still missing."

The words landed like a weight. Marcia saw Liam glance down at his notes, the flicker of realisation crossing his face. She knew immediately what had happened - the analytics endpoint had been dropped during the adapter rollout. It was a small omission, but a visible one to the client.

Marcia took a breath and spoke before anyone else could. "We missed the mark," she said plainly. "I failed to catch that the usage report hook wasn't included in the final build. That's on me."

The virtual room went silent. Then she continued, calm but firm. "Here's how we're fixing it: the team will add the endpoint back in, and we'll have it deployed within forty-eight hours. I'll also add a final verification checkpoint for all client-facing deliverables, so this doesn't happen again. But I wanted to tell you directly - we take full responsibility."

Malcolm breathed audibly on the other end. "Thank you for the honesty, Marcia. Keep me updated once it's deployed." The call ended without further discussion.

For a moment, no one in the Seattle office spoke. Marcia could feel the team's eyes on her.

Liam was the first to break the silence. *She had said we and I, but it was clear she meant me.* "You didn't have to do that," he said quietly. "It was my oversight. I knew that endpoint got de-scoped during the adapter change."

Marcia gave him a small, steady smile. "Maybe so. But

accountability isn't about blame - it's about focus. Now we can move on to fixing it instead of defending it."

He shook his head slightly, still processing. "I've never seen a manager just own it like that. Brett would've had us drafting excuses for a week."

Marcia's voice was calm, carrying the weight of experience. "That's the difference between protecting yourself and protecting the work. When leaders stop hiding mistakes, the team can too."

A few of the developers nodded. The tension that had hung over the room seemed to dissolve, replaced by quiet determination.

Later that evening, Marcia finalised the integration plan for London, her mind still on the day's events. The missed feature would be fixed by morning, but the real repair had already happened. The team had seen what ownership looked like - not deflection, not blame, but clarity and trust.

FIELD RULE: S.T.E.A.D.Y.
(Mini-OS)

- **S - Stand-ups (15 min 3-5/week):** *Today | Blocked* (Owner and When) | *Cleared* (one by midday); vary format.
- **T - Triage (15 min 2/week)**: Prioritise bugs/defects.
- **E - Embedded QA**: QA sits with squads; "facts, not theories" observer in incidents.
- **A - Async dashboards**: Shared wall for flow, defects, cycle time; snapshot at day's end.
- **D - Decision log**: Every decision gets decision ID, Context, Options, Owner, Revisit.
- **Y - Yes/No gates**: Clear entry/exit criteria for work; no silent scope creep; cross-office requirements refinement.

Do this tomorrow: Log one new decision needed; add Owner and When to every Blocked item.

Chapter 7
The Power of Ownership

Ownership is the turning point in every manager's story. It's the moment you stop waiting for permission and start carrying the weight yourself. When you say, "The outcome is mine," you unlock the authority - and the respect - that no title can give.

✧ ✧ ✧

Accountability that doesn't bounce.

✧ ✧ ✧

The view from GFP's London office swept across the Thames - modern towers rising beside weathered stone, the dome of St. Paul's to the northwest, and London Bridge carrying its stream of red buses to the southeast. From their high-rise on Queen Victoria Street, the City's financial district seemed to press against the windows, a collision of centuries-old facades and steel-and-glass ambition. Marcia hardly noticed, her attention fixed on the notes for the morning's kick-off with the European integration team.

"Nervous?" Liam asked, uncharacteristically early and surprisingly well-dressed in a button-down shirt and sport coat. His usual hoodie and jeans had been replaced for their international client meetings, though his comb-resistant hair still gave him away.

"Not nervous," Marcia replied, looking up from her laptop. "Just focused. The European integration adds layers of complexity we didn't face with the February milestone."

"Three acquisitions, three different technology stacks, three different corporate cultures," Liam said, a wry smile flickering across his face. "Plus, GDPR and country-specific regulations."

Their conversation was interrupted by the arrival of Noah, who had flown in from New York the previous day. He looked surprisingly fresh despite the jet lag.

Marcia waved him over. "London suits you," she said as he joined them in reception.

"Any city with decent tea suits me," Noah replied with a grin. "The New York office's idea of tea is borderline criminal."

Marcia and Liam shared a quick grin, then straightened as a tall man in an impeccable suit approached their small group. "Ms. Hughes? I'm Charles Worthington, GFP's European Operations Director. Welcome to London."

Marcia shook his hand. "Thank you for hosting us. This is Liam Everett, our Principal Architect, and Noah Vasques from our New York office."

"Ah yes - the connection patterns approach. I've heard rather a lot about it," Charles said, properly formal yet cordial. "Diana spoke well of the February milestone.

Elizabeth did too."

"We're looking forward to applying the same methodology here," Marcia said. "Though we recognise the European context presents different challenges."

"Indeed, it does," Charles confirmed, gesturing toward the conference room. "Our three recent acquisitions have created a rather... intricate integration landscape. Perhaps 'tangled web' would be more accurate. Shall we step inside?"

The conference room reflected GFP's global stature: a long table gleamed under recessed lighting, brushed steel and dark wood softened by the view of the river flowing below. The room was already filling with people - some in person, others joining virtually from Frankfurt, Paris, and Amsterdam. Marcia recognised Xavier Delgado's face on one of the screens, along with several GFP executives from Seattle she'd worked with during the February milestone.

"Quite the gathering," Noah murmured as they took their seats.

"High stakes," Liam replied quietly.

Charles called the meeting to order, introducing the key stakeholders from each acquisition: Fintech Solutions from Germany, PaySecure from France, and NetBank from the Netherlands. Each had been operating semi-autonomously since acquisition, creating silos that now impeded GFP's unified customer experience.

"Our challenge," Charles explained, "is to integrate these acquisitions while keeping their individual advantages intact - and, or course, working our way through the maze of EU-wide and national regulations."

He turned to Marcia with a polite incline of his head. "I suspect your connection patterns approach may be just the thing. Care you share your view?"

Marcia stood, taking in the mix of curious and sceptical faces around the room and on the screens. This wasn't just a technical presentation - it was a cultural bridging moment that would set the tone for the entire European integration effort.

"Thank you, Charles," she began. "The connection patterns approach isn't about forcing standardisation or eliminating differences. It's about identifying and strengthening the critical connection points that enable diverse systems to work together effectively."

She brought up a slide showing the results from the February milestone, highlighting the dramatic improvements in integration quality and customer experience.

"These results didn't come from a single breakthrough solution," she emphasised. "They emerged from systematic attention to the connection points that others often overlook - the interfaces between systems, the handoffs between teams, the translations between business needs and technical implementations."

As Marcia outlined the approach, she noticed the executives from the German and French acquisitions exchanging sceptical glances. The Dutch team appeared more receptive, leaning forward with interest.

"This all sounds impressive," said Klaus Richter, the former CEO of Fintech Solutions, now GFP's German operations head. "But our European regulatory environment is considerably more complex than the American context - as you know, every detail must be exact. How does your approach address these differences?"

It was a fair question - and one Marcia had anticipated. "You're absolutely right about the regulatory complexity," she acknowledged. "That's why we're not proposing to simply transplant the North American solutions. Instead, we'll apply the methodology to identify and strengthen the specific connection points relevant to your context."

She nodded to Liam, who stood and brought up a

diagram showing a preliminary analysis of the European regulatory landscape.

"We've mapped the key compliance requirements across jurisdictions," he explained, pointing to the interconnected nodes. "Rather than viewing regulations as constraints, we've incorporated them as design parameters for the connection patterns."

For the next twenty minutes, Liam walked through a technical framework that respected both the unified customer experience GFP wanted and the regulatory diversity the European operations required. It was impressively detailed for preliminary work, showing how thoroughly Liam had prepared for this meeting.

When he finished, there was a moment of silence before Marcel Dubois, the PaySecure leader, spoke up. "This is more sophisticated than I expected," he admitted. "You see, the real question is implementation - that is where such theories often falter. How do you propose to execute this approach across three different technical environments?"

Before Marcia could respond, Xavier jumped in from the video screen. "If I may - I had the same question about the February milestone. What convinced me was seeing their operational discipline in action. The Connection Patterns Approach isn't just a technical framework; it's a systematic methodology for integration excellence."

Marcia met his gaze on the screen, gratitude flickering across her face. "That's exactly right. The technology matters, but the operational practices matter more. We'll establish cross-functional teams with members from each acquisition, implement consistent connection verification protocols, and maintain transparent metrics that track integration quality in real-time."

As the meeting continued, Marcia could feel the initial scepticism gradually warming, particularly after Noah shared specific examples of how they'd overcome similar challenges in the New York-Seattle integration. His natural diplomatic skills bridged cultural gaps that might have otherwise hindered acceptance.

By the time Charles brought the kick-off meeting to a close, a tentative consensus had formed. They would proceed with the connection patterns approach, starting with a detailed analysis phase followed by implementation of the highest-priority integration points.

"Well navigated," Charles said quietly to Marcia as the room cleared. "European stakeholders are typically more sceptical of new methodologies than their American counterparts, especially when it's viewed as an American import."

"Scepticism is healthy," Marcia replied. "It leads to better solutions when channelled constructively."

"Indeed," Charles agreed. "Now, I should warn you - we've scheduled a rather intensive agenda for your visit. Diana wants momentum on this integration before you return to Seattle."

As they left the room, a notification from Elizabeth appeared on Marcia's phone: *How did the kick-off go? Malcolm is eager for updates.*

Positive start, Marcia replied. *Initial scepticism but growing interest. Liam's regulatory framework impressed them.*

She tucked her phone away.

Marcia noticed Liam deep in conversation with Klaus, the German operations head. They were examining something on Liam's laptop, both men focused intently on the screen. Liam's technical credibility was clearly cutting through cultural barriers that might have otherwise taken weeks to navigate.

"That's a good sign," Noah observed, following her gaze. "Klaus was the most sceptical during the presentation."

"Liam's expertise speaks a universal language," Marcia leaned forward a touch. "His preparation for this trip is paying dividends already."

Their European integration journey had begun more positively than Marcia had dared hope. The connection patterns approach had created a framework that respected local differences while enabling global integration - exactly what GFP needed for its European strategy.

Yet as they headed toward their next meeting with the technical teams, Marcia couldn't shake a lingering concern. Acceptance of the approach was one thing; successful implementation across such diverse environments would be another challenge entirely.

Later that afternoon, as Marcia reviewed integration plans with the Dutch technical team, she received an urgent message from Charles: *Security incident detected in German payment system. Potential impact on integration architecture. Emergency meeting in main conference room in 15 minutes.*

Marcia stared at the message a beat longer than she should have. Dashboards. Shareholders. Deadlines. A familiar tightness pressed beneath her collarbone, the old panic threatening to return. She inhaled slowly, once, exhaled, then in again, and reached for a pen.

One thing at a time.

The European integration had just become considerably more complicated.

✦ ✦ ✦

"What do we know so far?" Marcia asked as she entered the main conference room, finding it already filled with concerned faces. Liam and Noah had arrived moments before her, and Charles Worthington stood at the head of the table, his earlier composed demeanour now tense with worry.

Klaus Richter, the German operations head, was explaining the situation with characteristic precision. "The intrusion was detected exactly thirty minutes ago in our payment processing system. Initial assessment indicates the attack originated through a third-party API connection that was not properly secured during the last system update."

The room felt charged with anxiety. On the video screens, executives from Seattle had joined, including Xavier and Elizabeth. Malcolm's face appeared on another screen, his expression grim.

"Is customer data compromised?" Elizabeth asked immediately.

Klaus hesitated. "We are still determining the scope. The security team has isolated the affected systems, but we don't yet know if personal information was accessed."

Charles turned to Marcia. "I understand your team has only just arrived, but given that you're here to implement the connection patterns approach for our integration, this incident seems directly relevant."

Marcia felt the weight of all eyes in the room. This wasn't her system or her company's security breach. The logical response would be to position this as GFP's problem that needed solving before Alpha's integration work could continue. Yet she could see the opportunity - and responsibility - presented by this crisis.

"You're right, Charles," she said decisively. "This is absolutely relevant to our work. The security breach happened at an integration point - exactly the kind of connection our methodology is designed to strengthen."

She turned to Liam. "Can you work with Klaus's team to analyse how the breach occurred from a technical perspective?"

Liam didn't hesitate. "I'll need access to your security logs and API documentation," he said to Klaus.

The German executive looked momentarily taken aback by their willingness to dive into the problem. "You understand this is not your system or your responsibility?"

"It's an integration point in a system we're being asked to help connect," Marcia replied firmly. "That makes it relevant to our work, regardless of who built it or who maintains it."

She felt rather than saw Elizabeth's approving nod from the video screen.

"I appreciate your approach," Charles said, following Klaus's lead, "but we should clarify expectations. We brought Alpha in for the integration project, not incident response."

Marcia made a split-second decision that would shape everything that followed. "Charles, in our experience, successful integration isn't about connecting perfect systems - it's about creating robust connections between real systems with real challenges. This incident provides an opportunity to demonstrate how the connection patterns approach addresses security vulnerabilities at integration points."

She turned to the room at large. "We can view this as a roadblock to our integration work, or we can use it as a case study in how connection patterns strengthen system boundaries. I suggest the latter."

The tension in the room shifted subtly from anxiety to cautious optimism.

"Very well," Charles said evenly. "What, then, do you propose?"

Marcia didn't hesitate. "We form a joint incident response team - members from Alpha and each of the regional operations. We analyse the breach, identify the vulnerability, and develop both immediate fixes and systematic improvements to prevent similar issues across all integration points."

On the video screen, Malcolm spoke for the first time. "This changes our timeline, Ms. Hughes. The European integration was already on an aggressive schedule."

"Actually," Noah interjected, surprising everyone, "addressing this security vulnerability now might accelerate our timeline rather than delay it. By fixing this connection point properly, we establish a pattern that can be applied across similar integration points."

Over the next hour, they established a focused response team. Liam would work with Klaus's security specialists to analyse the technical aspects of the breach. Noah would coordinate with the French and Dutch teams to assess whether similar vulnerabilities existed in their systems. Marcia would ensure the response aligned with their broader integration methodology.

As the meeting disbanded, Charles held Marcia back. "That was unexpected," he said quietly. "Most consultants would have kept well clear of a client's security incident."

"Most consultants aren't implementing a connection patterns methodology," Marcia replied. "This incident provides a real-world test case for our approach."

Charles weighed her for a moment, then said. "Diana said you were different. I see what she meant, as it happens."

By late afternoon, Liam had established a makeshift command centre in a small conference room, surrounded by the German security team. Screens displayed logs and code snippets as they meticulously traced the path of the intrusion.

"Found it," Liam announced as Marcia entered. "The vulnerability is exactly where the payment processing system connects to the customer authentication service. During their last update, they implemented an API gateway but left a legacy connection active as a backup."

"And the attacker found the unprotected legacy path,"

Marcia surmised.

"Exactly," Liam confirmed. "It's a classic integration vulnerability - focusing on the new connection point while leaving an old one exposed."

On a group call the German security team had running, one of their application engineers raised a hand. "That fallback was mine," they said. "We left the legacy route live during cutover for rollback. It should have been removed afterwards."

"Thank you for flagging it," Marcia said. "No blame - let's close it now, document the decommissioning path, and add a legacy route removal step to the release checklist on your side and ours."

"We'll capture it in the connection-patterns library: deprecations must remove the old path, not just add the new one," Liam said.

Klaus, who had been listening nearby, approached with visible concern. "Have you determined if customer data was compromised?"

Liam looked up from his screen. "Based on the logs, the attacker accessed the payment processing system but didn't reach the customer database. They were detected before they could pivot to more sensitive systems."

The relief in Klaus's face was palpable. "So, no breach of personal information?"

"It appears not," Liam confirmed. "But if they'd found their way through, the potential damage would have been significant."

Marcia recognised the teaching opportunity. "This illustrates a core principle of our connection patterns approach. We don't just focus on the primary integration points - we systematically identify and secure all connection points, including legacy ones that might otherwise be overlooked."

Klaus's shoulders eased. "I see why Diana was so impressed with your methodology. You are not only fixing individual problems; you are addressing the underlying patterns that create them."

"Exactly," Marcia agreed. "And that's why this incident, while concerning, actually accelerates our integration work. It gives us a concrete example of what we're trying to prevent across all your systems."

An hour later, finding herself alone for the first time since the alert, Marcia stepped into a quiet corridor and opened the incident dashboard on her phone. Red. Red. Amber. The progress bars crawled, indifferent to pressure. The weight of it all settled on her - not just this incident, but what a failure here would signal about the whole recovery. *Have we built enough resilience - or is it still held together by willpower?*

✧ ✧ ✧

Her phone buzzed; the *#eu-incident* channel lit up. Alpha's New York AppSec team had packaged the German fix pattern and posted a quick scanner for the same legacy path. Paris Security had adapted the patch for their stack, and Paris QA had spun up a targeted regression set without waiting for assignment. Amsterdam Engineering posted a checklist for legacy endpoints that teammates were already filling in.

Marcia sighed, the tightness easing. They weren't waiting for orders. They were moving.

Before another hour was out, Marcia gathered with Liam, Noah, and key members of GFP's European security team to assess their progress. The immediate vulnerability had been identified and patched, and similar legacy connections were being audited across all three acquisitions.

"What I find most valuable," said Marcel from the French team, "is how quickly this identified similar risks in our systems. We had nearly identical legacy connections that could have been exploited."

"The connection patterns approach in action," Noah observed. "Once you recognise a vulnerability pattern, you can proactively address it across all similar integration points."

A message alert played on Marcia's phone - Elizabeth: *Malcolm and Diana have requested a briefing at 8 am London time tomorrow. They're impressed with how you've handled this incident.*

As the meeting wrapped up, Marcia noticed Liam in deep conversation with Klaus and the German security lead. They'd been working together intensely all day, and what had started as technical cooperation had evolved into genuine collaboration.

"Liam seems to have found his element," Noah commented as they walked back to their hotel through London's evening drizzle.

"He thrives on solving complex problems," Marcia replied. "And he's evolving beyond just technical solutions. Did you notice how he explained the security patterns to Klaus? Six months ago, he would have used technical jargon that only engineers would understand."

"The connection patterns approach has influenced him too," Noah observed. "He's thinking about how technical architectures connect to business operations and human processes."

✧   ✧   ✧

By the time Marcia reached her hotel, the London sky had slipped from silver to charcoal. She dropped her bag, set the kettle going, and opened her laptop on the small desk by the window. A calendar reminder blinked: *Platform/Payments handoff - DE throttling. 17:30 London / 09:30 Seattle.*

She slid in earbuds and checked the connection - good enough. Camera on. She'd planned to switch off for the evening, but this one mattered: the overlap between platform and payments was exactly where work went to die unless someone owned the outcome.

The meeting room tiles popped into place: Priya in Seattle on the platform floor, Daniel from the payments area. Marcia kept her square small and her notes open. Tonight she was there to observe, steady the room if needed, and make sure the work had somewhere to land.

The handoff meeting started tense and stayed there. Two leaders - Priya and Daniel - both looking at the same diagram shared on the call.

"My team will handle the rate-limit fix," Daniel said.

"That's platform," Priya replied, eyes steady. "We own the gateway."

"And the payment retries," Daniel added.

"Which hit the gateway," Priya said. "So failures look like ours."

The room tightened. Threads of the same problem ran through two backlogs, two stand-ups, and three Slack channels. Bugs bounced. Nothing landed.

Marcia let the overlap linger. "Okay," she said quietly. "Describe success - one sentence."

Daniel: "No payment fails due to throttling in Germany."

Priya: "Gateway protects upstreams without blocking good traffic."

"Great," Marcia said. "Now the uncomfortable bit: Who owns the outcome? Not the tasks - the outcome."

Silence.

She shared her screen, drew a rectangle on a fresh RealtimeBoard and wrote Owner at the top. "Single-threaded. One person. Priya or Daniel."

Daniel rubbed his forehead. "If we take it, we'll need

gateway tweaks."

"If we take it," Priya said, "we'll need payment retry changes."

"So either way," Marcia said, "one of you owns the outcome and borrows the other team's hands."

Priya studied Daniel's body language, then shook her head. "I'll own it."

Daniel nodded. "Okay."

Marcia typed on the board:

Owner: Priya (Directly Responsible Individual - DRI)
Outcome: Germany throttling → 18 Mar

"Say it out loud," Marcia said, knowing this would help her internalise this and build ownership.

Priya took a breath, glanced at Daniel, then back to the camera. "I own the outcome. No throttling-caused payment fails in Germany by 18 March."

"Good," Marcia said. "Now split the work without splitting the outcome."

Marcia dropped a link to the board in chat, and together they built two lists:

Gateway (Platform, Priya DRI)
- Dynamic burst window for DE merchant cluster
- Rule audit and observability hook (p95, p99)

Payments (Daniel support)
- Retry backoff tweak for 429s (DE only)
- Canary cohort and rollback guard

"Slack channel?" Marcia asked.

"#de-throttle," Priya said, recalling James's RACI-Lite training.

"Cadence?"

"Ten-minute sync at 4 p.m. PT; async updates in-channel," Daniel said.

"Escalation?"

"Me," Priya said. "If I'm blocked more than a day, I'll escalate to you."

Marcia added a text box. "One more line," she said, writing under the owner box:

Consulted: Daniel. Informed: Risk, Support. Decider: Priya.

Marcia stopped sharing, bringing their tiles back into focus. "This is where overlaps stop. We'll judge by the outcome, not who did which task."

"Thanks Marcia," Priya said.

"Thanks," from Daniel also.

"We're aligned," Marcia said. "Let's execute." She ended the call and the tiles winked out.

Jet lag tugged, but she drew on a thin reserve only leadership seemed to unlock.

She made tea, saved the handoff board link to her GFP folder, and sketched a note begin structuring her presentation for tomorrow:

What happened → what we changed → what to watch

The willingness to step forward when others might step back was the real magic for managers - turning challenges into opportunities and building trust through accountability rather than avoidance.

Tomorrow would test that approach again, this time with GFP's highest leadership watching closely.

"One owner. Outcome, not tasks."

✧ ✧ ✧

Marcia arrived early for the 8 am briefing, coffee in hand and notes organised. She took a sip - strong, hot, efficient. London coffee was serviceable, but it lacked the nuance she'd grown used to in Seattle, where baristas treated beans like fine wine. Here in the City, it was fuel more than culture, caffeine on the run between meetings.

London's pale March light settled over the Thames, a muted grey-green ribbon flowing directly below.

The conference room had been set up for a high-level meeting - water bottles at each place, notepads emblazoned with the GFP logo, and a large video wall where Malcolm and Diana would join virtually from Seattle.

Liam entered, looking surprisingly alert despite having worked until nearly midnight with the German security team.

"Ready for this?" Marcia asked, handing him an extra coffee she'd picked up.

"As ready as possible," he said with a tired grin, accepting the cup. "We've completed the full audit across all three acquisitions. Found similar vulnerabilities in the French system, but nothing in the Dutch implementation."

"That's good news," Marcia said. "Did you get any sleep?"

Liam almost smiled. "Enough. The German team is actually quite impressive once you get past their initial formality. Klaus stayed with us the entire time."

"That speaks volumes," Marcia noted. "Executive engagement makes all the difference in these situations." She realised Klaus was practicing the quiet power of presence last night - and that noticing it was, in its own way, her using the power of perspective.

The room began filling with key stakeholders. Charles

Worthington arrived with Klaus and Marcel, while the Dutch team lead joined virtually from Amsterdam, already a small tile on the video wall. Someone jabbed the remote; the panels woke from sleep with a grudging blink - they always did this at the least convenient moment.

The mood was sombre but not panicked - a good sign that yesterday's immediate crisis had transitioned to focused problem-solving.

Liam tapped out a quick message to Marcia on Slack: *I'll take root cause → remediation → prevention, plus the scanning pattern. You set the context and close with the next steps?*

Marcia replied: *Exactly. I'll cover context and current status then hand to you.*

A thumbs-up emoji appeared in reply.

At 8 am sharp, the main feed connected and the wall filled out with Diana Thompson and Malcolm Wright in GFP's Seattle boardroom despite the late hour there.

"Good morning, London," Diana greeted them. "I understand you've had an eventful first day."

"That's one way to put it," Charles replied with understated British humour. "As it happens, I believe Marcia has prepared a briefing for us."

Marcia stood, moving to the front of the room.

"Thank you for joining us, especially given the time difference," she began. "I'd like to start by addressing the security incident directly, then explain how this relates to our connection patterns approach for the European integration."

She proceeded to outline exactly what had happened - a legacy connection point left active during a system update, creating a vulnerability at the intersection of the payment processing and authentication systems. The attacker had exploited this path but had been detected before accessing customer data.

"The immediate vulnerability has been patched," she

continued, "and we've conducted a comprehensive audit across all three acquisitions to identify similar risks. Liam can speak to the technical details, but the key finding is that we discovered a pattern of vulnerability that existed in multiple systems."

Liam took over, explaining the technical aspects with surprising clarity. He avoided jargon and focused on the implications rather than technical minutiae.

"What's most significant," Liam concluded, "is that this vulnerability existed at an integration point - precisely the kind of connection our approach is designed to strengthen. It validates our methodology in ways a theoretical discussion never could."

Malcolm leaned forward on screen. "To be clear - no customer data was compromised?"

"Correct," Klaus confirmed. "The intruder accessed the payment processing system but not the customer database. They were detected and blocked before any personal information could be extracted."

"And you're confident you've identified all similar vulnerabilities across the European operations?" Diana asked.

"Yes," Liam replied, fielding the question. "We've implemented a systematic scanning process focused specifically on legacy connection points. The French system had similar issues which have now been addressed. The Dutch implementation was properly secured."

From the incident log, Marcia saw teams acting on their own initiative - Paris had applied the pattern to close related legacy paths, and Amsterdam had validated and documented the check. The connection-patterns mindset was clearly being adopted across offices.

Diana acknowledged with a brief, professional smile and turned her attention to Marcia. "I'm curious about something. When this incident occurred, you could have reasonably defined it as outside your project scope. Yet I understand you immediately stepped in to address it. Why?"

The question was direct but not confrontational. Marcia recognised it as an opportunity to articulate the leadership philosophy behind their approach.

"In our experience," she said, meeting Diana's gaze through the video link, "successful integration isn't about connecting perfect systems. It's about creating robust connections between real systems with real challenges."

She paused, choosing her next words carefully. "More fundamentally, I believe that ownership is where a leader's value truly emerges. We could have defined this as 'not our problem,' but that wouldn't have served GFP or advanced our shared goals for the European integration."

Diana's voice held crisp approval. "Exactly what I hoped you'd say. Charles, what's your assessment of Alpha's response to this incident?"

Charles straightened in his chair. "Remarkably proactive. They transformed what could have been a setback into a valuable case study. It has accelerated our understanding of the connection patterns approach in ways that would not have happened otherwise."

"And the timeline for our European integration?" Malcolm asked, ever focused on deliverables.

"Surprisingly, this incident may have accelerated rather than delayed our work," Marcia replied. "By addressing these vulnerabilities now, we've eliminated issues that would have surfaced later in the integration process. We've also strengthened our credibility and working relationships with the technical teams across all three acquisitions, which will streamline our collaboration moving forward."

The briefing continued for another thirty minutes, covering the detailed implementation plan for the connection patterns methodology across the European operations. By the time it concluded, the mood had transformed completely - what had begun as a crisis response had evolved into a strategic planning session with renewed confidence.

As people began filing out, Diana asked Marcia to stay on for a private conversation. When the room had cleared except for Malcolm on Diana's end and Charles in London, Diana spoke directly.

"What you demonstrated yesterday goes beyond technical expertise or methodology," she said. "It's a leadership philosophy that aligns perfectly with what GFP needs right now."

She leaned closer to the camera. "I'll be proposing to our board a significant expansion of Alpha's role in our global transformation. Malcolm has reservations about the timeline, but I believe your connection patterns approach - and more importantly, your leadership approach - could accelerate, not delay, our progress."

Malcolm said, reluctance edging his voice. "I remain concerned about the timeline, but I can't argue with results. Your handling of yesterday's incident was commendable."

"Thank you," Marcia said. "We believe ownership is fundamental to effective leadership. Problems don't respect organisational boundaries or project scopes - they emerge at the connections between systems and teams."

"Well said," Diana commented. "Charles, please ensure Marcia and her team have whatever resources they need. I want the European integration to become a showcase for this approach, just as the February release was."

After the call ended, Charles turned to Marcia. "I'm not sure you realise what just happened. Diana does not easily expand consultant engagements, yet she just essentially handed you the keys to our entire European integration strategy."

"We still need to deliver results," Marcia cautioned.

"Of course," Charles agreed. "But you've already delivered something valuable - a demonstration of what ownership looks like in a crisis. That is rare, in my experience."

Later that morning, Marcia gathered with Liam and Noah to realign their approach based on what they'd learned from the security incident. The vulnerability had revealed important patterns about how GFP's acquired companies had integrated their systems - patterns that would inform their broader methodology.

As they worked, Marcia noticed how naturally they were applying the ownership mindset that had guided their response to the security incident. They weren't just addressing the technical aspects of integration but taking responsibility for the entire system's integrity, regardless of which company had originally built each component.

By lunchtime, they had refined their approach and scheduled workshops with each acquisition's technical teams. The security incident had created a shared challenge that united the otherwise separate groups - a silver lining to yesterday's crisis.

✧ ✧ ✧

"You know what I find most interesting about all this?" Noah commented as they walked to a nearby pub for lunch. "How quickly the European teams went from sceptical to collaborative once they saw us own the problem instead of distancing ourselves from it."

"Trust is earned through actions, not assertions," Marcia replied. "Especially across cultural and organisational boundaries."

As they settled at a table and place their orders, her phone hummed - Elizabeth: *Diana just briefed me on this morning's call. She's impressively enthusiastic about expanding Alpha's role. What exactly did you do to generate that kind of response?*

Marcia zoned out of the conversation briefly while she tapped her reply: *We just owned the problem completely and brought our best thinking to solving it. Sometimes the most powerful leadership moves are also the simplest.*

Elizabeth's response came quickly: *Simple but not easy. That ownership mindset is exactly why Diana wants to expand our relationship.*

As Marcia put away her phone, she caught Liam watching her with an unusually perceptive expression.

"You know," he said, "I used to think leadership was mainly about technical knowledge and decision-making. But yesterday showed me something different."

"What's that?" Marcia asked.

"That ownership - really taking responsibility even when you could avoid it - creates possibilities that expertise alone never could. The German team opened up completely once they saw we were truly committed to solving the problem with them, not just advising from a distance or blaming them."

Marcia leaned a little to her left, making space for the server to set down the drinks. She reflected on how far Liam had come in his understanding of leadership. "That's the essence of it," she agreed. "Not avoiding problems or deflecting blame but stepping forward to own challenges completely. It's where a leader's true value emerges."

Liam broke a piece off his fish and took a sip of something sparkling. "By the way," he added, gesturing toward his plate, "this might be the most elegant version of fish and chips I've ever seen. Micro-herbs on the mushy peas. Very London."

Marcia lifted her fork in acknowledgement. "You know it's upscale when they stack the triple-cooked chips vertically," and they all shared a laugh.

As they continued their lunch, reviewing the workshop planned for the next day, Marcia realised how different she felt. The security incident yesterday could have rattled her months ago. Instead, she had responded almost on instinct - instinct she recognised had been built deliberately through practice, mentoring her team, and strengthening relationships with leaders like Diana. The ease she felt now wasn't accidental; it was earned.

What struck her most was how the sources of encouragement had changed. James and Robert were still there, but the steady reinforcement no longer came just from them. It came from Liam's growing confidence, from Noah's diplomacy, from Klaus and Marcel treating her as a peer, and from Diana's trust. Even her own voice felt steadier, as if she was finally learning to back herself. The lessons weren't only ones she was teaching - they were also being reflected back to her by the people around her.

✧ ✧ ✧

Two days after the security incident, Marcia stood before a packed room in GFP's London office. Representatives from all three European acquisitions had gathered for a workshop on the connection patterns methodology, and the energy was markedly different from their initial sceptical reception.

"The security vulnerability taught us something important," Marcia explained, gesturing to the diagram Liam had created on the whiteboard. "Integration isn't just about connecting systems - it's about understanding the patterns of connection that either strengthen or weaken the entire ecosystem."

Heads nodded around the room. Nothing builds credibility like successfully navigating a crisis together.

"Today we'll map the critical connection points across all three acquisitions," she continued. "Not just the technical interfaces, but the operational handoffs, the data flows, and the business process intersections."

The workshop format was deliberately collaborative. Instead of Alpha consultants presenting solutions, mixed teams from each acquisition worked together to identify connection points and potential vulnerabilities in their integrated environment.

Liam moved between tables, offering guidance without dominating. Marcia noted with satisfaction how naturally he engaged with the European technical leaders - a transformation from the somewhat isolated developer she'd first met six years ago.

"The German team has identified something interesting," Noah said quietly, joining Marcia at the back of the room. "The payment processing vulnerability we found? It appears in a slightly different form in the customer onboarding systems too."

"Another legacy connection point?" Marcia asked.

"Similar pattern but different cause," Noah explained. "In this case, it's duplicate data flows - the same customer information flowing through multiple paths with different validation rules."

"Which creates inconsistency risks," Marcia said, making a quick note. "Have they mapped the full impact?"

"Working on it now," Noah said. "But here's what's remarkable - they found it themselves, using the connection patterns approach we introduced. They've internalised the methodology."

This was exactly what Marcia had hoped for - not just fixing specific problems but building capability within GFP's teams to identify and address connection issues systematically.

By lunchtime, the workshop had produced detailed maps of critical connection points across all three acquisitions. The visual representation was powerful - showing how seemingly separate systems were actually deeply interconnected through dozens of data flows, API calls, and operational handoffs.

Klaus approached as Marcia studied the completed maps. "This is illuminating," he said, gesturing to the visualisation. "We've been trying to integrate these systems for months, but we never saw the patterns so clearly before."

"That's the value of the methodology," Marcia replied. "It makes visible what's often invisible - the connection points that determine how well the entire system functions."

"The security incident was actually fortunate timing," Klaus reflected. "It created a concrete example of why these connection patterns matter."

Marcia nodded. "Sometimes it takes a real-world problem to demonstrate the value of a systematic approach."

Charles Worthington joined them, looking pleased with the workshop's progress. "Diana just called," he informed Marcia. "The board has approved expanding Alpha's role in our global transformation program."

"That's excellent news," Marcia replied. "The European integration gives us an opportunity to demonstrate the connection patterns approach at global scale."

"Indeed," Charles agreed. "And speaking of global scale - Malcolm mentioned you'll be heading to our Singapore office next quarter to assess the Asia-Pacific expansion opportunities."

This was news to Marcia. "Singapore?"

Charles looked surprised. "I thought you knew. Diana wants to apply the connection patterns approach across all our global operations. Asia-Pacific is the next frontier after Europe."

As Charles walked away, Noah raised an eyebrow. "Singapore? The methodology is going global faster than expected."

"One step at a time," Marcia cautioned. "Let's make sure we deliver success in Europe before we start thinking about Asia."

The afternoon session focused on prioritising integration points and developing specific connection patterns for each high-risk area. By the end of the day, they had a comprehensive integration roadmap that incorporated both technical architecture and operational practices.

"This is what ownership looks like in practice," Marcia observed to Liam as they reviewed the day's output. "Every team contributing to a shared solution rather than protecting their individual domains."

Liam took in her words, expression intent. "The security incident changed everything. Before that, each acquisition was guarding their territory. Now they're collectively focused on strengthening connections."

"Crisis often reveals what matters most," Marcia agreed. "In this case, it showed that successful integration depends on collaboration, not control."

✧ ✧ ✧

That evening, the leadership team gathered for dinner at a restaurant near Tower Bridge. The setting was informal but the conversation substantial as they reflected on the week's progress and planned next steps.

"When I arrived in London," Marcia told the assembled group, "I expected our biggest challenges would be technical complexity and cultural differences. Instead, we found that ownership - taking collective responsibility for integration challenges - was the critical factor."

"The security incident was the turning point," Marcel observed, raising his glass. "You see, when you and Liam stepped forward to address our vulnerability instead of stepping back to protect your project scope, it changed how we viewed the entire partnership."

Klaus inclined his head once. "In my experience, consultants do not usually take responsibility for client's problems. Your approach was, as you say, refreshingly different."

"We've learned that integration success depends on blurring those boundaries," Marcia explained. "The biggest opportunities emerge when organisations, systems, and teams connect."

"A philosophy that aligns perfectly with our needs," Charles said warmly, raising his glass. "GFP's future depends on bringing these strong companies together into a cohesive whole while preserving their unique strengths."

As dinner continued, Marcia noticed Liam engaged in animated conversation with the German and Dutch technical leads - gesturing with uncharacteristic enthusiasm as he explained a concept. Noah caught her watching and smiled knowingly.

"He's come a long way," Noah observed quietly.

"We all have," Marcia replied. "This project has stretched everyone in different ways."

Later, as they walked back to their hotel through London's chilly evening, Marcia reflected on how far they'd come since inheriting the troubled GFP project months ago.

"Do you think we're ready for Singapore?" Noah asked, breaking into her thoughts.

"Honestly? I'm not sure," Marcia admitted. "The Asia-Pacific context brings new dimensions of complexity -

different regulatory environments, cultural considerations, market maturity variations."

"But the core principle remains the same," Liam said unexpectedly. "Identify the critical connection points, establish clear patterns for integration, and - most importantly - take ownership of the challenges regardless of where they originate."

Marcia looked at him with surprise. "That's exactly right. The context changes, but the approach remains consistent."

When they reached the hotel, Marcia found an email from Robert Miller waiting for her:

Marcia,

Diana Thompson called today to express her appreciation for how you handled the European security incident. She's approved a significant expansion of our engagement, including the Asia-Pacific assessment, which I would like you to lead next quarter.

More importantly, she mentioned something that resonated with me. She said your team "demonstrated what ownership truly means in a crisis - stepping forward when others would step back, taking responsibility without hesitation or deflection."

That's precisely the leadership philosophy Alpha was founded on. The connection patterns methodology you've developed is valuable, but this ownership mindset is what truly differentiates our approach in the market.

We'll discuss the Singapore trip when you return, but I wanted you to know how proud I am of what you and your team have accomplished. You've transformed a troubled project into a showcase of Alpha's values and capabilities.

Safe travels, Robert

Marcia closed her eyes and took in a long breath as she finished reading. The acknowledgment was gratifying, but more meaningful was seeing how the ownership mindset had permeated both their team and their approach to complex integration challenges.

The power of ownership had proven itself repeatedly throughout this journey - from the initial rescue of the troubled GFP project to the handling of the European security incident. Each time, the willingness to step forward and take responsibility had created possibilities that technical expertise alone never could.

As she prepared for bed, Marcia updated her project journal:

Ownership (GFP Europe trip)
Ownership isn't just accountability - it's stepping in early, even when it's outside your lane.
Security incident could've been a setback; owning it turned it into progress.
Trust deepens when you show up in the problem, not just after.
The value of a leader shows up most in the moments we could reasonably step back - but don't.

As Marcia tried to sleep, the unfamiliar sounds in her hotel room kept her awake. Her thoughts turned to the Asia-Pacific expansion on the horizon. Singapore would bring new tests of their approach, new integration challenges to navigate, new opportunities to demonstrate the power of the connection patterns methodology.

But whatever specific challenges emerged, the core principle would remain the same: own problems completely, especially when they cross boundaries that others use to deflect responsibility.

For the first time, Marcia realised she no longer saw

leadership as something she had to prove - it was something she could practice, refine, and own.

✧ ✧ ✧

Marcia had seen the daily in-channel updates from Priya and Daniel, and nothing had been escalated to her since the handoff meeting.

The canary chart showed the first clean hour in Germany. Daniel DM'd: *Backoff fix shipped; seeing fewer 429s.* Priya posted the dashboard in #de-throttle with a single caption: *Green. Holding steady.*

Marcia posted in #gfp-updates: *Win: first clean hour of Germany checkout traffic - no throttling-caused failures. Impact: checkout stability restored; unblocks core-banking milestone, sets up user-training prep, and keeps Week-12 transition on track. Credit: Priya owned the outcome to 18 March; Daniel partnered on retries; platform and payments delivered together. Thanks, all.*

Bugs stopped bouncing. Updates stopped duplicating. The work had somewhere to land.

"Show the win - and why it matters."

✧ ✧ ✧

The flight from London to Seattle gave Marcia much-needed time to reflect. As the plane cruised at 38,000 feet somewhere over Greenland, she reviewed her notes from the week in London, organising her thoughts for the debrief with Robert and the leadership team tomorrow.

"Working on the Singapore plan already?" Noah asked, glancing over from the seat beside her.

Marcia let out a quiet breath of amusement. "Getting my

thoughts in order for tomorrow's debrief. Singapore planning comes after we deliver solid progress in Europe."

"One step at a time," Noah said with an understanding nod. "Though I have to admit, I'm intrigued by the Asia-Pacific expansion. The cultural dimensions alone will test our methodology in new ways."

Across the aisle, Liam was sound asleep - a rare sight. He had worked tirelessly in London, particularly during the security incident response. His evolution throughout this project continued to impress Marcia. The technically brilliant but difficult developer had transformed into a collaborative leader who understood that problems don't respect organisational boundaries.

"Liam's earned that rest," Marcia observed quietly.

"He has," Noah agreed. "I never would have imagined him volunteering to fly to London, let alone becoming so engaged with the European teams. That security crisis showed a side of him I didn't know existed."

"Crisis reveals character," Marcia said. "But I think it's more than that. The connection patterns approach resonates with his natural way of thinking. He sees systems in terms of their interactions, not just their components."

"Like you do," Noah pointed out. "That's why the methodology works - it matches how you naturally approach complex challenges."

Marcia hadn't considered that before, but Noah's observation rang true. She had always focused on connections and relationships rather than isolated components, whether working with technical systems or people. The connection patterns methodology had formalised that intuitive approach.

"I suppose you're right," she acknowledged. "Though formalising it into a methodology that others can apply has been the real challenge."

"A challenge you've met impressively," Noah said. "The European teams aren't just accepting the methodology; they're actively applying it. That's the true measure of success."

As the flight continued westward, Marcia turned her attention to the global expansion strategy Diana had hinted at. GFP clearly saw the connection patterns approach as a framework for their entire global integration strategy. That represented both an opportunity and a responsibility for Alpha.

When they finally landed in Seattle, the familiar grey drizzle felt oddly welcoming after London's winter chill. James was waiting in the arrivals area, a welcome sight after a long international flight.

"Welcome back," he greeted them. "How was the European adventure?"

"Eventful," Marcia replied with a smile. "Much more so than we anticipated."

"So I heard," James said. "Robert's been fielding calls from Diana all week. Something about a security incident that turned into a showcase for our methodology?"

"That's one way to put it," Liam chimed in, surprisingly alert despite having just woken up on the plane. "We found a vulnerability that validated our entire approach to connection patterns."

James raised an eyebrow at Liam's enthusiasm. "I'm looking forward to hearing the full story. Robert's called an expanded leadership meeting tomorrow morning. Apparently, this has implications beyond the GFP project."

On the drive back to Alpha's offices, James updated them on developments during their absence. The recovery plan implementation was progressing smoothly, with customers already responding positively to the authentication improvements. The core banking module delivery was on track.

"The GFP success has created significant interest," James explained. "Other clients with complex integration challenges are asking if we can apply similar approaches to their projects."

"That's both exciting and concerning," Marcia commented. "The methodology is still evolving, and its success depends greatly on the mindset of the people implementing it."

"Exactly what Robert said," James nodded. "That's why tomorrow's meeting is so important. He wants your perspective on what elements are truly transferable versus what depends on specific project contexts or team capabilities."

When they arrived at Alpha's building, Marcia was surprised to find Robert waiting in the lobby despite the late hour.

"I couldn't wait until tomorrow to hear about London," he explained, greeting them warmly. "Diana's been raving about your handling of the security incident."

"It was a team effort," Marcia said, glancing at Liam and Noah. "And honestly, it demonstrated the value of our methodology better than any planned presentation could have."

Robert's expression brightened as they crossed the lobby together. "Nothing validates an approach like applying it to an unexpected real-world challenge. Come up to my office - I want to hear the details before tomorrow's formal debrief."

In Robert's corner office, with Seattle's night skyline glittering through the windows, they recounted the European experience - from the initial scepticism to the security incident that changed everything. Liam explained the technical aspects with unexpected clarity, while Noah highlighted the cross-cultural dimensions that had influenced their approach.

"What strikes me most," Robert observed when they finished, "is how this ownership mindset created opportunities that simply wouldn't have existed otherwise. By stepping into the security problem rather than stepping away from it, you transformed a potential setback into a powerful demonstration of our methodology."

"It wasn't a conscious strategy at first," Marcia admitted. "It was a values-based response. We saw a problem at a connection point - exactly the kind of issue our methodology is designed to address - and we couldn't ignore it simply because it wasn't in our original scope."

"That's exactly why it worked," Robert said. "Authentic leadership isn't calculated; it's a natural expression of values. The European teams responded to your genuine commitment to solving their problem, not to clever tactics or positioning."

He leaned back in his chair, studying the three of them with obvious pride. "You've created something significant here - not just a technical methodology but a leadership approach that addresses the complex, boundary-spanning challenges our clients face."

"It's still evolving," Marcia cautioned. "The European integration will test it in new ways, and the Asia-Pacific expansion even more so."

"Of course," Robert agreed. "But that's the beauty of what you've built. It's not a rigid framework; it's an adaptive approach that gains strength from each new challenge it encounters."

James glanced around. "Nice work, all - it sounds like the truth, scope, fix, prevention structure served you well."

As they prepared to leave, Robert held Marcia back. "Diana mentioned Singapore in June," he said quietly. "Are you comfortable with that timeline?"

"As long as we have a solid foundation in Europe first," she replied. "I don't want to expand too quickly at the cost of quality."

Robert's approval was evident. "Wise approach. We'll discuss the details tomorrow, but I wanted you to know that this has become a significant strategic opportunity for Alpha. The GFP relationship alone would be valuable, but the methodology you've developed has potential applications across our entire client portfolio."

As Marcia finally made her way home, exhausted but satisfied, she reflected on how far they'd come since she'd inherited the troubled GFP project months ago.

The ownership mindset had transformed not just the GFP project but the team itself. Liam's evolution from isolated technical expert to collaborative leader. Noah's growth as a cross-cultural bridge builder. The European teams' shift from scepticism to active engagement with the methodology.

As Marcia felt the familiar comfort of her own bed, she also felt a deep sense of satisfaction. *Own problems completely, and magic happens.*

Then the thought sharpened: one person - one team - can't carry this. *Ownership lit the fuse; connection carries the flame.*

**FIELD RULE: RACI-Lite
(One Owner, Clear Chorus)**

- Owner (Directly Responsible Individual - DRI): one person owns the outcome.
- Decider (default Owner).
- Consulted; Informed; channel and cadence.
- Say it out loud with a date.

RACI = Responsible Accountable Consulted Informed

Do this tomorrow: Add "Owner / Decider / Consulted / Informed" to one bouncing ticket.

Chapter 8
The Power of Team Synergy

Every breakthrough story has the same twist: the misfits win by combining what makes them different. Alone, their edges clash. Together, those same edges lock into something unbreakable. Team synergy isn't cooperation - it's alchemy.

✧ ✧ ✧

Make progress visible and shared.

✧ ✧ ✧

The next morning came sooner than Marcia expected. Despite the late-night debrief in Robert's office and the long flight home, she felt a steady clarity as she arrived at Alpha's headquarters. GFP's board had already approved expanding Alpha's involvement across Asia-Pacific and into global operations - an extraordinary opportunity that now demanded discipline and sobriety from Alpha's leadership.

Today wasn't about permission.

It was about readiness.

Before anything moved forward, the executive team needed a clear-eyed assessment of what the Europe incident had exposed - and whether Marcia's proposed stabilisation track could support the weight of global expansion.

Marcia straightened her blazer, gathered her notes, and stepped into the executive conference room.

The room was already full. Elizabeth reviewed notes on her tablet, her expression unreadable. Malcolm sat with his arms crossed, posture taut. Two directors from GFP's European acquisition appeared on the wall displays, the grainy video frames unable to soften the tension in their faces.

Conversation tapered off as Marcia took her seat. Everyone understood the stakes.

Elizabeth nodded once. "Let's begin. Europe raised concerns about the integration approach. Before we scale further, we need clarity on what the incident revealed. Marcia - walk us through your findings."

This was the moment the entire trip had been building toward.

Marcia met their eyes one by one. "Europe wasn't resisting the approach. They were reacting to missing context - some of which we didn't realise they lacked until we were on the ground."

Malcolm leaned forward. "The Frankfurt team said the integration work destabilised production. That's not a misunderstanding. That's a risk."

"It was," Marcia agreed. "Because we treated the acquired companies as though they shared baseline operational practices. They don't. Their release processes, data governance, and access controls differ significantly. Our connection patterns exposed these inconsistencies - they didn't create them."

A flicker of surprise rippled through the room. Not defensive - attentive.

She continued, steady and composed. "Production instability was the symptom. Fragmented operating models were the cause. And unless we address that now, the next year of integration work will repeat this pattern."

She paused, letting the truth land.

"Ownership is a posture, not a job description," she said softly.

"And in Europe, we finally saw what happens when everyone adopts that posture at the same time."

One of the European directors spoke through the speaker. "So, you're saying the fault isn't exclusively ours."

"No," Marcia said. "I'm saying it belongs to all of us - including Alpha. We assumed alignment that didn't exist. That's on us. Now that we see it clearly, we can fix it."

The room shifted. Shoulders lowered. Malcolm's posture eased; he was no longer bracing for a defence but listening for a solution.

Elizabeth tapped her pen lightly. "What does fixing it look like?"

Marcia drew a breath. "We run a stabilisation track alongside integration. A small cross-office team - one lead from each acquisition and one from Alpha - maps operational differences through real incidents, not theoretical exercises. The unified operating model emerges from live work, not pre-written documentation."

The Frankfurt director nodded slowly. "You're proposing we build the operating model as we go, grounded in practice."

"Yes," Marcia said. "Because building it beforehand

would be guesswork."

Malcolm sat back, tension leaving his shoulders. "That would have prevented the incident."

"It will prevent the next one."

Silence followed - this time evaluative, not sceptical.

Elizabeth closed her tablet. "This aligns with what we need. One question: can you lead both stabilisation and integration?"

Marcia didn't break eye contact. "Yes. With the right people and clear boundaries."

The room held still for half a heartbeat.

Then Elizabeth nodded. "Ok, let's do the stabilisation."

A warm, grounded resolve rose in Marcia's chest. As the meeting dissolved into follow-up discussions, James caught her eye and gave a small, knowing nod.

You did it.

For the first time, Marcia didn't feel like she was surviving leadership.

She felt like she was owning it.

"Ownership is a posture, not a job description."

✧ ✧ ✧

The stabilisation track had been approved. The path forward was clear. Now it was about execution.

Marcia stood at the front of the room again, this time to articulate the next steps

"So that's the European implementation plan," Marcia said, concluding her presentation to Alpha's leadership team. The conference room fell silent as Robert Miller studied the slides still displayed on the screen, his expression thoughtful.

A week had passed since their return from London. The

European security incident had been fully resolved, and GFP's board had formally approved expanding Alpha's role in their global transformation.

"This is impressive work," Robert said finally, looking up from his notes. "You've developed it into a comprehensive methodology that addresses both technical and human dimensions."

Murmurs of agreement came from around the table. Other delivery managers who had initially viewed the GFP project as an outlier were now leaning forward with obvious interest.

"What I find most valuable," said Alan Meadows, Alpha's VP of Delivery, "is how you've documented the patterns so they're transferable to other contexts. The authentication consolidation pattern alone could solve integration headaches for at least three of my clients."

Liam, who sat beside Marcia, looked quietly pleased at this acknowledgment. The connection patterns library he'd helped build had grown into a valuable company asset.

But across the table, Michael Winters - a veteran delivery manager with a reputation for skepticism - folded his arms. "I've seen fixes come and go," he said, cutting in with a frown. "What makes you think this one will be any different? From where I sit, it hinges on teams breaking out of their silos. Not every team - or every client - is ready for that." His tone carried enough doubt to draw a few nods around the room.

Marcia forced herself to meet his gaze. "You're right, Michael. This isn't about a quick fix or a silver bullet. It's about creating the conditions for teams to collaborate across boundaries. That takes both methodology and mindset - and that's what we're proving here."

Robert clasped one hand in the other, his gaze circling the table. "Which brings us to the next phase of our discussion. Diana has requested that we extend this approach to GFP's Asia-Pacific operations, starting with a preliminary assessment in Singapore in June."

This news created a ripple of reaction around the table.

"Are we ready for that scale of expansion?" James Anderson asked, voicing what several others were clearly thinking.

"That's what I want to explore today," Robert replied. "Marcia, you've been closest to the methodology's development. What's your assessment?"

Marcia took a moment to gather her thoughts, aware that her response would shape Alpha's strategy moving forward.

"The methodology itself is ready," she said carefully. "The connection patterns we've documented are applicable across diverse contexts. But successful implementation depends on having the right team - people who understand both the technical patterns and the collaborative mindset required to apply them effectively."

"Exactly my concern," Michael interjected. "You've had the advantage of working with Liam, Noah, and others who've gradually bought into this approach. Scaling requires people who can implement it without that evolutionary journey."

Liam surprised everyone by speaking up. "That's why we've been documenting not just the patterns but the implementation approach. The European security incident taught us something important - real-world challenges actually accelerate understanding better than theoretical explanations."

Heads turned toward Liam, many clearly startled by his unprompted contribution.

"Liam makes an excellent point," Marcia agreed. "The methodology gains strength when applied to concrete challenges. That's why I believe a phased expansion makes sense. Solidify our European implementation first, then apply those learnings to the Asia-Pacific assessment."

Robert leaned in. "What would that phased approach look like specifically?"

Over an animated twenty minutes, Marcia outlined a strategic expansion plan. They would establish a core team that understood both the methodology and the mindset, then gradually expand as they developed more practitioners through real-world implementation. The European integration would serve as a training ground, with team members cycling through before joining the Asia-Pacific initiative.

"This isn't just about technical skills," she emphasised. "It's about developing people who understand that ownership transcends traditional boundaries - people willing to step forward when others might step back."

As the discussion continued, Marcia noticed the energy in the room shifting. Scepticism about scaling the approach was evolving into practical planning for implementation. Michael, initially the most vocal sceptic, was now suggesting specific consultants who might have the right combination of technical skills and collaborative mindset.

"I'm seeing something important happen here," Robert observed as the conversation flowed. "You're demonstrating exactly what makes this methodology powerful - the ability to integrate diverse perspectives into a stronger whole."

He was right. The leadership team was modelling the very connection patterns they were discussing - identifying integration points between different viewpoints, establishing clear communication channels, and building on each other's ideas rather than defending separate positions.

"Let's take this a step further," Robert continued. "I'd like each delivery manager to identify potential candidates for the expanded GFP team - people with both the technical capabilities and the collaborative mindset Marcia described. We'll create a development program to prepare them for implementing the connection patterns approach across GFP's global operations."

As the meeting concluded, people lingered in small groups, continuing the discussion with new energy. Liam found himself surrounded by technical directors eager to understand the authentication connection pattern in more detail. Noah, who had initially said little during the formal presentation, was now engaged with the international operations team discussing cultural considerations for the Asia-Pacific assessment.

"That went better than expected," James commented, joining Marcia as she gathered her materials. "Especially Michael's shift to practical support."

"The methodology itself helped," Marcia replied with a smile. "When we frame integration challenges in terms of connection patterns, people naturally move from defending positions to seeking integration points."

Robert approached looking pleased, slipping his phone back into his jacket pocket. "Diana just confirmed the Singapore assessment for June 13th. She's arranged for representatives from their Australia, Japan, and Singapore operations to participate."

"That timeline works well with our European implementation," Marcia said. "We'll have established the core patterns in London before exploring the Asia-Pacific context."

✧ ✧ ✧

Later that afternoon, as the building began to quiet, Marcia received an email from Diana Thompson:

Marcia,

Robert shared your European implementation plan and preliminary thoughts on the Asia-Pacific assessment. Your phased approach makes perfect sense - build on success rather than dilute it through overly rapid expansion.

What strikes me most is how your team embodies the very methodology you've developed. The connection patterns approach isn't just a process; it's become part of who you are as a team. That authentic alignment between methodology and mindset is what gives me confidence in expanding our engagement.

I look forward to seeing you in Singapore in June. The Asia-Pacific leadership team is eager to experience firsthand what their European colleagues have been raving about.
Diana

Marcia felt appreciated as she read it again. Diana had captured something essential about their journey - the methodology hadn't just changed how they worked; it had transformed the team itself. Liam's evolution from isolated technical expert to collaborative leader. Noah's growth as a cross-cultural bridge builder. Her own development as a leader who created space for others to contribute their unique perspectives.

Beyond individual growth, their synergy - the weaving together of diverse viewpoints into a stronger whole - was the most powerful pattern they had discovered.

✧   ✧   ✧

"It's like conducting an orchestra," Marcia explained, standing before the whiteboard in Alpha's training room. "Each instrument sounds beautiful on its own, but the magic happens when they play together."

Twenty consultants - handpicked from across Alpha's offices - watched attentively as she sketched a simple diagram showing how different specialties intersected in the connection patterns approach. This was the first formal training session for what Robert had dubbed the "Connection Patterns Practice Group," and Marcia could feel both excitement and trepidation in the room.

"For years, we've organised ourselves by technical specialty," she continued. "Developers in one group, business analysts in another, QA in yet another. But the most challenging problems our clients face don't respect those boundaries - they emerge at the connections between specialties."

A hand went up near the back. "So you're saying we should abandon specialised teams?" The question came from Alicia Mendez, a senior developer and front-end lead, known for her technical precision.

"Not at all," Marcia smiled. "We need deep expertise. But we also need to strengthen how those specialised areas connect. Think of it as having both solo performances and ensemble pieces in the same concert."

Liam, who stood near the whiteboard, stepped forward. "Let me share a concrete example," he said, uncapping a marker. "During the February milestone work, we discovered that our authentication issues weren't just technical problems - they emerged at the connection points between security architecture, user experience design, and business requirements."

He drew a simple diagram showing three overlapping circles. "Traditional approaches would have each specialty optimising their piece in isolation. Our connection patterns approach identified the integration points where these specialties needed to align."

Marcia watched quietly as Liam explained the technical patterns with practiced clarity.

"What about client boundaries?" asked Thomas Kim from the international practice. "Most of our clients expect clear scope definitions between their responsibilities and ours."

"That's where ownership becomes crucial," Noah replied from his seat near the front. "The European security incident taught us that maintaining rigid boundaries often prevents effective solutions. When we stepped forward to address an issue that technically wasn't 'our problem,' we created trust that transformed the entire engagement."

For the next hour, the group explored practical examples from the GFP project - how they'd identified critical connection points, established integration patterns, and fostered the collaborative mindset needed to implement them effectively.

"The methodology is powerful," Marcia acknowledged as they neared the end of the session. "But it only works when we bring both technical expertise and human connection to the table. That's why you've been selected for this practice group - you each bring unique perspectives that, when connected properly, create something greater than any individual contribution."

As the session concluded, people clustered in small groups, continuing discussions that had begun during the formal presentation. Alicia was shoulder-to-shoulder with a financial-services analyst, sketching on a tablet: a login flow boxed in blue, arrows re-routed to a single authentication check - building on each other's ideas rather than defending separate positions.

"The seeds are taking root," Robert observed, joining Marcia as the room gradually emptied.

"It's early days," she cautioned. "Understanding the

concept is one thing; applying it in the messy reality of client projects is another."

"True," Robert tapped his pen rhythmically. "But look at what's happening already." He gestured toward a corner where Liam was walking three technical architects through the authentication connection pattern in detail.

Marcia followed his gaze. No one was asking permission or waiting for orders - people just jumped in to help wherever a problem popped up. *This is what synergy looks like,* she thought, a swell of pride rising in her chest. Months ago, these same individuals had been working in silos, even at odds. Now the factions had truly fused into one team. She could see it in their ease of communication and the speed at which they solved issues together. This was the climax of everything they'd built: not a miracle performed by one hero, but a triumph created *together.*

"I never expected Liam to become such an advocate," Marcia admitted. "When I first inherited the GFP project, he was the most resistant to collaborative approaches."

"People rise to meaningful challenges," Robert said. "Liam's always cared about getting the tech right - he just never had a reason to care as much about the people side. The connection patterns showed him the two can actually strengthen each other."

As they left the training room, Marcia reflected on how the team itself had evolved throughout the project.

"The European implementation team is nearly complete," Robert said as they walked. "I've approved all your recommended transfers from other projects. They'll start transitioning next week."

"Excellent," Marcia replied. "That gives us time to build the team dynamics before the critical integration points in May."

Back in her office, Marcia found Tessa waiting with a

tablet full of charts. "The connection patterns library is gaining traction," Tessa reported, showing usage metrics from Alpha's internal knowledge base. "The authentication pattern has been downloaded seventy-three times since we published it last week."

"That's encouraging," Marcia said, studying the data. "Are people adding their own patterns or just consuming the existing ones?"

"Both," Tessa replied with satisfaction. "Liam created a submission process that encourages collaborative development. People propose patterns, others build on them, and a review team evaluates them for inclusion in the official library."

"Another example of connection patterns in action," Marcia observed. "By creating a structured process for collaboration, Liam has enabled collective intelligence that no individual could match."

After Tessa left, Marcia turned her attention to the European implementation plan. The team was taking shape, combining veterans from the February milestone work with fresh perspectives from other projects.

Later in the afternoon, Marcia gathered with Liam, Noah, and Sarah to review the European implementation strategy.

"The key integration points are clear," Liam explained, showing a diagram of the European systems landscape. "We've mapped the critical connections between the three acquisitions and identified the patterns needed for each."

"The technical patterns are solid," Sarah agreed, "but we need to ensure the operational practices support them. Each connection point needs verification protocols and quality gates."

Noah spread his hands lightly. "And the cross-cultural dimensions can't be overlooked. The German, French, and

Dutch teams have different working styles that affect how we implement these patterns."

Marcia watched their interaction with satisfaction. Each perspective added depth to the approach, creating a strategy far stronger than any individual could have developed alone.

"This is exactly how the team needs to function in Europe," she observed.

"It didn't always work this way," Liam pointed out, a hint of self-awareness in his tone. "Six months ago, I would have focused exclusively on the technical architecture without considering the operational or cultural dimensions."

"We've all evolved," Marcia acknowledged. "The GFP project pushed us to think beyond our specialties and see the connections between them."

As they continued refining the European strategy, Marcia reflected on how their working relationship had transformed. The initial friction between different perspectives had given way to productive integration.

That evening, as Marcia prepared to leave, Robert stopped by her office. "I've been thinking about something Diana said," he remarked, settling into a chair. "She mentioned that your team embodies the very methodology you've developed - that the connection patterns approach isn't just something you do; it's become who you are as a team."

Marcia nodded. "That's perceptive of her. The methodology has changed how we work together, breaking down the barriers between our specialised areas."

"Which raises an important question for our broader rollout," Robert continued. "How do we cultivate that same integration in teams that haven't been through the evolutionary journey yours has?"

"I think it requires both structure and experience," Marcia said thoughtfully. "The structured methodology provides a framework, but people need to experience the power of integrated perspectives firsthand. That's why I believe in starting with small, cross-functional teams on concrete challenges before expanding."

"Like a chamber orchestra before a full symphony," Robert suggested, picking up on her earlier metaphor.

Marcia lifted a hand as if cueing a section. "Exactly. Let people experience the magic of true collaboration on a smaller scale first. Once they feel that power, scaling becomes more natural."

After Robert left, Marcia stayed late updating her project journal. The metaphor of the orchestra had resonated more deeply than she'd initially realised. Each team member brought a unique instrument, a specialised skill that had value on its own. But the true magic emerged when those instruments played together in harmony, creating music that no soloist could achieve alone.

That was the essence of team synergy.

As she finally headed home, Marcia felt a sense of purpose about the next phase of their journey. Building the European implementation team would test their ability to foster that synergy at a larger scale, blending seasoned veterans with fresh perspectives to create a cohesive whole.

The orchestra was assembling. Soon they would begin to play.

✧ ✧ ✧

The European implementation team gathered in Alpha's largest conference room, transformed for the occasion with tables arranged in clusters rather than the usual rows. Three weeks had passed since the first training session and today marked the official kick-off for the GFP European integration project.

Marcia stood near the entrance, observing as people found their places. The careful team composition she'd designed was visible in the diversity of the gathering - veterans from the February milestone work mixed with specialists from other projects, technical experts alongside business analysts, Seattle-based consultants next to those who'd transferred from New York.

"Nervous?" James asked, appearing at her side with two cups of coffee.

"Cautiously optimistic," Marcia replied, accepting one of the cups. "We've done the preparation. Now we see if the synergy actually develops."

On the video wall, the London, Frankfurt, and Paris teams were connecting, creating a virtual workspace that spanned four cities and two continents. Liam was already engaged with the technical teams, walking them through the authentication patterns that would form the foundation of their integration work.

"I still can't believe that's the same Liam who used to avoid team meetings," James remarked quietly.

Marcia kept her tone light. "Well, he had a bit of help - the same way I did."

At 9:00 am precisely, Marcia moved to the front of the room. Conversations quieted as she took her position, all eyes turning toward her, both in person and on the screens.

"Good morning, everyone," she began. "Today we launch the European implementation phase of GFP's global transformation program. What we're attempting is among the most complex integrations GFP has ever undertaken - bringing together three distinct acquisitions across multiple countries while maintaining both their unique strengths and a unified customer experience."

She gestured to the room at large and to the teams on the screens. "Look around. You've been selected not just for your individual expertise but for how your perspectives complement each other. The technical architects, business analysts, quality specialists, cultural liaisons - each of you brings a crucial instrument to this orchestra."

A sense of purpose seemed to settle over the room as Marcia continued, "The connection patterns methodology provides our framework, but the magic happens when your diverse perspectives integrate together."

She clicked to a slide showing the critical connection points they'd identified across GFP's European operations - the technical interfaces, process handoffs, and cultural bridges that would determine success or failure.

"These are our priorities for the next twelve weeks," she explained. "Not just implementing technical solutions but establishing sustainable connection patterns that will enable ongoing integration."

For the next hour, the team worked through the implementation roadmap, with leaders from each specialty adding their perspectives. Sarah outlined the quality verification protocol for each connection point. Noah explained the cross-cultural considerations for the German, French, and Dutch operations. Liam walked through the technical architecture that would enable secure, scalable integration.

What impressed Marcia most was how naturally they built on each other's ideas - Sarah suggesting quality checkpoints for Liam's authentication patterns, Noah highlighting cultural nuances that affected implementation timing, specialists from each location adding context that strengthened the overall approach.

As the teams broke into their working groups, Marcia circulated through the room, observing the dynamics taking shape. In one corner, a technical architect from Seattle and a business analyst from Paris were mapping integration points for the customer onboarding process.

Near the windows, Liam had gathered a cross-functional group to address the security architecture that had caused issues during their London visit. Rather than dominating the conversation as he might have months ago, he was facilitating - drawing out insights from others, synthesising diverse perspectives into a cohesive approach.

"It's working rather better than I expected," Charles Worthington commented, joining Marcia as she watched the teams in action. The GFP European Operations Director had flown in from London for the kick-off. "I've seen many integration attempts over the years, but this feels different."

"How so?" Marcia asked.

"Most approaches either enforce standardisation that destroys what made the acquisitions valuable, or preserve so much autonomy that integration never truly happens," Charles explained. "What I'm seeing here is a proper synthesis - respecting differences whilst creating connections that make the whole stronger than its parts."

By lunchtime, the momentum hadn't slowed. Teams had established clear goals for the first implementation phase, with ownership and dependencies clearly mapped. The video connections remained active, with virtual teams as engaged as those physically present.

Marcia checked the afternoon agenda. "Noah, can you lead the cross-office design call at 3 pm. You don't need me in the room - align the handoffs and decisions, and send me the notes."

"Copy," Noah said. "I'll run it."

She glanced around the table. "If I join every call, we'll slow down. You've got this."

"I'd say the orchestra is finding its rhythm," James observed as they stepped out for a brief break.

"The first notes, at least," Marcia agreed. "The true test

comes when we hit our first significant obstacles."

That test came sooner than expected. As they reconvened after lunch, an urgent message arrived from Klaus in Germany: the regulatory approval they'd been counting on for the unified authentication approach had been delayed, potentially jeopardising their core integration pattern.

Marcia watched closely as the teams processed this news. Rather than fragmenting into separate perspectives - technical blaming regulatory, Seattle blaming Germany - they naturally moved into problem-solving mode, bringing their diverse viewpoints to bear on the challenge.

"This is exactly why we designed the multiple-pathway authentication pattern," Liam pointed out. "We anticipated regulatory variations and built flexibility into the architecture."

"We can implement the core pattern in phases," Sarah added. "Starting with the Netherlands and France while we work through the German regulatory requirements."

Within thirty minutes, they had developed a modified approach that maintained the timeline while addressing the regulatory constraints. And they did it without her.

"They are working well together," Marcia said quietly to Charles as the groups returned to their work with renewed focus.

"Indeed," he agreed. "And precisely what GFP needs for our integration to succeed."

As the day progressed, Marcia noticed something remarkable happening. The carefully designed team structure was beginning to fade into the background as people naturally formed connections based on the challenges they were addressing. Organisational boundaries - between Alpha and GFP, between different offices and acquisitions - were becoming less relevant than the shared purpose of creating effective integration patterns.

This was the essence of team cohesion - a collaborative organism that could adapt, integrate diverse perspectives, and create successful outcomes.

As the kick-off day drew to a close, Marcia gathered everyone for a final reflection. "What we've demonstrated today is just the beginning," she told them. "It's your collective intelligence that will ultimately determine our success."

Looking around the room and at the faces on the screens, Marcia felt a steady, hard-won confidence. The European implementation would face many challenges in the weeks ahead, but the foundation they'd established today - the team synergy they'd begun to build - provided a strong starting point.

As the teams in each location signed off, promising to reconnect early tomorrow, Marcia realised they were building something that extended far beyond this specific project.

The orchestra was indeed beginning to play. And the music was even richer than she had dared to hope.

✧　✧　✧

Six weeks into the European implementation, Marcia stood by the window of the London office, watching rain lash against the glass. The Thames was a grey, sullen presence below, mirroring the mood that had settled over the project in the past forty-eight hours.

"Three critical integration points all hitting obstacles simultaneously," she murmured, more to herself than to James who stood nearby reviewing the incident reports. "Murphy's Law in full effect."

What had been progressing smoothly - remarkably so - had suddenly hit turbulence. The authentication pattern implementation had encountered unexpected compatibility issues with the German legacy systems. The customer data integration between the French and Dutch operations had revealed regulatory conflicts that their initial analysis had missed. And most concerning, the unified reporting framework had produced inconsistent results across the three acquisitions, creating confusion rather than clarity.

"Bad timing with the Asia-Pacific assessment just two weeks away," James observed, setting down the reports. "Malcolm's already expressing concerns about expanding a methodology that's hitting roadblocks in Europe."

Marcia turned from the window. "Malcolm's always looking for reasons to slow down. But I'm not as worried about these obstacles as you might think."

"No?" James raised an eyebrow.

"No," she confirmed with quiet certainty. "Because I'm seeing something remarkable in how the team is responding. Watch the team meeting and you'll understand."

As they walked to the main conference room, the space was already filling with team members both in person and on the video screens connecting Seattle, Frankfurt, Paris, and Amsterdam. Despite the challenges, there was no sense of panic or finger-pointing - just focused determination and an unusual amount of cross-functional conversation.

Liam was huddled with Klaus and the German technical team, laptops displaying code and architecture diagrams between them. Sarah was deep in conversation with the French regulatory specialists. Tessa had gathered a mixed group of business analysts from all three acquisitions, comparing output from the reporting framework against source data.

"Notice anything unusual?" Marcia asked James quietly.

"They're not waiting for direction," he observed. "Everyone's already working the problems."

"And not just within their specialties," Marcia added. "Look at the groupings."

Each cluster represented a diverse mix - technical architects working alongside business analysts, quality specialists collaborating with regulatory experts, team members from different acquisitions naturally forming problem-solving units rather than retreating to their separate domains.

As Marcia called the meeting to order, she felt a subtle swell of admiration for the group. "I know we're facing significant challenges across three critical integration points," she began. "Rather than addressing each separately, I'd like us to step back and look for patterns across these issues. What common factors might be influencing all three?"

Without hesitation, voices from across the room and on the screens began contributing perspectives. Liam pointed out that all three issues involved translation between different data models. Klaus noted regulatory interpretation variations affecting each challenge. Marcel from France highlighted temporal factors - how data timing affected integration outcomes.

Instead of competing or talking past each other, they were building a shared understanding, each perspective adding depth to their collective analysis. No individual had the complete picture, but together they were assembling insights that transcended specialty boundaries.

"I think I see the connection," said Miguel from the user experience team, surprising everyone. As a UX specialist, they rarely spoke on technical integration issues. "All three problems involve asynchronous processes that are being treated as synchronous."

A moment of silence followed as technical teams processed Miguel's observation. Then Liam straightened, something lighting in his eyes. "They're right," Liam said, nodding to Miguel. "We're assuming simultaneous data states across systems that are actually operating on different refresh cycles."

"Which explains the reporting inconsistencies," added Tessa excitedly. "We're comparing snapshots from different moments in time and expecting them to reconcile."

"And the authentication conflicts," Klaus said, recognition sparkling in his eyes. "The German system refreshes security tokens on a different schedule than the unified framework expects."

Carlos - the integration lead - gave Miguel a quick nod. "Good catch. That changes how we model the handoffs."

Within thirty minutes, they had not only identified the common pattern underlying all three issues but had developed an integrated approach to address it - a new connection pattern specifically designed for asynchronous integration points.

As the teams broke into implementation groups, James leaned toward Marcia. "That was remarkable. No individual would have made that connection - not even Liam. It emerged from their collective intelligence."

"That's the power of team synergy," Marcia replied. "It's the opposite of groupthink. Not just cooperation, but the productive integration of diverse perspectives into something greater than any individual contribution could produce."

She watched as Miguel, the UX specialist whose insight had sparked the breakthrough, was now fully integrated into the technical implementation planning. Six months ago, they would have been politely sidelined once the "real technical work" began. Now their perspective was valued precisely because it differed from the dominant technical viewpoint.

By late afternoon, the teams had developed implementation plans for all three integration points based on the new asynchronous connection pattern. What had seemed like separate crises that morning had transformed into an opportunity to strengthen their overall methodology.

Charles Worthington found Marcia as she was preparing the update for GFP's executive team. "I have just come from watching the authentication team," he said, obvious admiration in his voice. "They have not only solved the German compatibility issue but have developed an approach that will simplify our future integration with any asynchronous system."

"That's great," Marcia said with a smile. "They've really earned that breakthrough."

Charles leaned back, his tone less formal than usual. "But it's more than the methodology, isn't it? It's the way this lot work together. I can't recall seeing such a smooth blending of perspectives, particularly across organisational and cultural lines. Quite something, really."

"They're clicking in a way that feels natural now," Marcia said. "It just builds once people start to trust each other."

As they walked to the executive briefing, Marcia reflected on how far they'd come. Where most teams would have splintered, this one had come together.

That evening, as Marcia updated Robert on the day's developments, she emphasised this point. "The technical solutions are impressive," she told him over the video call, "but the team dynamics are the real breakthrough. They're functioning as a unified organism rather than a collection of specialists."

"Which makes me more confident about the Asia-Pacific expansion," Robert replied thoughtfully. "If this team synergy is transferable, we have something truly exceptional."

"That's what we need to determine," Marcia agreed. "Can we create the conditions for this kind of integration in new contexts, or is it specific to this team and their shared history?"

"A question Diana will certainly ask in Singapore," Robert noted.

After finishing her call with Robert, Marcia walked through the now-quiet London office. Most team members had departed, but Liam remained, working with a small group that included people from all three European acquisitions. They were documenting the new asynchronous connection pattern, building it into the library for future applications.

"Don't stay too late," she advised as she stopped by their workspace. This triggered memories of the many times James had shown her similar care.

Liam looked up, a hint of a smile on his normally serious face. "We're almost finished. This pattern has applications far beyond today's issues - it addresses a whole category of integration challenges."

As Marcia left the office and hailed a black cab back to her hotel, she reflected on the day's events. What had started as a potential crisis had transformed into a powerful demonstration of team synergy.

The obstacles weren't fully resolved yet, but she had complete confidence in the team's ability to implement their solutions. More importantly, they had strengthened both their methodology and their collaborative capacity in ways that would serve them well beyond these specific challenges.

The Asia-Pacific assessment loomed just two weeks away, bringing new complexities and stakeholders. But today had reinforced Marcia's belief that their approach was fundamentally sound.

As her cab navigated London's evening traffic, Marcia began mentally preparing for Singapore. The Asia-Pacific context would test their methodology in new ways, but the core principle would remain the same: integration excellence emerged when diverse perspectives combined into a greater whole.

✧ ✧ ✧

The aircraft banked gently over the South China Sea, and Marcia pressed closer to the window. Below, dozens of ships were scattered across the water in orderly lines - tankers, freighters, container vessels waiting their turn at one of the world's busiest ports. Beyond the shoreline, the island of Singapore appeared through a veil of morning haze, its dense greenery broken by high-rise towers and the first glint of glass from the financial district.

Following a smooth landing, the wide-body jet rolled along the runway past lines of neatly parked aircraft. Disembarking was orderly and immigration moved quickly, the efficiency almost startling.

"Quite the change from London," Noah commented, loosening his tie as they walked through Changi's gardens. Orchids and palms lined the walkways, the scent of greenery mixing with the sterile chill of air conditioning. "Though I swear this air-con can't keep up."

Marcia smiled. "Better get used to it. Europe was about refinement. Here we're starting from scratch."

Liam, walking a step ahead, glanced back. "And not a simple start. Three markets, three levels of maturity, three sets of rules."

"Singapore, Australia, Japan," Noah ticked off on his fingers. "Strict, relaxed, and… well, a mix of robots and samurai tradition."

That earned a small laugh, even from Liam.

Marcia shook her head, still smiling. "Perfect stress test for our connection patterns. If we can make it work here, we can make it work anywhere."

Singapore's humidity hit Marcia like a wall the moment they stepped out of the terminal. Only two weeks ago she'd been walking through London's cool drizzle, her coat still necessary against the spring chill. Here the air felt thick and damp, clinging to her skin. Even the light seemed different - sharper, more saturated - glinting off palm leaves and glass facades glimpsed beyond the airport roadways.

Marcia drew a breath. "Well, that's one way to wake up."

Their driver was waiting at the kerb, holding a discreet sign with GFP's logo and Marcia's name. He ushered them toward a gleaming black Toyota Alphard; its tinted windows and leather interior clearly intended for corporate travellers. Soon they were gliding onto the East Coast Parkway, the air-conditioning a welcome relief as the Alphard hummed through the morning traffic.

The ride into the city stretched close to half an hour, the coastline sliding past in flashes of bougainvillea and palm trees. As the expressway curved toward the city, the skyline slowly emerged - first the silhouette of Marina Bay Sands, then the clustered towers rising out of the humid air.

Noah leaned forward, looking out the window. "Hard to believe all this is just one city. London feels almost provincial by comparison."

Liam glanced up from his notes. "London is bigger by population and area. Singapore just compresses more into less space. That density makes it feel larger."

Noah smirked. "Trust you to fact-check my wonder."

Even Marcia chuckled, grateful for the lightness before the meetings ahead, and for the friendships that had grown alongside her leadership. What had started as a team to manage was now a circle she relied on.

By the time the Alphard pulled up outside GFP Singapore's headquarters, a glass tower in the heart of the financial district, Marcia felt the shift from airport arrival to boardroom expectation. The team was quickly escorted upstairs, where Diana Thompson was already waiting in the conference room along with leaders from GFP's Singapore, Tokyo, and Sydney operations.

"Perfect timing," Diana said, greeting them warmly. "We were just discussing how the European implementation might translate to Asia-Pacific."

As introductions proceeded around the table, Marcia noted the scepticism in some faces - particularly Hiroshi Fujimoto from GFP's Tokyo office, whose polite smile didn't reach his eyes. She'd expected this; success in Europe didn't automatically translate to credibility in Asia.

"Before we dive into specifics," Marcia began, "I'd like to acknowledge something important. The connection patterns approach we've developed in North America and Europe isn't a template we intend to impose here. Rather, it's a methodology we hope to adapt collaboratively to your unique contexts."

Several faces registered surprise at this opening - they'd clearly expected a more prescriptive approach.

"Our experience has taught us that integration excellence emerges when diverse perspectives combine into a greater whole," she continued. "That's why we're here to listen and learn before we suggest applications."

For the next two hours, Marcia, Liam, and Noah primarily asked questions and listened as the regional leaders described their operations, challenges, and integration priorities. The dynamics gradually shifted as the local leaders realised this wasn't a standard consulting presentation but a genuine exchange of perspectives.

"Your approach in Europe addressed asynchronous data flows between systems," Hiroshi noted, finally engaging more actively. "We face similar challenges between our legacy mainframes and modern cloud applications in Japan."

"That pattern might transfer well," Liam agreed, "though we'd need to understand the specific cultural and regulatory constraints that shape your operations."

By lunchtime, the atmosphere had warmed considerably. The regional leaders began offering insights rather than just responding to questions, and genuine dialogue emerged around shared challenges.

"This is exactly what we hoped would happen," Diana commented quietly to Marcia as they broke for lunch. "You're building bridges before proposing solutions."

"It's fundamental to the connection patterns approach," Marcia replied. "Integration begins with understanding, not implementation."

After lunch, they divided into focused groups, with Liam working with the technical teams, Noah addressing cross-cultural considerations, and Marcia discussing strategic alignment with Diana and the regional executives.

"What strikes me most about your approach," said Clarissa Tan, GFP's Singapore managing director, "is how it integrates technical and human dimensions. Most methodologies focus exclusively on one or the other."

"That integration is deliberate," Marcia explained, providing an example from her experience.

As afternoon turned to evening, the teams reconvened to share initial impressions. The doubt that had greeted them that morning had transformed into cautious enthusiasm, with regional leaders identifying potential applications for connection patterns within their operations.

"I believe we have a foundation to build upon," Diana said as they wrapped up. "Tomorrow we'll explore specific integration opportunities across our Asia-Pacific operations."

Later, as Marcia reviewed her notes in the hotel, she

reflected on how differently this assessment was unfolding compared to their early days with the GFP project. The team now moved with confident purpose, naturally integrating diverse perspectives into a coherent approach. Liam engaged easily with technical leaders across cultural boundaries. Noah bridged communication gaps that might have derailed progress. And she found herself focusing less on specific solutions and more on creating conditions where collaborative innovation could flourish.

The power of team synergy had become core to their identity - not just something they talked about but something they embodied in every interaction.

Her screen blinked with a message from Robert: *How's Singapore? Malcolm anxious about expansion timeline.*

First day exceeded expectations, she replied. *Regional leaders engaging meaningfully. Building foundation for successful assessment. Malcolm can relax.*

She set the phone face down and squared her shoulders. Six months ago, she would have qualified her response with caveats and contingencies. Now she trusted both the methodology and the team. The connection patterns approach had proven itself repeatedly, becoming stronger with each new challenge it encountered.

Tomorrow promised deeper discussions about specific integration priorities across GFP's Asia-Pacific operations - conversations that would begin over breakfast, high above the bay, where the Supertrees rose like living architecture from the gardens below.

As Singapore's lights glittered outside her window, Marcia felt a humbling awe, as though she were watching herself from outside her own story. Only weeks ago she'd been walking through London's drizzle, months before that fighting fires in Seattle. Now she was here - guiding a global transformation.

The orchestra was playing beautifully now, each section adding its voice to a harmony no individual could create alone.

We've proven the approach - but can we make it scale?

**FIELD RULE: Make Momentum Visible
(so A-players want to join and stay)**

- Show the win and why it matters: share a 60-second before/after and invite stakeholders to a 10-min demo.
- Run a recognition loop: public shout-outs tied to a specific behaviour and impact.
- Make growth visible: each person has a "next skill" with a target date tracked in 1:1s.
- Keep it sustainable: publish on-call and after-hours rotation; set a no-heroics norm.
- Hold the A-player bar (no brilliant jerks): hire slow, coach fast, and part ways kindly.

Do this tomorrow: Share one *Cleared* win with context and owner in chat, and ask one stay-interview question in a 1:1 (e.g., "What would make you more excited to stay for the next two years?").

Chapter 9
Moving Forward with Confidence

"So, Singapore was a success?" Robert asked, leaning back in his chair as the morning sun streamed through his office windows. Three days had passed since Marcia's return from Asia, and this was their first chance for a proper debrief.

Marcia rolled her shoulders once, still feeling the lingering effects of jet lag. "Better than we expected. The regional leaders moved from scepticism to engagement within the first day. By the end of the assessment, they were identifying connection patterns specific to their markets."

"Diana mentioned that in our call yesterday," Robert said. "She was particularly impressed with how you adapted the approach to their cultural contexts rather than imposing a standardised model."

"That's been our learning throughout this journey," Marcia replied. "The connection patterns methodology works precisely because it's adaptive, not prescriptive. It provides a framework while respecting the unique characteristics of each environment."

Robert regarded her, a faint smile forming. "You've come a long way since inheriting the troubled GFP project. Remember that meeting when I handed you the business card holder with your new title?"

Marcia recalled the memory, forming wrinkles under her eyes. "I was terrified but trying desperately not to show it."

"And now you're confidently leading global implementations and developing methodologies that are transforming how we approach complex integration." Robert's voice carried genuine pride. "The Board is taking notice. They've approved establishing a formal Connection Patterns Practice Group with you as the global lead."

Marcia paused, genuinely surprised. "That's far beyond what I imagined when we started this journey."

"It's well-deserved," Robert assured her. "You've not only rescued a troubled project but developed an approach that's creating significant competitive advantage for Alpha."

He slid a folder across the desk. "These are the initial scope and structure documents for the practice group. I'd like your input before we finalise anything."

As Marcia flipped through the material, she saw that Robert had outlined an ambitious vision - a global team focused on complex integration challenges, with specialists trained in the connection patterns methodology working across Alpha's client portfolio.

"This is comprehensive," she said, looking up from the documents. "But I have one concern - scaling the approach without diluting what makes it work."

"Which is?"

"The mindset more than the mechanics," Marcia explained. "The connection patterns library and technical frameworks are valuable, but what truly transforms outcomes is the integration of diverse perspectives."

Robert folded his arms, thinking. "Team synergy can't be bottled and distributed like a technical solution. So how do we scale it?"

"By demonstration and experience," Marcia said. "Just like we did for GFP."

She leaned forward. "What if we created integration teams with at least one veteran from the GFP project paired with new practitioners? Let people *experience* the approach rather than just reading about it in a playbook."

"A mentorship model," Robert mused. "That could work. We create connections between experienced practitioners and newcomers, modelling the very approach we're teaching."

"Exactly. We establish connection patterns within our own organisation, not just for our clients."

They spent the next hour refining the structure for the practice group, creating a framework that balanced formal methodology with experiential learning. By the time they finished, the vision had evolved from a traditional practice structure to a more interconnected community of practitioners.

"I'll revise the proposal based on our discussion," Robert said as they wrapped up. "One more thing before you go - Diana has requested a formal board presentation on the connection patterns approach next month. She wants her entire leadership team to understand the methodology that's transforming their organisation."

Marcia felt a flicker of nervousness but also a solid confidence that hadn't been there months ago. "We'll be ready."

As she walked back to her office, Marcia found James waiting with a cup of coffee. "From your expression, I'm guessing Robert shared the practice group news?"

"He did," Marcia confirmed, accepting the coffee gratefully. "It's exciting but also daunting. We're moving from project success to organisational transformation."

"That's been happening for months," James pointed out as they settled into her office. "The GFP work has already influenced how other teams approach integration challenges. Liam's connection patterns library has become one of the most accessed resources in our knowledge base."

"Speaking of Liam," Marcia said, "have you seen the mentoring program he's started with the technical architects?"

James laughed softly. "That might be your most impressive transformation."

"It's not my transformation," Marcia corrected gently. "It's his. That's what happens when people experience the power of team synergy - they naturally want to recreate it."

Her phone vibrated softly - Tessa: *European implementation team just completed successful integration of the German, French, and Dutch payment systems using the asynchronous connection pattern. Client calling it a 'breakthrough moment' in their digital transformation. Liam's pattern library deserves most of the credit.*

Marcia showed the message to James. "This is what gives me confidence about scaling the approach. The patterns work across diverse contexts when implemented with the right mindset."

"Which is exactly what your practice group will need to cultivate," James observed.

As they continued discussing the practice group structure, Marcia felt a growing sense of purpose. She was helping to transform Alpha itself.

Later that afternoon, Marcia gathered with Liam, Noah, and Sarah to discuss the GFP board presentation Diana had requested. Each brought unique perspectives to the planning.

"We should emphasise the measurable outcomes," Sarah suggested. "The authentication improvements alone have reduced customer complaints by 78% since implementation."

"And the cross-border integration metrics from Europe," Noah added. "The payment processing times between acquisitions have improved from daily to hourly."

Liam, who was sketching connection patterns on a

laptop, looked up. "The technical results matter, but I think we should focus equally on the methodology's adaptability across contexts. The patterns we developed for North America evolved in Europe and are now being applied in Asia-Pacific, each time becoming more robust."

Marcia clicked her pen closed, struck again by how naturally they integrated their diverse perspectives. "That's exactly right," she said noting down the ideas.

As they continued planning, Marcia reflected on how far they'd come - not just in the GFP project but in their growth as leaders. With each application, the methodology grew stronger, and their confidence in its transformative potential deepened.

The connection patterns approach was becoming a movement within Alpha - a new way of thinking about integration that recognised the power of diverse perspectives properly connected.

Marcia, once uncertain about her sudden promotion to Delivery Manager, now moved forward with inner confidence, ready to lead this transformation with the team that had made it possible.

✧ ✧ ✧

Marcia leaned over the table, glancing at Noah's slides. "Looks solid," she said, her tone encouraging. "Remember - we're not just showing results, we're showing what's possible when we work this way." Her calm assurance set the tone in the small conference room they'd commandeered to finalise preparations for GFP's board presentation, starting in thirty minutes.

The door opened as Sarah joined them, carrying printouts of the latest connection pattern metrics. "The European implementation team just sent updated data.

Customer experience scores have improved another 12% since the last survey."

"Perfect timing," Marcia said, taking the reports. "These will strengthen our case even further."

As they made final tweaks, Marcia reflected on how naturally they worked together now. Liam fine-tuned the technical architecture slides. Noah polished the cross-cultural implementation narrative. Sarah organised the quality and user experience metrics. Each focused on their areas of expertise while maintaining awareness of how their pieces fit into the larger presentation.

"Five-minute warning," James announced, poking his head through the doorway. "Diana just arrived with the board members. They're settling in now."

Marcia paused outside GFP's boardroom, the hum of conversation audible through the door. A year ago, walking into a room like this - with Diana Thompson, Malcolm Wright, and a dozen regional heads - would have tied her stomach in knots. She caught her reflection in the glass and was struck by what she saw: a calm, self-assured manager in a navy blazer, not the anxious newcomer she once was.

Noah nudged her elbow softly, balancing a stack of handouts. "Ready?" he whispered, a hint of a grin on his face.

Marcia smiled back. "Ready," and this time she truly meant it. The self-doubt that once jabbed at her before big meetings was gone. In its place was increasingly consistent confidence, earned through months of hard-won lessons. Whatever happened in the next hour, she knew she could handle it, especially with her team at her side.

The boardroom fell silent as they entered. Around the massive table sat GFP's most senior leaders - Diana Thompson at the head, with Malcolm Wright beside her. Regional executives from Europe, Asia-Pacific, and North America filled the remaining seats, with Robert representing

Alpha's leadership.

"Thank you for joining us today," Diana began after introductions were complete. "Over the past nine months, Alpha Consulting has partnered with GFP on what began as a troubled implementation project. What emerged was something far more significant - a methodology that has transformed not just our technology integration but how our global operations work together."

She turned to Marcia. "I've asked Marcia and her team to present the connection patterns approach and its impact across our organisation. This isn't just a project update but a strategic discussion about how we approach integration going forward."

Marcia moved to the front of the room, feeling all eyes upon her. "Nine months ago, I inherited a project that was behind schedule, over budget, and facing significant quality issues. Today, I'm here to share not just how we solved those specific challenges but how we developed a methodology that's creating breakthrough results across your global operations."

She clicked to the first slide, showing the dramatic improvements in authentication services, customer experience metrics, and cross-border integration times.

"These results aren't just technical achievements," she continued. "They represent a fundamental shift in how we approach integration - focusing not on components in isolation but on the connections between them."

For the next twenty minutes, Marcia outlined the connection patterns methodology, explaining how it had evolved from addressing specific technical challenges to providing a framework for integration excellence across diverse contexts.

Liam then stepped forward, walking the board through key technical patterns they'd developed - the authentication consolidation that had transformed customer experience, the asynchronous integration pattern that had enabled European payment processing, the cross-border data exchange protocols being implemented in Asia-Pacific.

What continued to impress Marcia most was how Liam engaged the non-technical board members, explaining complex concepts in accessible language while maintaining the precision technical leaders required. Liam was now commanding the room with confident expertise.

Noah followed, highlighting how the methodology adapted to different cultural contexts - the process-oriented approach that resonated in Germany, the relationship-based implementation in France, the harmony-focused adaptation for Japan.

Sarah concluded the technical portion with impact metrics - how each connection pattern had improved quality, reduced maintenance costs, and enhanced customer experience across markets.

As Marcia returned to the front for the closing, she noticed the engaged expressions around the table. Even Malcolm, typically sceptical of consultants, was leaning forward with interest.

"What makes the connection patterns approach different," Marcia emphasised, "isn't just its technical architecture but its recognition that integration excellence emerges when diverse perspectives combine into something greater than individual contributions."

She paused, making eye contact with key board members. "This isn't a methodology that can simply be purchased and implemented. It requires a mindset shift - from viewing integration as technical alignment to seeing it as the strengthening of connections across both systems and organisations."

Diana spoke up. "What you're describing goes beyond

our digital transformation. It addresses one of our greatest challenges as a global organisation - how to function as a unified enterprise while honouring the unique strengths of our regional operations."

"Precisely," Marcia agreed. "The connection patterns approach provides a framework for that balance - strengthening integration while respecting diversity."

The discussion that followed was remarkably strategic, with board members asking thoughtful questions about application beyond technology to organisational structure, governance, and cultural integration.

"What would implementation across our global organisation look like?" asked the Asia-Pacific regional president. "We've seen the benefits in specific markets, but scaling this approach would be complex."

Marcia had anticipated this question. "We recommend a phased approach - establishing connection pattern teams in each region, trained in both the methodology and mindset. These teams would identify critical integration points specific to their markets while maintaining global alignment through a shared framework."

"Essentially creating connection patterns between our regional operations," Diana observed.

"Exactly," Marcia kept her tone even. "The methodology applies to organisational integration just as effectively as it does to technical systems."

As the presentation concluded, Diana turned to her board. "I've been convinced of this approach's value through direct observation. What are your thoughts on expanding implementation across our global operations?"

What followed surprised even Marcia. The board members, typically cautious about large-scale initiatives, expressed unanimous support for expanding the connection patterns approach globally. Even Malcolm acknowledged the compelling results and strategic potential.

"I believe we've found not just a methodology but a framework for how GFP operates as a global organisation," Diana concluded. "I'll work with Marcia and Robert to develop a formal expansion proposal for our next meeting."

When the board members filed out, Diana lingered behind to speak with Marcia and her team. "That was exceptional," she said warmly. "You've transformed how our most senior leaders think about integration - not an easy feat."

"The results made a compelling case," Marcia replied modestly.

"It wasn't just the results," Diana corrected. "It was how your team presented - each bringing distinct expertise while maintaining a unified message. You embodied the very approach you were describing."

As Diana left to join the other executives, Marcia gathered her things. Her team was already moving toward the corridor when James touched her arm, holding her back briefly. There was a shine in his eyes that she rarely saw.

"You nailed it," he said warmly. "I've sat through more 'big initiative' presentations than I can count, but I've never seen a board so energised."

They walked side by side down the hallway, having a private conversation behind the hum of voices.

Marcia felt relief and happiness welling up. "Thank you. I wasn't sure how they'd respond to our approach," she admitted with a laugh. Now that it was over, the nervous energy was washing out of her.

James shook his head in admiration. "I'll confess - I wondered if letting the team share the stage would dilute the message. But it unified it instead." He lowered his voice and added, "Marcia, watching you these past months has taught me a few things. I used to believe a manager always needed to be the smartest person in the room with a polished plan. But you... you've shown it's even more powerful to bring others into the plan, to trust them and even let them lead."

Marcia blinked, contemplating. James was someone she had looked up to for years; hearing that she had influenced his thinking was a milestone she hadn't expected. "That means a lot, James," she replied, her voice quiet but full of gratitude.

He patted her on the upper arm, smiling. "You earned it. And clearly the board agrees - they're not just approving the global rollout; they're excited about it."

This was more than just a project victory; it was proof that leadership built on trust and connection could energise even the most sceptical boardroom. And the mentor who had started her on this journey had just acknowledged he'd learned from how she had travelled it.

✧　✧　✧

Back at Alpha's offices, Robert gathered them in his room for a quick debrief. "Diana called me before you even made it back," he said, looking pleased. "The board wants a comprehensive proposal within two weeks."

"That's faster than we expected," Marcia said, surprised by the timeline.

"Success creates its own momentum," Robert replied. "They're seeing transformative results and want to accelerate. The question is - are we ready to scale this approach at that pace?"

Marcia exchanged glances with her team. Nine months ago, she would have hesitated.

"We're ready," she said simply. "We'll need to expand the core team, establish regional connection pattern practices, and develop training programs - but the foundation is solid."

As they began outlining the expansion approach, Marcia reflected on how differently she now approached leadership challenges. Where once she'd sought certainty before acting, she now moved forward with confident adaptability, trusting both the methodology they'd developed and the team they'd built.

Global implementation would test the team in new ways. But Marcia no longer feared the unknown. She welcomed it as an opportunity to further refine their approach.

✧ ✧ ✧

"Can't we just clone you and your team?" Robert said with a wry smile, gesturing to the whiteboard covered with expansion plans. Two days had passed since the GFP board presentation, and they were deep into planning the global implementation.

Marcia laughed. "If only it were that simple."

The conference room crackled with energy as key leaders from across Alpha collaborated on scaling the connection patterns approach. Liam had commandeered one wall, mapping technical integration points between regional practices. Sarah organised quality standards and verification protocols. Noah sketched cultural adaptation frameworks for diverse markets.

"The challenge isn't the methodology itself," Marcia continued, turning serious. "It's cultivating the mindset that makes it work - the willingness to integrate diverse perspectives rather than defending turf."

From across the table, Michael Winters cleared his throat. "I'll admit it - I didn't believe in this at first." He gave Marcia a small nod, his eyes glinting with reluctant respect. "But you proved me wrong. We now look at things from angles we'd usually ignore."

"It didn't start that way," Liam confessed, surprising those who didn't know his history. "I used to think my technical perspective was the only one that mattered."

"And I kept business and technical concerns too separate," Marcia added. "We learned to integrate our viewpoints through facing real challenges together."

Robert tapped his pen thoughtfully against the table. "So, we need to create conditions where that integration can happen for new practitioners, not just teach them the technical patterns."

"That's right," Marcia agreed. "I've been thinking about expanding the mentorship model where GFP project team members pair with newcomers on real implementation challenges. Just like the approach of expanding the team from GFP Europe integration to Asia-Pacific, but internally."

As they continued refining the expansion approach, Marcia noticed people were naturally building on each other's ideas. Technical leads engaged with cultural specialists. Operations directors found common ground with innovation teams. The connection patterns mindset was already spreading beyond the original group.

By lunchtime, they had outlined a three-phase global implementation:

1. Core Team Expansion: Identifying key practitioners with both technical expertise and collaborative mindsets
2. Regional Practice Establishment: Creating connection pattern teams tailored to market-specific challenges
3. Client Implementation: Applying the methodology to GFP's global integration priorities

"This is ambitious," James observed as they reviewed the timeline. "Establishing regional Alpha practices while simultaneously implementing at GFP will stretch our resources."

"We don't have much choice," Robert replied. "Diana's board approved the approach based on expanding immediately, not waiting for perfect conditions."

Marcia took it in her stride. "We faced the same pressure with the February milestone. Sometimes the timeline forces creative solutions."

"Speaking of creative solutions," Liam interjected, "I've been thinking about how to accelerate knowledge transfer." He pulled up a diagram on his tablet.

"I think Liam's onto something," Marcia said. "We could structure the GFP implementation to serve both client outcomes and practitioner development simultaneously."

They spent the afternoon refining this approach, designing integrated teams that balanced experienced connection pattern practitioners with newcomers across all required specialties. By late afternoon, they had a comprehensive expansion plan that addressed both the immediate GFP implementation and the longer-term development of Alpha's connection patterns practice.

"This feels right," Robert said as they wrapped up. "Not just expanding a methodology but growing a community of practice."

As the group dispersed, Marcia found herself alone with Robert.

"You know," he said thoughtfully, "when I promoted you to take over the troubled GFP project, I had confidence in your abilities, but I never imagined it would lead to this."

"Neither did I," Marcia admitted. "I was just trying to fix a broken project, not create a new methodology."

"That's often how the most valuable innovations

happen," Robert observed. "They emerge from practical problem-solving rather than abstract theorising."

He gathered his materials, then paused at the door. "Diana called earlier. GFP's executive committee has formally approved phases one of global implementation. They want to announce it at their leadership summit next month - with you presenting the vision."

After Robert left, Marcia remained in the conference room, studying the expansion plans covering the whiteboards.

Marcia's phone interrupted her thoughts with a message from Elizabeth Parker: *Diana just shared the expansion plans with me. Ambitious but exactly what GFP needs. You've created something remarkable, Marcia.*

✧   ✧   ✧

The next morning, Marcia found Liam and Noah already working when she arrived.

"We've been thinking about the leadership summit presentation," Noah explained. "If we're asking GFP's global leaders to embrace the connection patterns mindset, we need to demonstrate it in how we present."

"What do you have in mind?" Marcia asked, setting down her coffee.

"Instead of a traditional presentation, we create an experience," Noah suggested. "We design integration challenges that require the leaders to apply connection patterns thinking in real-time."

"An immersive demonstration rather than a passive explanation," Liam added. "Show them the power of integrating diverse perspectives by having them experience it firsthand."

Marcia smiled at their enthusiasm. "That's brilliant. And

perfectly aligned with our expansion approach."

As they began sketching ideas for the leadership summit, Sarah joined them, adding considerations for measuring the experience's effectiveness. Then Tessa arrived with insights about structuring the integration challenges to resonate across different cultural contexts.

Marcia listened at first, then let her focus drift - not out of disinterest, but from a sudden sense of distance, like watching the scene unfold from just outside herself, like she had felt in Singapore.

Watching her team work, Marcia felt a deep satisfaction. A satisfaction that settled in her chest - not just at the success of the project, but at something deeper. Marcia no longer saw leadership as a weight she had to carry alone.

She had discovered the seven hidden powers of effective managers, and in doing so, had reshaped not just the GFP project, not just Alpha's approach to integration - but herself.

✧ ✧ ✧

Two weeks later, the evening sky over Seattle had turned a deep purple as Marcia stood at the windows of Robert's corner office. The impromptu celebration had been his idea - gathering the core team for a quiet moment of acknowledgment before the whirlwind of global implementation fully engulfed them.

"I still remember how terrified I was that first day," she said, accepting a glass of sparkling from James. "Inheriting a project in crisis, a disjointed team, and an impossible deadline."

"Yet here we are," Liam remarked, surprising everyone with his relaxed demeanour. The usually intense developer had shed his hoodie for a casual button-down, his hair slightly more cooperative than usual, hinting at an effort to look the part.

The room held an atmosphere of measured achievement. Robert had kept the gathering small - just the core team that had transformed a troubled project into a global methodology. Liam, Noah, Sarah, Tessa, James, and Marcia - the architects of the connection patterns approach that was reshaping both Alpha and GFP.

"The leadership summit plans are brilliant," Robert said, raising his glass. "Having GFP's executives experience the methodology rather than just hear about it - that's exactly the approach that makes this work so transformative."

"It was Liam and Noah's idea," Marcia acknowledged, nodding toward them. "They recognised that the connection patterns mindset can't just be explained - it has to be experienced."

"Something I wouldn't have understood nine months ago," Liam admitted with surprising candour. "I used to think technical solutions were all that mattered."

Noah turned a palm up, conceding his part. "And I focused too much on people and process without appreciating the technical architecture. We each had pieces of the puzzle - "

"But it was only when we connected them that the full picture emerged," Tessa finished.

Robert looked around the room. "That's the essence of what you've created - not just a methodology but a mindset that transforms how organisations approach complex integration. The board is beyond impressed."

"Speaking of the board," James said, checking his phone. "Diana just confirmed that GFP has approved the *full* budget for global implementation. All three phases, no cuts."

A wave of satisfaction passed through the room. Full funding represented more than just resources - it was validation of the approach they'd developed through months of challenging work.

"Well then," Robert said, raising his glass higher, "to the Connection Patterns Practice Group and the team that made it possible."

As glasses clinked, Marcia felt a moment of perfect clarity. The journey hadn't been easy - from the initial rescue efforts to the innovation sprint, from the European security crisis to the Singapore assessment. Each challenge had tested them in different ways, revealing the powers they needed to develop: the power to convene, to take calculated risks, to see patterns others missed, to maintain presence amid chaos, to drive operational excellence, to own problems completely, and to foster team synergy.

Later, as the small gathering wound down, Marcia found herself standing with Liam by the windows, looking out at Seattle's glittering skyline.

"I almost took that job with GFP," he said quietly.

"I know," Marcia replied. "What made you stay?"

Liam let the question hang, then said, "I realised that what we were building here wasn't just about technical architecture. It was about creating connections - between systems, yes, but more importantly, between people with different perspectives." He gave a small, self-deprecating smile. "Something I'd spent most of my career avoiding."

"Well, I'm glad you stayed," Marcia said sincerely. "Your technical vision has been crucial to the connection patterns approach."

"It's not just my vision anymore," Liam pointed out. "That's what makes it valuable - it's evolved through the integration of diverse perspectives."

As they gathered their things to leave, Robert caught Marcia's attention. "Diana mentioned that Malcolm is finally, fully on board. Apparently, he told the board that the connection patterns approach is 'the most significant methodology advancement he's seen in a decade.'"

Marcia laughed. "From Malcolm, that's practically a love letter."

"Indeed," Robert agreed. "The leadership summit will be the real test - getting all of GFP's regional leaders to embrace it."

"We're ready," Marcia said with steady confidence. "Not because we have everything figured out, but because we've learned how to navigate challenges together."

Walking to her car through the cool evening air, Marcia reflected on the transformation she'd experienced - from reluctant delivery manager to confident leader.

Her mind turned, as it often did, to the work ahead: planning the summit, building regional teams, and scaling their approach. But tonight she let those thoughts drift to the background. Tonight she would simply savour the satisfaction of what they'd already accomplished.

✧ ✧ ✧

The GFP Leadership Summit venue buzzed with activity as executives from across the globe gathered in Singapore's Marina Bay Convention Centre. Floor-to-ceiling windows offered spectacular views of the harbour, but Marcia barely noticed as she made final adjustments to the room setup with Noah and Liam.

"Nervous?" Noah asked, arranging the last of the materials at each table.

"Focused," Marcia replied with a smile. "There's a difference."

Unlike a traditional conference setup with rows of chairs facing a podium, they had transformed the space into collaboration zones. Each area featured round tables with interactive displays, whiteboard surfaces nearby, participant name cards for allocated seating, and carefully designed integration challenges specific to different regions.

"Final tech check," Liam reported, tapping his laptop. "All systems connected. The simulation is ready to run."

Marcia took in the scene. What they'd designed wasn't a presentation but an experience - one that would require GFP's global leaders to apply connection patterns thinking to solve integration challenges in real-time.

"They're arriving," Noah said quietly as the doors opened and executives began to file in.

Diana Thompson entered first, followed by regional presidents, country directors, and technology leaders from across GFP's global operations. Malcolm Wright offered a brief incline of the head to Marcia as he passed, a gesture that would have seemed impossible only months ago.

"Welcome to the Connection Patterns Experience," Diana began once everyone had found their assigned tables. "Rather than tell you about the approach that's transforming our organisation, we've asked Marcia and her team to show you - by having you experience it firsthand."

As Diana yielded the floor, Marcia moved to the centre of the room. This was the moment they'd been preparing for - the official launch of the global implementation that would reshape GFP's approach to integration across all markets.

"For the next three hours," Marcia explained, "you'll face integration challenges modelled on real situations from across GFP's global operations. Each challenge requires connecting diverse perspectives to develop effective solutions."

She gestured to the mixed regional groupings at each table. "You've been deliberately placed with colleagues from different markets and functions. That diversity isn't accidental - it's essential to the connection patterns approach."

The executives exchanged curious glances as Liam stepped forward.

"The simulation is now live," he announced, triggering the interactive displays at each table. "You're facing a global authentication challenge with different regulatory requirements across regions. Your goal isn't standardisation but effective integration that respects regional differences."

What followed was remarkable to watch. Initially, the executives approached the challenges from their specialised perspectives - technical leaders focusing on architecture, regional directors emphasising market differences, operations heads prioritising efficiency. But as they engaged with the simulation, something shifted.

Marcia moved between tables, observing the dynamics. At the Asia-Pacific table, she watched as the Japan country director and the Australian technology lead found unexpected common ground on a regulatory approach. At the European table, a breakthrough emerged when a technical architect incorporated a cultural insight from the French operations director.

"They're getting it," Noah murmured as he joined Marcia. "Not just solving the challenges but experiencing the power of integrated perspectives."

By the midpoint break, the energy in the room had transformed. Executives who typically interacted through formal channels were engaged in animated discussion, building on each other's ideas rather than defending separate positions. The artificial boundaries between regions, functions, and specialties were giving way to collaborative problem-solving.

"This is remarkable," Diana said quietly, joining Marcia as refreshments were served. "I've never seen our leadership team engage like this across regional boundaries."

"It's the power of the connection patterns approach,"

Marcia explained. "When people experience how diverse perspectives strengthen rather than weaken solutions, they naturally seek integration rather than protection."

For the final hour, they increased the complexity, introducing challenges that required coordination across all regional teams. Without prompting, the executives reorganised themselves, creating cross-regional working groups that fluidly shared insights.

When the simulation concluded, Diana called for everyone's attention. "Before we hear from Marcia about what we've just experienced, I'd like your impressions. What did you notice about this approach compared to our typical methods?"

The Asia-Pacific regional president spoke first. "We solved problems we might have struggling with for weeks in just a few hours because we connected perspectives that are usually kept separate."

"The solutions we developed respect regional differences," added the European operations director. "That's been our greatest challenge in previous approaches."

"And the technical architecture is more robust because it incorporated cultural and regulatory considerations from the beginning," observed the technology lead from Latin America. "We usually address those as constraints after the design is complete."

Marcia stepped forward as the discussion continued. "What you've experienced is the essence of the connection patterns approach - integration excellence emerges when diverse perspectives combine into something greater than any individual contribution."

She clicked to a slide showing the global implementation plan. "Over the next six months, we'll establish regional connection pattern practices across GFP's operations, each tailored to your specific integration challenges while maintaining global alignment."

"This isn't just another methodology," Diana emphasised, joining Marcia. "It's a fundamental shift in how we approach integration across our global organisation. Connecting not just systems but perspectives, markets, and teams."

As the summit transitioned to implementation planning sessions, Marcia found a moment to step back and observe. Regional leaders who had jealously guarded their autonomy were now actively seeking connections with colleagues from other markets. Technical directors were engaged with business stakeholders rather than retreating to separate discussions.

"I think we've officially moved beyond project success to organisational transformation," Robert said, appearing beside her. He had flown in that morning to observe the summit. "The board will be more than satisfied."

"The foundation is solid," Marcia agreed. "Now comes the real work of sustaining this approach as we scale."

Later, as the summit concluded, Diana gathered Marcia's team for a brief private moment. "Today you've launched a transformation that will reshape GFP's future. Thank you for showing us a better way forward."

As Marcia looked at her team - Liam, Noah, Sarah, and the others who had joined their journey, she felt a profound sense of accomplishment - as did they all.

Walking out into Singapore's warm evening, a notification from James back in Seattle appeared: *How did it go?*

Beyond expectations, she tapped out in reply. *The global implementation is officially launched. Connection patterns are now part of GFP's DNA.*

The seven powers she had developed through this journey weren't isolated skills but an interconnected system.

Each one strengthened and sharpened the others, creating a deep reservoir she could now draw from instinctively.

As Marcia joined her team for a celebration dinner overlooking Singapore's spectacular skyline, she realised perhaps this was the greatest insight of all: these powers had always been there - hidden, until someone gave them a name, modelled them in action, and showed her how to use them with intent.

Leadership excellence emerged not from raw instinct alone, but from knowing which tool to reach for, even before the need became conscious. And once you see them - really see them - you can't *not* see when they're needed.

Momentum's here - now we have to keep it.

Chapter 10
Momentum Secured

"Welcome back, conquering hero," James said with a smile as Marcia stepped off the elevator. Two days had passed since the triumphant Singapore leadership summit, and Alpha's Seattle office buzzed with energy as news of their success spread throughout the company.

Marcia laughed, adjusting her bag on her shoulder. "Hardly a hero. Just doing my job."

"Your 'just doing my job' has transformed two organisations and created Alpha's signature methodology," James countered, falling into step beside her. "Robert's been fielding calls from the board all morning. Apparently, news of the GFP success is making waves in the consulting world."

The familiar hallways of Alpha felt both unchanged and entirely different after her time in Singapore. As Marcia walked toward her office, she noticed colleagues watching her with new interest, nodding in recognition as she passed. Success, it seemed, altered how people saw you.

"How's the jet lag?" James asked as they reached her door.

"Still catching up with me," she admitted. "Singapore to Seattle is a brutal time shift."

Inside her office, Marcia found a small welcome gift on her desk - a model of the Singapore skyline with a note from Robert: "From troubled project to global transformation. Remarkable journey, even more remarkable leader."

She placed the model on her shelf next to the business card holder Robert had given her when she first became Delivery Manager nine months ago. The contrast between those two moments - the terrified new manager and the confident leader who had just launched a global implementation - could hardly be more striking.

"The Connection Patterns Practice Group is generating significant interest," James reported, as he took a chair across from her desk. "Seven client inquiries already this week, all asking if we can apply the approach to their integration challenges."

"That's encouraging," Marcia said, organising the items on her desk. "But we need to be careful about expansion."

"Which is exactly what Robert said in the leadership meeting yesterday," James settled back, forearms resting on the chair arms, a thoughtful crease forming between his brows. "He's insisting on careful practitioner development before we scale too quickly."

Marcia's phone buzzed with a message from Liam who had stayed on longer: *Back in Seattle. Team gathering at 2 pm to review Singapore outcomes and plan next steps for European implementation.*

"Liam's already planning the next phase," she told James with a smile. "No rest for the weary."

"He's not the only one eager to move forward," James replied. "The European team has been sending daily updates on their implementation progress. They've applied the asynchronous connection pattern to the French payment systems with impressive results."

As James left to attend another meeting, Marcia took a moment to absorb the quiet of her office. The past months had been a whirlwind of activity - from crisis management to innovation sprints, from London security incidents to Singapore leadership summits. Now, briefly back in Seattle before the next phase began, she had a rare moment to reflect.

Her gaze fell on the notebook James had given her at the beginning of her journey - the same one she'd started on her very first day on the GFP project. She opened it, flipping through pages that traced her evolution as a leader. Near the front, she found a page with scrawled worries: *No trust from execs... Team divided... Impossible deadline?* with half a dozen question marks. She could almost feel the stress radiating off the ink. That version of Marcia had felt overwhelmed and underqualified.

She turned to the most recent pages. They were filled with bullet points about practice launch tasks, names of colleagues from three continents, and bold asterisks next to *share lessons learned*. It read more like a playbook than a panic journal. Marcia couldn't help but smile. The problems that once kept her up at night had become case studies she now used to teach others.

Closing the notebook, Marcia exhaled deeply. She allowed herself a brief, satisfying acknowledgement: *I've come a long way.* The nervous new manager from nine months ago was gone. In her place stood someone who had earned the trust of her team and clients - and, more importantly, had learned to trust herself.

A knock at her door interrupted her thoughts. It was Tessa, tablet in hand.

"Sorry to disturb your first day back," she said, "but I thought you'd want to see the latest metrics from the European implementation."

"Never apologise for good news," Marcia replied warmly, gesturing for her to enter. She stood and offered a handshake that lingered just long enough to show real appreciation. "It's good to see you."

Tessa placed the tablet on Marcia's desk, bringing up

charts that showed remarkable improvements in integration quality and processing times. "The connection patterns approach is delivering even better results as the teams gain experience with it," she explained. "They're not just following the methodology; they're enhancing it with their own insights."

"That's exactly what we hoped would happen," Marcia leaned forward a touch, encouragement threading her voice.

As they reviewed the data, Marcia noticed something interesting. "The team composition in Frankfurt has changed," she observed, studying the implementation reports.

"Yes," Tessa confirmed. "They've adapted the structure based on what they learned during the security incident. More cross-functional integration from the start, rather than specialised teams that collaborate later."

"A great adaptation," Marcia said with satisfaction.

Tessa paused at the doorway. "Thanks for trusting me with the change log and the cross-office metrics," she said quietly.

"You earned it," Marcia replied. "You kept it simple, consistent, and visible."

After Tessa left, Marcia spent an hour catching up on emails and reports that had accumulated during her Singapore trip. The sheer volume was daunting, but she tackled it methodically, prioritising items that needed immediate attention.

Among them was a message from Diana Thompson:

Regional directors are already competing for who gets to implement connection patterns first in their markets. You've created something that's transforming GFP from the inside out.

As lunchtime approached, Marcia decided to step out for

fresh air. Seattle's spring was in full bloom, a stark contrast to Singapore's tropical climate. Walking toward her favourite café, she reflected on how her perspective had changed throughout this journey.

Nine months ago, she had carried leadership like a weight - heavy with responsibility, shaped by the belief that success or failure rested entirely on her shoulders. Now, she understood it differently.

She pushed open the door to the café and immediately spotted Nelson at a corner table. The same spot where they'd shared coffee and sketched wild ideas on napkins - one of which had sparked the innovation sprint. Today, he was already halfway through a sandwich, a laptop open beside him.

"Perfect timing," Nelson said, standing to greet her. "I was just thinking about that mad idea we cooked up here back in January. I've been dying to know - how did the sprint go?"

Marcia set her bag down, her tone bright. "Better than either of us could've imagined. It kicked off a chain of momentum we're still riding."

Nelson leaned back, clearly pleased. "So, I get partial credit?"

"You get a lunch and a thank you," she replied, grinning. "Seriously, that conversation changed everything."

They ate as Marcia shared updates from the past several months: how teams had adapted and evolved the methodology, how the European teams had made it their own, and how the Asia-Pacific rollout was revealing new dimensions of the model.

As the conversation wound down, Marcia glanced at the time. The team meeting at 2 pm would start planning the next phase of work, but for now, she lingered a moment longer.

"Thanks again," she said, finishing her tea. "You saw something back then that I hadn't quite found words for yet."

Nelson smiled. "Sometimes all it takes is someone to name it."

✧ ✧ ✧

The conference room buzzed with energy as Marcia's team gathered for their 2 pm meeting. Maps and diagrams from the Singapore summit covered one wall, while implementation plans for Europe and Asia-Pacific filled whiteboards on the others. The faces around the table showed a mix of jet lag and excitement - the aftermath of breakthrough success combined with anticipation for what came next.

"I think we can officially say the connection patterns approach has moved beyond experimental to proven," Marcia began, taking her place at the head of the table. "The question now is how we scale effectively without losing what makes it work."

Liam, looking surprisingly rested despite the long flight from Singapore, pulled up a diagram on the main screen. "I've been thinking about that. The key is maintaining the balance between structured methodology and adaptive mindset."

The diagram showed how the connection patterns library had evolved from initial technical patterns for the February milestone to the comprehensive framework now guiding implementations across multiple regions.

"What works in North America doesn't necessarily work in Europe or Asia," Noah added, gesturing toward his cultural adaptation framework on a side screen. "But the core principles translate remarkably well when we respect local contexts."

"Exactly," Sarah brought up performance metrics from the European implementation. "The German team modified our testing protocols to match their regulatory requirements, but the connection verification approach remains consistent. Results are actually better than our initial implementation."

Marcia watched as her team built on each other's ideas. The synergy they'd developed now operating smoothly without her direction.

"We have a significant opportunity here," she said when the initial updates concluded. "GFP's board has approved the full global implementation budget. Diana reports that regional directors are competing to be first in line."

"I'm not surprised," Tessa commented. "The Singapore summit demonstrated what's possible when regional leaders experience the approach firsthand. Nothing convinces like results they can personally verify."

As they discussed implementation priorities for the next quarter, Marcia noticed Robert hovering outside the conference room. He caught her eye through the glass wall and motioned that he needed a word.

"Take five minutes," she told the team, stepping out to join him in the hallway.

"Sorry to interrupt," Robert said quietly, "but I thought you should know - Alpha's board just approved establishing the Connection Patterns Practice Group as a formal division within the company," He paused to let her absorb the information. "With you as Associate Director."

Marcia blinked in surprise. "That's... un-expected." Marcia's leadership in establishing this practice was now being officially recognised.

"Success creates its own momentum," Robert said, approval unmistakable. "They want to announce it at next week's company meeting. The GFP contract alone justifies the investment, and the seven client inquiries this week demonstrate broader market potential."

"What about the GFP implementation? I need to stay involved."

"You will be," Robert assured her. "The new role gives you authority to shape how we implement globally, not just at GFP. You'll need to build leadership teams for each region, of course."

As Marcia processed this unexpected development, she found herself thinking not about herself but about her team. "Liam should lead the technical architecture practice," she said. "He's ready for formal leadership, even if he might not realise it yet."

Robert's approving look deepened into a knowing half-smile, the kind that suggested he'd seen this coming. "And Noah for cross-cultural integration. Sarah for quality verification. You're already thinking about the team structure."

"They've earned it," Marcia said simply. "None of this would exist without their contributions."

Back in the conference room, Marcia decided to hold the news until the end of their planning session. The team was deeply engaged in mapping implementation priorities, with Liam and Noah debating the sequencing of Asian markets while Sarah and Tessa refined the quality verification approach.

"Japan presents unique challenges with their legacy mainframe systems," Liam was explaining, "but the asynchronous connection pattern we developed for Europe provides a starting framework."

"We'll need to adjust for cultural factors," Noah countered. "The Japanese approach to consensus decision-making affects how we structure implementation teams."

"Which is exactly why we've built adaptability into the

methodology," Marcia interjected. "The patterns provide structure while allowing for cultural and technical variation."

By the time they reached the end of their agenda, the implementation roadmap for the next six months had taken clear shape. Regional teams would extend the European success model, with core patterns adapted to local contexts. Knowledge transfer would happen through integrated teams rather than formal training programs, allowing the approach to evolve through application.

"Before we wrap up," Marcia said, "I have some news to share." She explained Robert's announcement about the new practice division and her role as Associate Director.

The team's reactions were immediate and supportive.

"About time," Liam said matter-of-factly. "The methodology deserves formal recognition within Alpha's structure."

"This opens up career paths for connection pattern practitioners," Sarah observed. "A dedicated division creates opportunities for advancement."

"And gives us more influence in shaping Alpha's approach to complex integration," Noah added. "We can establish standards across the company."

Marcia smiled at their enthusiasm. "There will be leadership roles for each of you, of course. This isn't just my success - it's something we've built together."

As the meeting concluded and people began to disperse, Liam lingered behind, seemingly hesitant to speak.

"Something on your mind?" Marcia asked.

"I've been offered the Technical Director role at GFP," he said, surprising her. "Xavier renewed his offer after the Singapore summit. He wants me to lead their internal connection patterns practice."

For a moment, Marcia felt a pang of concern. Losing Liam would be a significant blow to their team. But she quickly realised that this represented success in a different form - the methodology spreading through GFP's internal leadership, not just Alpha's consulting approach.

"That's a fantastic opportunity," she said sincerely. "You'd be ideally positioned to ensure the connection patterns approach becomes embedded in their organisation."

Liam studied her reaction. "I haven't decided yet. There's important work to do here too."

"The methodology is designed to create connections across organisational boundaries," Marcia pointed out. "Having you lead from within GFP while we support from Alpha would strengthen those connections, not weaken them."

"I hadn't thought of it that way," Liam admitted. "As extending the patterns, not breaking them."

That evening, as Marcia prepared to leave the office she paused, fingertips resting on the silver card holder Robert had given her when she first became Delivery Manager. On that rainy day, she could never have imagined how far the role would take her. Tonight, she could.

A small, knowing smile touched her lips as she remembered the steadiness Robert had shown throughout the project. It wasn't until after the Singapore summit that she learned he had already spoken with Xavier, quietly, after that first unexpected offer to Liam.

"Did you ever talk to Xavier about the offer?" she'd asked, unable to hide the lingering question.

"Of course," Robert replied evenly. "I reminded him that consultants aren't currency to be traded. But in the end..." He paused, calm and unhurried. "Liam will make his own decision. That's how it should be."

She had been struck then by how lightly Robert carried the conversation. He hadn't panicked, hadn't confronted Liam, hadn't tried to force an outcome. Instead, he treated it as part of the natural talent fluidity in their world - something to be managed with respect rather than fear.

Looking back now, she saw the real lesson: leadership wasn't about blocking every threat in the moment, but about shaping the field so people could see their best path clearly. Robert had played the long game, steady and invisible, like a chess master who moved only when the board required it.

Her phone vibrated - Diana: *Just heard about Alpha's new practice division. Congratulations! This partnership continues to exceed expectations on both sides.*

As Marcia headed home through Seattle's evening traffic, she reflected on the unexpected ways this journey had unfolded.

There would be new challenges as she built a formal division around the methodology they'd created. But those challenges felt different now - opportunities to extend what they'd created rather than obstacles to overcome.

✧   ✧   ✧

The company-wide meeting was scheduled for 11 am, but Marcia arrived at the office by 7 am. She wanted quiet time to organise her thoughts before the announcement of the new Connection Patterns Practice Group became official.

As she arranged materials in her office - now adorned with mementos from their journey, including the Singapore skyline model and a framed photo of the team from the leadership summit - she heard a knock at her door.

"You're here early," Robert said, resting casually against the doorframe. "Nervous about the announcement?"

"Not nervous," Marcia replied with a smile. "Just making sure we're set up for success from day one."

Robert studied her whiteboard, taking in the implementation plans. "You've come a long way from the day when I handed you the GFP project."

"We've come a long way," Marcia corrected gently. "None of this would exist without the support you and James provided along the journey."

As they discussed final details for the announcement, Marcia's phone pinged - Liam: *Decision made. Accepting GFP's Technical Director role. Will strengthen connection patterns from the inside. Let's discuss transition plans.*

She showed the message to Robert, who took it in, thoughtful. "That's actually perfect. Having Liam inside GFP creates a direct connection between our organisations. The methodology working as intended."

"My thoughts exactly," Marcia agreed. "Though we'll need to adjust our technical leadership plans."

By 10:50 am, the large conference room was filling with Alpha employees from across the company. The buzz of conversation reflected the rumours that had been circulating all week - something significant was about to be announced.

James found Marcia near the entrance. "Ready for the spotlight?"

"As ready as I'll ever be," she replied. "Though I'm still getting used to the idea of running a whole practice division instead delivery teams."

"The title changes, but the core work remains the same," James said wisely. "Creating connections that strengthen the whole system."

At exactly 11:00 am, Robert called the meeting to order. The room quieted as he took his place at the front.

"Nine months ago," he began, "Alpha inherited a troubled project that many considered unsalvageable. Today, I'm pleased to announce that what emerged from that challenge has become our company's signature approach to complex integration."

He gestured toward a screen showing the connection

patterns framework. "The methodology developed by Marcia and her team has transformed not just the GFP project but how both our organisations approach integration across boundaries of all kinds."

A ripple of interest moved through the room as Robert continued. "The board has unanimously approved establishing the Connection Patterns Practice Group as a formal division within Alpha, with Marcia as Associate Director."

Applause broke out, surprisingly enthusiastic. Marcia realised that news of their success had spread throughout the company, creating genuine appreciation for what they'd accomplished.

"This represents more than just a new service offering," Robert explained as the applause subsided. "It's a fundamental shift in how we approach complex integration challenges - focusing on the connections between components rather than the components themselves."

He invited Marcia to join him at the front. As she moved through the crowd, colleagues nodded in recognition and respect - a far cry from the scepticism that had greeted her early efforts nine months ago.

"The connection patterns approach wasn't created in isolation," Marcia said when she reached the front. "It emerged from real-world challenges and the integration of diverse perspectives."

She described how the methodology had evolved from addressing specific technical problems to providing a framework for integration excellence across diverse contexts.

As she outlined the structure of the new practice group, Marcia noticed many taking notes - an encouraging sign that they saw value in the approach beyond the GFP success story.

"We'll be establishing regional practices led by

experienced practitioners," she explained. "And we'll be recruiting both from within Alpha and externally for those with the right combination of technical expertise and collaborative mindset."

When the formal presentation concluded, Robert opened the floor for questions. The first came from Michael Winters. He leaned forward with an expression Marcia now recognised as deliberate rather than doubtful.

"How does one know if they have the right mindset for this approach?" he asked, his tone inviting rather than challenging. "It seems to require a different way of thinking than traditional consulting."

Marcia caught the subtle shift - Michael wasn't asking for himself. He already knew the answer. He was giving her the chance to set the tone for the discussion.

"That's an excellent question," Marcia replied, taking his lead. "The connection patterns practitioner isn't just technically skilled but actively seeks diverse perspectives to strengthen solutions. They see boundaries as opportunities for integration rather than lines of separation."

She looked around the room. "Many of you already have this mindset, even if you haven't labelled it that way. It's about valuing the space between specialties as much as the specialties themselves."

More questions followed - about implementation methodology, client selection criteria, and career paths within the new division. Marcia answered each one directly, drawing on years of hard-earned wisdom at Alpha.

As the meeting transitioned to a casual reception, colleagues approached Marcia individually, expressing interest in the new practice group. Some shared integration challenges they were facing on current projects, seeing potential applications for the connection patterns approach.

"You've created quite a following," James observed as

the reception continued. "People are genuinely excited about the methodology."

"It resonates because it addresses a universal challenge," Marcia replied. "Everyone has experienced the pain of disconnection - between departments, disciplines, or organisations. The connection patterns approach offers a bridge."

✧ ✧ ✧

Later that afternoon, Marcia met with Liam to discuss his transition to GFP.

"Xavier wants me to build an internal connection patterns practice," Liam explained. "GFP sees this as strategic, not just project-specific."

"That aligns perfectly with our vision," Marcia kept her voice even, assured. "The methodology becomes more robust when it's implemented from both sides of the client-consultant relationship."

They discussed knowledge transfer, ongoing collaboration structures, and how to maintain the technical integrity of the approach as it expanded.

"I never expected to be taking a leadership role," Liam admitted as their meeting concluded.

"We've all grown through this journey," Marcia said with a smile. "The connection patterns approach transformed not just the project, but everyone involved with it."

As the day drew to a close, Marcia found herself alone in her office, reflecting on how rapidly everything was changing. The practice group would officially launch next week. Liam would transition to GFP the week after. Implementation teams were already forming for the next phase of global expansion.

Amidst this whirlwind of activity, she opened her

notebook - the one James had given her at the start of her delivery manager journey - and began a new entry:

First Day as Associate Director
Can't quite believe I'm writing that title down.
Not because I didn't earn it - but because of how much has changed.
This isn't about solving everything myself anymore. It's about enabling others.
What I'm most proud of: seeing people like Liam, Tessa, and Sarah step into bigger versions of themselves.
That's the best part of the job now - growing people alongside me.

As Marcia closed her notebook, she looked out at the Seattle skyline now bathed in evening light. She couldn't wait to see what her new team would create together next.

✧   ✧   ✧

One month after the official launch of the Connection Patterns Practice Group, Marcia stood in the doorway of what had once been her office. The space looked different now - the walls adorned with framework diagrams, the whiteboard covered with implementation timelines for new clients, the desk organised with a precision that wasn't her style.

"Having second thoughts about the promotion?" James asked, joining her in the doorway.

Marcia shook her head, a brief laugh in her voice. "Not at all. Just appreciating how quickly things evolve." She gestured inside the office. "Kelly's already made it her own."

Kelly Yamamoto, the newly appointed Delivery Manager, assigned to GFP's North American account, was due back from a client meeting any minute. Marcia had handpicked her from Alpha's financial services division -

recognising in the younger consultant the key combination of technical insight and people skills that the role required.

"She's a good choice," James said, reading her thoughts. "She reminds me of someone else who stepped up to rescue a troubled project not so long ago."

"Let's hope her journey is slightly less dramatic than mine was," Marcia laughed.

They turned as footsteps approached - Kelly walking briskly down the hallway, tablet in hand and purpose in her stride.

"Sorry I'm late," she said, slightly breathless. "The client meeting ran over. They had a million questions about the authentication implementation."

"No apology needed," Marcia assured her. "How did it go?"

"Really well," Kelly replied, ushering them into her office. "Once I showed them the performance metrics from GFP's implementation, they stopped questioning the approach and started asking how quickly we could get started."

Marcia caught the shift in Kelly's tone, noting how confidently Kelly discussed the connection patterns methodology. After just four weeks of immersion, she spoke about the approach with the conviction of personal experience rather than borrowed knowledge.

"You've clearly made the framework your own," Marcia observed as they settled into chairs. She noted a sleek silver business card holder on Kelly's desk and smiled.

"It resonates with how I naturally think," Kelly admitted. "I've always been frustrated by how traditional methodologies create artificial boundaries between technical and business concerns."

"That's exactly why I recommended you for this role," Marcia said. "The connection patterns approach works best when led by people who intuitively think in terms of integration rather than separation."

They spent the next hour reviewing Kelly's transition plan. The GFP North American operations were now stable, with the February milestone implementation successfully completed and the connection patterns approach firmly established. Kelly's role was to maintain this foundation while supporting expansion to new clients.

"I have one concern," Kelly said as they wrapped up. "Liam's departure to GFP leaves a significant gap in our technical leadership. He was the architect of many core patterns."

"It's a valid concern," Marcia acknowledged. "But remember that Liam's move actually strengthens our connection to GFP rather than weakening it. And Sarah has stepped up impressively to lead the technical documentation effort."

"Plus," James added, "the methodology is designed to evolve through application across diverse contexts. New practitioners will contribute their own insights, making the patterns more robust over time."

As their meeting concluded, Marcia stood by her old window, looking out at the familiar Seattle skyline. "When I inherited this role ten months ago, I was terrified of failing. The project seemed impossible, the team was fractured, and the deadline was imminent."

"And now?" Kelly asked.

"Now I understand that leadership isn't about having perfect answers from the start. It's about building teams that find them together."

She turned to face Kelly directly. "That's what I hope for you - not that you'll avoid challenges, but that you'll discover how those challenges reveal possibilities you couldn't have imagined at the outset."

Later that afternoon, Marcia led her first official strategy meeting as Associate Director of the Connection Patterns Practice Group. The conference room was filled with practice leaders from across Alpha - some veterans from the original GFP project, others new recruits drawn by the approach's growing reputation.

"We stand at an important inflection point," Marcia began. "What started as a project-specific solution has evolved into Alpha's signature approach to complex integration. Our challenge now is to scale without losing what makes the methodology effective."

Noah, recently appointed as Cultural Integration Lead, brought up the implementation map on the main screen. "We're now active in twelve countries across three continents. Each implementation teaches us something new about how the patterns adapt to different contexts."

"Which is exactly as it should be," Marcia noted. "The methodology isn't static - it evolves through application."

Tessa stood at the whiteboard, sketching a simplified flow of how user feedback from regional pilots was being looped into the design phase. "We're seeing early signs that integration quality correlates strongly with how soon local teams are involved in connection mapping - not just process owners, but frontline contributors."

Sarah, now officially the QA Lead, nodded thoughtfully. "That makes sense. The earlier we embed context into test cases, the fewer blind spots show up downstream. Most defects lately have been gaps in understanding, not gaps in logic."

"So, we're not just testing the system - we're testing alignment," Tessa said.

"Exactly. And alignment's a moving target," Sarah replied, circling one of the feedback loops. "I've started having my team attend the local alignment sessions before they write test scenarios. It's adding a half-day up front, but saving two days of rework later."

Marcia, didn't interrupt. This was exactly what she'd hoped for when they restructured the team - leaders who could challenge each other constructively, grounded in a shared understanding of the work.

"I'll update the connection guidelines to reflect that," Tessa said, finding her stride in her new Business Connection Architect role. "Cross-discipline presence during early mapping - it's more than optional now."

Sarah raised her coffee. "I'll drink to that."

As the team discussed expansion priorities, Marcia observed how naturally they integrated diverse perspectives. Technical architects built on cultural insights. Quality specialists contributed to governance frameworks. Recent recruits offered fresh viewpoints that seasoned practitioners incorporated without defensiveness.

Halfway through the meeting, Marcia's phone vibrated with a message from Diana Thompson: *Just met with Liam and Xavier. The internal practice is taking shape. Thank you for helping us get here.*

Marcia shared the message with the group. "This is what success looks like - when the methodology becomes embedded in the client's own approach, not just our consulting engagement."

As the meeting continued, Marcia found herself thinking about the journey that had brought them here.

None of it had been planned. The methodology had emerged organically through their efforts to solve real problems.

As Marcia prepared to leave for the day, she found James waiting by the elevator.

"Robert mentioned you might be visiting London next month," he said as they descended to the lobby. "Checking in on the European practice?"

"That, and meeting with potential clients who've heard about our approach," Marcia confirmed. "The connection patterns methodology is generating significant interest, especially for cross-border mergers and acquisitions."

Outside, the evening was unusually clear, the setting sun casting a golden glow across Elliott Bay. As they walked toward the parking garage, James asked, "Does it feel strange, stepping back from direct management to lead the practice group?"

"It did at first," Marcia admitted. "But I've realised that the same principles apply - creating conditions where diverse perspectives can combine effectively, just at a larger scale."

"And Kelly?"

"She's going to be excellent," Marcia said with confidence. "She has the right combination of technical understanding and people skills. And she naturally thinks in terms of connections rather than boundaries."

As they reached their cars, James paused. "You know, when Robert first suggested promoting you to rescue the GFP project, I was concerned it might be too much too soon. I've never been happier to be proven wrong."

Marcia waved it off. "It wasn't just me. It was the team we built, the methodology we developed together, and the support you and Robert provided throughout."

"True," James acknowledged. "But it took your leadership to make that possible. You never made it about you - you gave ownership to your people."

Driving home on autopilot, Marcia reflected on how completely her perspective had changed over the past ten months. The seven powers she'd developed along the way weren't separate tools but part of one integrated approach.

As she pulled into her driveway, she felt not an ending but a surge of momentum - progress secured, with the promise of more to come. The foundation was strong, the direction clear, and she couldn't wait to see how far they could go.

✧ ✧ ✧

Marcia stood at the podium, looking out over the crowd gathered for Alpha's annual client summit. The ballroom of Seattle's Grand Hotel was filled to capacity - executives and technology leaders from across industries, all drawn by the growing reputation of the connection patterns approach.

"Integration excellence," she began, "isn't about perfect components or flawless plans. It emerges when we strengthen the connections between diverse perspectives, technologies, and organisations."

Six months had passed since the launch of the Connection Patterns Practice Group. Alpha's signature methodology had grown, with implementations now spanning fifteen countries and twenty-three major clients.

"The journey that brought us here wasn't straightforward," Marcia continued, clicking to a slide showing the original GFP project timeline with its impossible February milestone. "It began with a crisis - a project behind schedule, over budget, and failing to meet client expectations."

She paused, allowing the audience to absorb the familiar scenario. The ballroom stayed hushed, then a ripple of nods moved across the room - many had faced similar challenges in their own organisations.

"At first, we didn't realise we were uncovering anything special," Marcia said, looking out at the sea of conference attendees. "In fact, some of the things we tried felt almost too simple or even counterintuitive."

Her mind flashed back to that seemingly basic daily

stand-up that had jump-started trust, and the risky three-day sprint that had achieved more than months of grinding. She let the silence stretch a beat, then continued.

"But as our story unfolded, we discovered that the greatest powers a manager can tap into aren't about technical wizardry or authority." She paused, meeting a few sceptical eyes in the crowd, and offered a small, knowing smile. "They turned out to be things that were there all along, hidden in plain sight - bringing the right people together, asking candid questions, listening, learning, and giving others ownership of the solution. None of it was magic. It was about seeing old challenges in a new light."

A murmur of agreement spread across the room. Marcia saw heads tilting as the point landed.

"Each time we used one of these 'hidden powers,' it felt surprising because it went against the grain of how we normally operate under pressure. Slowing down to listen when you're behind schedule, admitting a mistake to your client, letting your team lead in areas where they know more than you - those aren't typical management instincts. But they made all the difference."

"That crisis became an opportunity not through revolutionary technology or individual brilliance, but through a shift in how we approached integration - focusing not on components in isolation but on the connections between them."

As Marcia outlined the methodology that had emerged from that initial challenge, she noticed familiar faces in the audience. Diana Thompson sat at a front row table, nodding occasionally. Robert and James watched from the side of the room, quiet pride in their expressions. Even Malcolm Wright was present, his traditional scepticism replaced by genuine interest.

"The connection patterns approach isn't just a technical

framework," Marcia emphasised. "It's a mindset that recognises integration excellence emerges when diverse perspectives combine into something greater than any individual contribution."

She clicked to a slide showing results from across implementations - dramatic improvements in system performance, user experience, and business outcomes. "These aren't isolated successes. They represent a consistent pattern across diverse contexts - from financial services to healthcare, from North America to Asia."

As she concluded her keynote, Marcia introduced the panel that would follow - practitioners from different organisations who had implemented the connection patterns approach in their own contexts. Kelly Yamamoto would represent the GFP implementation. A healthcare CIO would discuss how they'd applied the methodology to electronic medical record integration. A manufacturing executive would share how connection patterns had transformed their supply chain systems.

"What you'll hear from these leaders isn't a single standard implementation," Marcia explained. "Each has adapted the approach to their specific challenges while maintaining the core principle - strengthening connections across both technical and human systems."

As applause filled the room Marcia stepped away from the podium. As she descended the stage stairs to return to her table, Diana approached.

"Impressive turnout," she commented, gesturing toward the packed ballroom. "Word has spread about what you've created."

"What we've created," Marcia corrected gently. "The GFP project was where it all began."

Diana's voice held a note of approval. "Have you spoken with Liam recently?"

"We have a standing weekly call," Marcia said. "The cross-organisation practice leaders meet to ensure the methodology continues evolving consistently."

"He's transformed our internal approach to integration," Diana said. "The connection patterns practice he's built has become central to our global strategy."

They moved to a quiet corner as the panel discussion began, Kelly confidently explaining how the methodology had transformed GFP's customer experience.

"I've been thinking about our first meeting," Diana said. "When you inherited that troubled project and promised honest assessment rather than comfortable fiction."

"I remember being terrified," Marcia admitted with a laugh. "But unable to pretend the situation was better than it was."

"That honesty was the foundation of everything that followed," Diana observed. "You created space for real solutions instead of temporary patches. You and your team never passed the buck."

As the summit continued through the day, Marcia moved between sessions, connecting with clients and colleagues. The practice group she now led had grown to sixty consultants across three continents, with demand still outpacing their capacity to deliver.

✧   ✧   ✧

That evening, Alpha hosted a private dinner for key clients and practice leaders. As servers cleared the main course, Robert stood to offer a toast.

Robert clinked his glass, waiting for the table to quiet. "I don't need to make any announcements tonight," he said with a smile. "You've all already heard the news about Marcia's new role. What I do want to do is acknowledge what made it possible. When our work with GFP hit its toughest stretch, Marcia stepped in. She steadied the team, rebuilt confidence, and transformed a difficult engagement into one of our strongest partnerships."

He raised his glass toward her. "That's the kind of leadership that earns trust - not just inside Alpha, but with the clients who matter most. Here's to Marcia."

A warm round of applause rippled around the table, with several GFP leaders lifting their glasses in agreement. Marcia felt her face flush, humbled by the praise. This time it wasn't about an announcement or a title - it was about being seen, in front of clients and colleagues alike, as the leader she had become.

As the room settled, James lifted his glass lightly in salute. "I have to thank you, Marcia. You've reminded me of something I'd almost forgotten - that even those of us mentoring others can still learn. Watching you navigate this project has changed how I think about leadership."

Coming from James, in front of the group, the words struck deep. Her cheeks warmed further, pride welling in her chest.

In the toasts that followed, as others began to chime in, Sarah raised her glass with a grin. "To the project that reminded us why we love this work," she said, drawing warm laughter.

After dinner, as conversations flowed around the room, Marcia found a quiet moment with James near the windows overlooking Seattle's twinkling skyline.

"Do you remember that first coffee at Analog, just after I was appointed Delivery Manager?" she asked.

"Vividly," James smiled. "You were determined, but unsure - wondering if you had what it took to rescue a project that looked unsalvageable."

"I was convinced I'd be fired within weeks," Marcia said

with a laugh. "The February milestone seemed impossible. The team was fractured. I didn't even know where to start."

"And now look," James gestured toward the room, alive with conversation and possibility. "You haven't just succeeded. You've built something that's changing how organisations think about transformation."

Marcia shook her head slightly. "It didn't come from me alone. It came from all of us."

"Which is exactly what made you the right leader," James said. "You didn't solve the problem. You created the conditions where people could."

As the evening drew to a close, Marcia was gathering her things when Diana approached.

"Before you go," she said, "I wanted to let you know - the GFP board reviewed our transformation efforts last month. The connection patterns approach was named the single most valuable investment we've made in years."

Marcia's eyebrows lifted. "That's good to hear."

"They've asked me to explore how we might apply it more broadly - across org design, talent strategy, even post-merger integration. It's bigger than tech now."

Marcia's eyes warmed. "It always was. We just needed the right language - and the right proof."

As she stepped out into the crisp night air, Marcia felt her satisfaction settle into something deeper: a readiness.

Leadership, she had come to realise, wasn't about control - it was about unlocking the strength that exists between people.

And the seven hidden powers? They weren't tools to carry alone. They were shared keys - to systems, to teams, to transformation itself.

As she drove home beneath the stars, Marcia wasn't sure what the next chapter would bring.

But she knew this: the biggest changes hadn't come from

grand gestures, but from daily habits, deliberate choices, and quiet conviction.

She didn't need a map anymore. She had a compass.

And for the first time, it truly felt like enough.

Epilogue

- Two Months Later -

The cohort was small - six new managers in a quiet training room. Kelly stood at the back with a notebook, watching closely; today wasn't just training, it was a handover. Marcia would model the session, and next quarter Kelly would run it herself.

"You've read the pre-read," Marcia said, "but this bit doesn't fit in a report." She drew a long line, then split it into three, and listed seven levers below them.

Stabilise →	**Accelerate** →	**Sustain**
Convene	Calculated Risk	Ownership
Presence	Perspective	Team Synergy
Process		

"Every recovery we've lived moved through these three phases," she said. "We didn't start with names. We started with pain. The names came later."

"These weren't theories. We discovered them through experience."

She tapped the first segment. "**Stabilise**: we made the work visible and met on purpose. That was **Convene**. When panic hit, we borrowed each other's nervous systems - **Presence**. And we replaced heroics with small, repeatable rituals - **Process**."

"**Accelerate**: once steady, we pushed safely. **Calculated Risk** gave us guardrails - what we would try, what we wouldn't, and how we'd roll back. **Perspective** kept us from winning locally and losing globally."

"**Sustain**: speed sticks when someone owns the outcome

- **Ownership** - and when the culture makes people want to stay - **Team Synergy**."

She paused. "If one is missing, you feel it. No **Convene**? Decisions scatter. No **Presence**? Panic eats time. No **Process**? You ship on luck. Skip **Calculated Risk**? You stall. Lose **Perspective**? Local wins harm the whole. Fuzzy **Ownership**? Tasks bounce and die. Ignore **Team Synergy**? You burn bright, then burn out."

"We didn't solve everything at once. We triaged, then healed, then built strength." She underlined a final line at the bottom of the board:

Small things. Done well. Every day.

She capped the marker.

Jason, a manager in the front row raised a hand. "Where do we start?"

"Map where you are on the line," Marcia said, tapping the board. "Then fix the missing power first. Make it visible. Make it weekly. And don't skip phases because you're impatient," she glanced at the students. "The work remembers shortcuts."

The group laughed softly. Someone snapped a photo of the board.

"You'll build your own version of this," she said. "That's the point." She stepped back from the whiteboard. "Alright - let's talk about your teams."

✧ ✧ ✧

The last of the workshop attendees drifted out of the Seattle training room, leaving behind half-erased whiteboards and the faint smell of coffee.

Marcia stacked the name badges while Kelly wiped down the table beside her and tucked her *facilitator notebook* into her bag.

"Full circle," Kelly said, smiling. "Watching you model it was gold."

Marcia laughed. "You're ready. You reset the room by bringing us back on task and parked the derailment by assigning an owner and a date."

Kelly nodded toward the doorway, where a young delivery manager lingered, laptop tucked under his arm.

"He's got potential," she murmured.

Marcia motioned him in. "Come on in, Jason - what's on your mind? "

He hesitated, still half in the hall. "I tried using the cross-office cadence you showed us, but New York keeps drifting off schedule. I can't keep both sides aligned."

Marcia spoke instinctively. "Start by listening - listen first, solutions later. You're trying to manage certainty; try managing rhythm instead. Focus on the people, not the plan."

Jason frowned, thinking it through. "Easier said than done."

"You'll get there," Marcia said. "Remember when you were coding all night with your iPhone buzzing and Messenger lighting up on the second screen? You debugged systems then. Now you're just debugging humans - same logic, more variables."

Jason chuckled, the tension easing from his shoulders. "That's fair. Thanks, Marcia."

As he left, Kelly turned back with a grin. "You really did know him back when."

Marcia smiled. "I did. And watching him grow reminds me why this matters."

Kelly laughed, tilting her head. "You never stop, do

you?"

Marcia shook her head. "Neither did James."

She glanced at the empty chairs, picturing the next group who would sit there - the next questions, the next breakthroughs.

Leadership, she realised, wasn't a finish line. It was a relay - each person learning, running their stretch, then passing the baton forward.

And somewhere out there, the next runner was already stepping onto the track.

You've made it to the end - but Marcia's story is only part of the journey.

Why not take a moment to help the next manager find this book?

If a sentence or two from you could give another leader the clarity or encouragement they need right now… would you write it?

To leave a review

💬 Go *to your Amazon Orders* → *find this book* → *"Write a Product Review"*

Thank you for reading.
And for leading beyond your own team.

With gratitude,

Stephen J. McIntyre

About the Author

Stephen J. McIntyre began writing *The 7 Hidden Powers of Effective Managers* in 2018 under the working title Magic for Managers. The original idea was simple: that great managers seem to have "special powers" - the ability to create alignment, spark momentum, and influence outcomes - often in subtle, invisible ways. Powers like conjuring clarity from chaos, possessing ownership of problems, and charming people into alignment. Before long, the metaphor expanded into a deeper reflection on leadership, influence, and the shift from being a leader to becoming a manager.

Stephen realised something important: to reach more people with the message, he needed to wrap these ideas inside a story. The result is this business parable - a practical tale woven with subtle metaphors, crafted to speak to first-time managers, mid-career professionals, and anyone navigating the complex transition from technical doer, to trusted leader, to enlightened manager.

Professionally, Stephen has worked at the intersection of software, strategy, and transformation. He's led cross-functional teams in multinational product companies and guided post-acquisition system assimilation across global offices. He's helped hardware-first companies evolve into software-led enterprises and supported national organ-isations - including universities and fast-scaling businesses - through strategic IT and asset management transformations.

The 7 Hidden Powers of Effective Managers was written as part of Stephen's own transition: from a team leader focused on culture and influence, to a delivery manager responsible for scale, structure, and cross-site coordination. The lessons captured here reflect not only what he learned - but what he wished someone had told him earlier.

The turning point came when three friends, within

months of each other, were promoted into leadership roles. Each of them called Stephen with the same question: *What do I do now?*

Instead of giving a checklist, he sent them an early version of the manuscript. One friend read it over a weekend and applied it in his new role. When checking in a week later, the feedback was: *This was really useful. My boss says there's more order, and productivity is increasing.*

That moment reframed the purpose of the book. It wasn't just a collection of insights - it was a way to pay it forward - to share the insights learned from mentors, from experience on the job, and from self-realisation.

Stephen lives in Auckland with his wife and daughter, and believes great leadership is less about having all the answers - and more about building teams that find them together.

Other Books by Stephen J. McIntyre

Lead With Confidence™ Series

Book 1 - *Team Leaders Toolbox*

Book 2 - *The 7 Hidden Powers of Effective Managers*

Book 3 - *Delivery Mindset* (coming soon)

Book 4 - *Leading Change* (coming soon)

Book 5 - *Lessons Learned* (coming soon)

The 7 Hidden Powers™ Framework

1. The Power to Convene
    (decisions have a home; using meetings strategically)

2. The Power of Calculated Risk
    (speed, inside guardrails; controlled risk-taking to achieve breakthroughs)

3. The Power of Perspective
    (Street → Skyline → Systems; identifying underlying patterns)

4. The Power of Presence
    (steady is faster; leadership presence and influence)

5. The Power of Process
    (habits that survive bad days; operational excellence through attention to detail)

6. The Power of Ownership
    (one owner, one outcome; accountability without blame)

7. The Power of Team Synergy
    (edges that lock, not clash; enabling collective intelligence)

Resources

Bring the story to life with editable templates and practical tools inspired by *The 7 Hidden Powers of Effective Managers*. These resources are designed to help you apply what Marcia used: right in your own team.

1-Page Summary: The 7 Hidden Powers™
Quick reference guide for applying each power.

Power-by-power Toolkits
- **The Power to Convene**
  - **Calendar as a Decision Engine** (meeting objective, pre-read, FYI → Async)
  - **Decision Log** (decision id) and examples
  - **Momentum Board & Rule of Three** - setup & Daily use (*Today* | *Blocked* (Owner and When) | *Cleared*)
- **The Power of Calculated Risk**
  - **Controlled Chaos Pre-Brief** (30 min) - goal, risk budget, rollback signal, owner, Go/Test/No-Go
  - **Rollback Guard checklist** (signal, threshold, owner, action)
- **The Power of Perspective**
  - **Perspective Reset: Street → Skyline → Systems** (3 one-liner prompts)
- **The Power of Presence**
  - **Presence Under Fire** (10 min) - still room, facts, narrow path, observer, timebox

- **The Power of Process**
  - **S.T.E.A.D.Y. (Mini-OS)** - Stand-ups, Triage, Embedded QA, Async dashboards, Decision Log, Yes/No gates
  - **Change-Impact Email** (6 lines)
- **The Power of Ownership**
  - **RACI-Lite (One Owner, Clear Chorus)** - owner, decider, consulted, informed, channel & cadence
  - **Outcome statement examples** ("I own \<the outcome\> until \<date\>")
- **The Power of Team Synergy**
  - **Win & Impact note template** (what changed, why it matters, owner)
  - **Recognition loop guide** (specific behaviour plus impact)
  - **Next-Skill tracker** (growth signal in 1:1s)

Extras & Behind-the-Scenes
- **How to Introduce the 7 Powers to Your Team** - A mini-facilitator guide
- **Self-Assessment: Which Power Needs Strengthening?** - Quick quiz and resource recommendations
- **Sneak Peek:** *Delivery Mindset*
- **Upcoming Titles** – Early access to *Leading Change* and *Lessons Learned* for subscribers
- **Monthly manager's Letter** (via email) – Actionable tips, reader stories, and exclusive previews from future books

☞ Download at: *https://echostorymedia.com/7powers*

Recommended Reading

Recommended books to deepen your management journey beyond *The 7 Hidden Powers of Effective Managers*:

Convene (decisions have a home)
- *Turn the Ship Around!* by L. David Marquet - Language and mechanisms that move authority to where the information is.
- *The Motive* by Patrick Lencioni - Why meetings stall: a leader's job is not optional.

Calculated Risk (speed, inside guardrails)
- *The Goal* by Eliyahu Goldratt - Throughput thinking for real-world constraints.
- *Checklist Manifesto* by Atul Gawande - Cheap guardrails that save expensive mistakes.

Perspective (Street → Skyline → Systems)
- *Thinking in Systems* by Donella Meadows - See the hidden levers and feedback loops.
- *Start with Why* by Simon Sinek - Re-anchor teams to purpose when tactics sprawl.

Presence (steady is faster)
- *High Output Management* by Andy Grove - Calm cadence: 1:1s, OKRs, and decision hygiene.
- *Essentialism* by Greg McKeown - Create margin so your presence actually signals, not adds noise.

Process (habits that survive bad days)

- *The Manager's Path* by Camille Fournier - From IC to org-scale rituals that actually stick.
- *They Ask, You Answer* by Marcus Sheridan - A practical operating rhythm for clarity and trust.

Ownership (one owner, outcome not tasks)

- *The Hard Thing About Hard Things* by Ben Horowitz - Owning the ugly problems in public.
- *Drive* by Daniel H. Pink - Motivation as autonomy, mastery, purpose-ownership's backbone.

Team Synergy (edges that lock, not clash)

- *Radical Candor* by Kim Scott - Caring personally and challenging directly.
- *The Five Dysfunctions of a Team* by Patrick Lencioni - Trust, conflict, commitment, accountability, results.

Referenced Frameworks & Concepts

The story incorporates several well-established workplace, leadership, and management approaches, which are acknowledged here for context and clarity:

Agency - The belief that managers can intentionally shape outcomes - not through control, but through thoughtful action, structure, and presence.

Chaos Engineering - From software to management: sometimes introducing small doses of "chaos" (noise) helps reveal system weaknesses and increase resilience.

Design Thinking - Popularised by Tim Brown's *Change by Design*. Teaches us to approach change with empathy, iteration, and visualisation. Marcia uses similar approaches in the way she leads change.

Eisenhower Matrix - The urgency vs. importance matrix helped shape the ideas of presence, prioritisation, and non-reactive leadership.

Empowerment through Structure - Structure isn't rigidity. When done right, it enables clarity, autonomy, and flow - just as Marcia discovers in her delivery mindset.

Feedback Loops - Common in systems thinking and Agile practices - visible in the team retrospectives, cross-office reviews, and client updates that tighten the learn-and-adapt cycle.

First-Principles Thinking - Marcia breaks down complex problems into fundamental truths before rebuilding.

Focused Work - Cal Newport's *Deep Work* emphasises the value of focused, uninterrupted time to tackle complex problems - mirrored in how Marcia clears space to think clearly and act deliberately.

Influence without Authority - Managers often rely more on informal influence than formal power. This concept shaped how powers like Power of Presence and The Power to Convene operate.

Leadership Presence - Inspired by Amy Cuddy and others, presence isn't about charisma - it's about calm, clarity, and showing up fully when it counts.

Magic as Metaphor - Ordinary actions (e.g., booking a meeting) as "small spells" that shift systems and outcomes.

Operational Excellence - This concept is visible in the structural tools and lean concepts, like momentum boards for visibility, clear goals, and structured meetings.

Precession (*Buckminster Fuller*) - The idea that small actions can create effects at right angles to the effort - for example when you design an innovation sprint, the most valuable result might not be the innovation sprint at all - but building lasting connection, a side-effect that emerges through interaction, visibility, or alignment.

Psychological Safety - Rooted in the research of *Amy Edmondson*; Marcia's demonstrates a focus on team trust, communication, and productive conflict.

Rituals as Culture - Regular standups, retrospectives, and one-on-ones act as shared rituals that shape team identity and reinforce expectations.

Systems Thinking - Donella Meadows *Thinking in Systems* and Peter Senge *The Fifth Discipline*, frame organisations as living systems - where cause and effect aren't always obvious and deeper patterns drive behaviour.

Vulnerability as Strength - *Brené Brown*'s work highlights the courage to say "I don't know yet" or ask hard questions as a hallmark of true leadership. Marcia's exhibits vulnerability as part of her growth.

Note: Concept names are used descriptively; all trademarks and copyrights belong to their respective owners.

Thanks & Acknowledgements

Special thanks to the leaders, teams, mentors, and clients - past and present - whose real-world challenges helped shape this story.